The
BATTLE OF
Copenhagen
1801

The BATTLE OF *Copenhagen* 1801

OLE FELDBÆK

Translated by TONY WEDGWOOD

Pen & Sword
MARITIME

First published in 1985 in Denmark by Politikens Forlag A/S
under the title *Slaget på Reden*

First published in Great Britain in 2002 by Leo Cooper
Reprinted in this format in 2016 by
Pen & Sword MARITIME
An imprint of
Pen & Sword Books Ltd
47 Church Street, Barnsley
South Yorkshire
S70 2AS

ISBN 978 1 47388 661 2

Typeset in 11/13pt Plantin by
Phoenix Typesetting, Auldgirth, Dumfriesshire

Printed and bound in England
By CPI Group (UK) Ltd, Croydon, CR0 4YY

Pen & Sword Books Ltd incorporates the Imprints of Pen & Sword Aviation,
Pen & Sword Family History, Pen & Sword Maritime, Pen & Sword Military,
Pen & Sword Discovery, Pen & Sword Politics, Pen & Sword Atlas,
Pen & Sword Archaeology, Wharncliffe Local History, Leo Cooper,
Wharncliffe True Crime, Wharncliffe Transport, Pen & Sword Select,
Pen & Sword Military Classics, The Praetorian Press, Claymore Press,
Remember When, Seaforth Publishing and Frontline Publishing

For a complete list of Pen & Sword titles please contact
PEN & SWORD BOOKS LIMITED
47 Church Street, Barnsley, South Yorkshire, S70 2AS, England
E-mail: enquiries@pen-and-sword.co.uk
Website: www.pen-and-sword.co.uk

CONTENTS

Author's Preface

This book is based on considerably more sources, published and unpublished, than any previous account of the events culminating in the Battle of Copenhagen. The British and Danish sources are, naturally enough, the most prominent; but also included are Swedish, French, Russian and Prussian sources. They explain the complex major politics of the time, without which 2 April 1801 has no meaningful explanation.

The book was first published in Danish in 1985 and reprinted in 2001. HM Queen Margrethe II graciously awarded me the Amalienborg Medal and generously provided funds for the book's translation into English.

There are others to whom I should like to express my thanks. The British Ambassador to Denmark, Philip Astley, and his Defence Attaché, Commander Andrew Gordon Lennox, for all their support, and the committee of the 1805 Club in England for their encouragement and enthusiasm.

Maps and illustrations have been generously provided by the Royal Danish Naval Museum and by an anonymous fund; to them I also express my thanks.

And finally, to Tony Wedgwood for convincing me that the book should be translated. With his ability to keep one eye on detail and the other on the overall picture, his sure instinct for my language and mastery of his own, and his naval interest and background, he has succeeded in turning a Danish book into an English book.

TRANSLATOR'S PREFACE

We learn through stories, we remember things through stories and we view established facts in a different way through stories. This story, this history, has long been sadly lacking from the shelves if the Battle of Copenhagen, and the events leading up to it, were to be fully understood; it tells the same story but from a different viewpoint, that of the Danes, using source material that has never before been published. It is particularly fitting that the English translation was completed on 2 April 2001, the 200th anniversary of the battle.

Without the help, support and encouragement of many people, it would never have seen the light of day – and to them I extend my sincere thanks.

First and foremost to Professor Ole Feldbæk for allowing a job of work to become a game and being so generous in the freedom he gave me to relate his story in a different language.

And to my dear friend Commander Andrew Gordon Lennox RN, to whom I dedicate this work. He simply refused to accept that it would not happen and persuaded a chain of people, including Philip Astley, the British Ambassador to the Court of Denmark, to turn every stone to find financial support.

This duly came from Her Majesty Queen Margrethe II and Prince Henrik's Foundation, to whom I offer my undying thanks.

To Colin White, then Deputy Director of the Royal Naval Museum in Portsmouth, for correcting my greatest blunders and sharing his encyclopaedic knowledge.

Finally, to Lieutenant Commander Ted Atkinson RNR, to whom naval history is an obsession, for locating Pen & Sword Books.

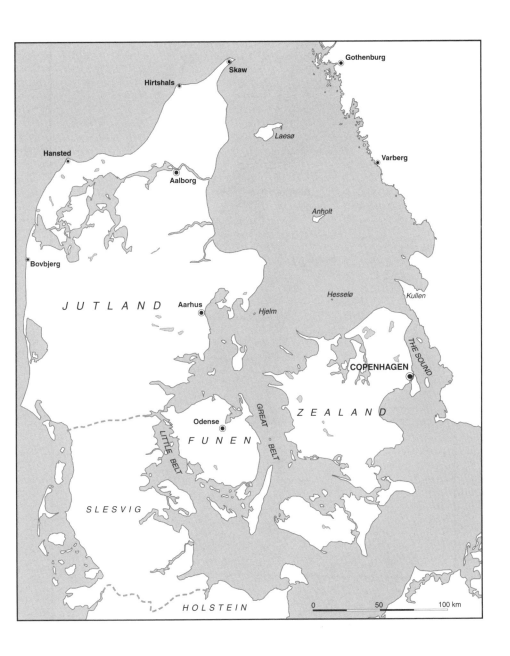

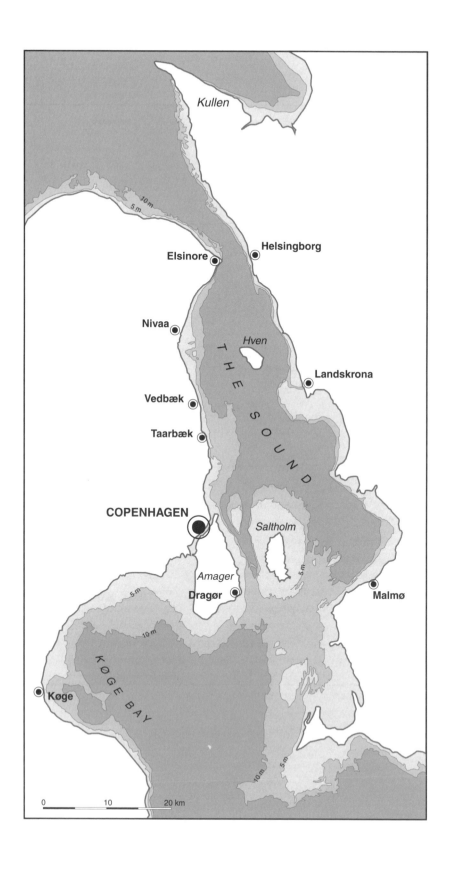

Kullen

Helsingborg

Elsinore

Nivaa

Hven

Landskrona

Vedbæk

THE SOUND

Taarbæk

COPENHAGEN

Saltholm

Amager

Dragør

Malmø

KØGE BAY

Køge

0   10   20 km

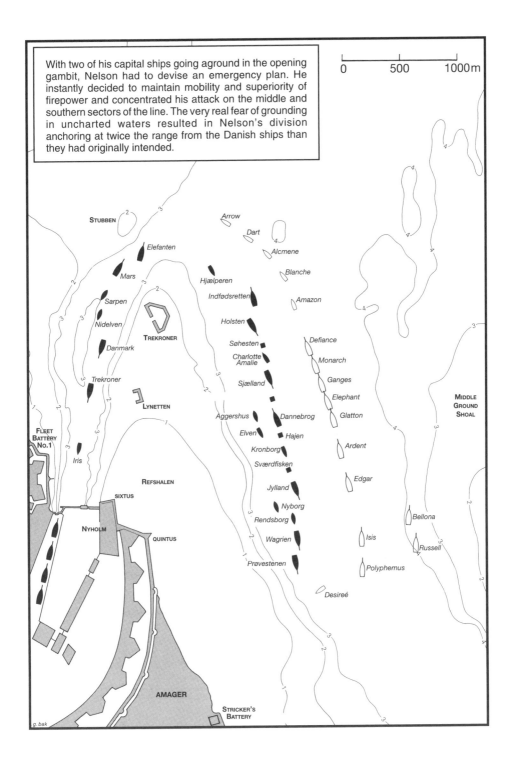

With two of his capital ships going aground in the opening gambit, Nelson had to devise an emergency plan. He instantly decided to maintain mobility and superiority of firepower and concentrated his attack on the middle and southern sectors of the line. The very real fear of grounding in uncharted waters resulted in Nelson's division anchoring at twice the range from the Danish ships than they had originally intended.

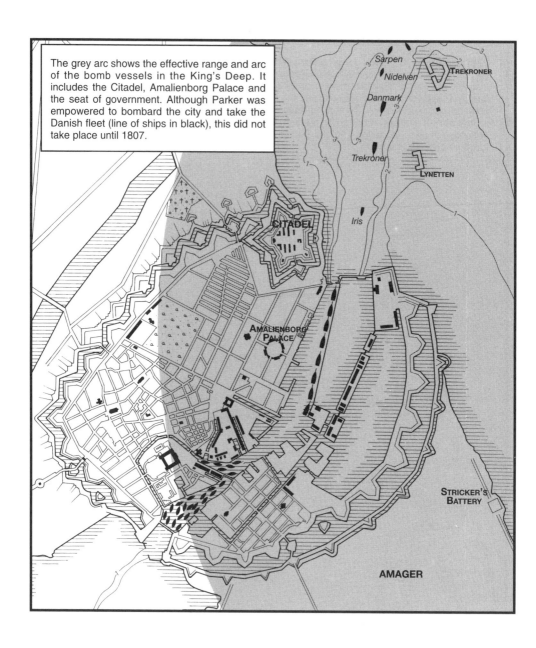

The grey arc shows the effective range and arc of the bomb vessels in the King's Deep. It includes the Citadel, Amalienborg Palace and the seat of government. Although Parker was empowered to bombard the city and take the Danish fleet (line of ships in black), this did not take place until 1807.

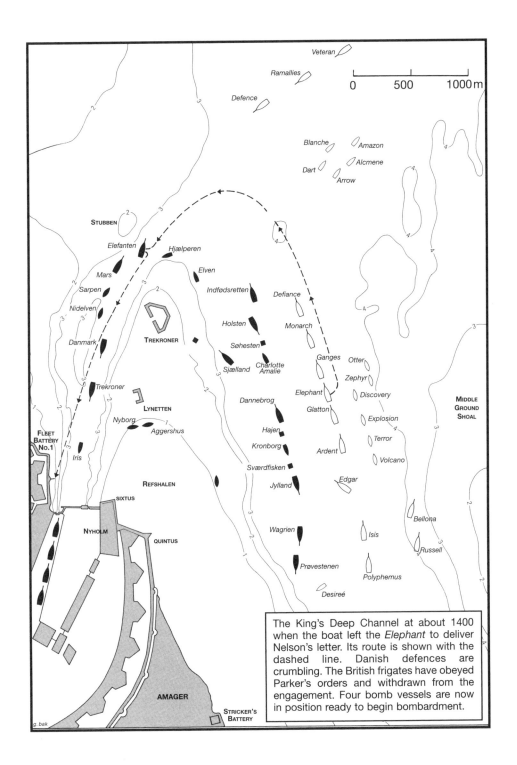

The King's Deep Channel at about 1400 when the boat left the *Elephant* to deliver Nelson's letter. Its route is shown with the dashed line. Danish defences are crumbling. The British frigates have obeyed Parker's orders and withdrawn from the engagement. Four bomb vessels are now in position ready to begin bombardment.

Chapter 1

ONE GREY MORNING IN MARCH

The morning watch on Monday 30 March was cold and grey on board the hulk *Prøvestenen*. As was normal for the time of year, temperatures during the night had hovered uncertainly around freezing point. And the officer of the day, 31-year-old Lieutenant Michael Bille, was thanking his lucky stars for the providence he had shown in equipping himself with a thick, fur-lined coat a week before when he received orders to make himself ready, at an hour's notice, to go to war.

He had appeared on deck at four, just as the guard ship *Elefanten*, moored in Kronløbet, had fired her duty shot to welcome the morning. At that time the ship's company was still abed, slumbering in their hammocks, shortly to be rudely awakened to a new day. The people were shaken, hammocks lashed and stowed and breakfast almost over. There was a fresh wind blowing from the north. The sun was not yet up – that trivial astronomical event would not take place until shortly before six – but it was light enough to get one's bearings. Normally, at this time of year, Copenhagen Roads would be deserted; in the last month, however, it had become the arena of hectic activity.

In 1801 the *Prøvestenen* was a reminder of glorious days long gone. She had been launched in 1767 from the Nyholm slips, with great festivity and celebration, the only three-decker in the fleet, a ship of power and pomp and pride bearing the name of the young king, Christian VII. Just over twenty-five years later, in 1793, the mighty 90-gunner was decommissioned; the upper gun deck was removed and the massive hull converted to a floating battery with an upper and lower gun deck. When the decision was made to moor her in the King's Deep, the Admiralty had not seen it fitting for the ship to bear the king's name any longer and she was renamed

1

Prøvestenen. Which did not for one moment make her any the weaker – she still had the most powerful artillery of any vessel moored in the King's Deep. On the upper deck she sported twenty-eight 24-pounders. On the lower deck, where Michael Bille took charge at action stations, there were twenty-eight of the navy's heaviest artillery pieces, the massive 36-pounders.

The ship's company matched the size of the weapons arsenal – 529 men. Only one ship in the King's Deep line had more men, the ship-of-the-line *Sjælland*. Seen from a naval officer's viewpoint, however, the *Prøvestenen* was poorly manned. There were only three naval officers aboard – the commanding officer, Commander Lassen, the second-in-command, Lieutenant Commander Ravn and Lieutenant Bille himself. The remaining four officers were young mates from the merchant fleet, seconded just a few weeks before on monthly contracts. In terms of ratings in the Navy's permanent employ, that is petty officers, gunnery ratings, carpenters and seamen carrying out their national service, there were no more than 179. The largest group aboard was the 225 volunteers who had arrived the week before. Most of them were craftsmen and workmen from Copenhagen. There was also a touch of the exotic – twenty-three Lascars, seamen from the Danish colony of Tranquebar on the coast of south-east India, who had recently arrived with the East Indiaman *General Abbestée*. The *Prøvestenen*'s numbers had also been boosted with six of the men pressed by Copenhagen's Chief of Police and his constables on the city streets and in the alehouses. Finally, there was the ship's military detachment, 110 red-coated musketeers from the 1st Jutland Infantry, under the command of two young lieutenants whose names Bille had not yet heard. This was hardly a crew in accordance with the Admiralty's manning regulations, but it was what they had managed to scrape together. And Bille knew that things were not much better aboard the other ships.

The *Prøvestenen* was the most southerly ship in the line stretching almost two miles up to Trekroner Fort on the northern tip of Refshale Shoal. The light had gradually improved enough for Bille to see the nearest blockships, the *Wagrien*, *Jylland* and *Kronborg*, and beyond her the vague outline of the *Dannebrog*, from which the Commander-in-Chief of the defence line, Commodore Olfert Fischer, flew his broad pennant. That was his limit of visibility from the upper deck of the *Prøvestenen*, but he knew the line continued north, with the ship-of-the-line *Sjælland*, the blockship *Charlotte*

Amalie (on board which his close friend and neighbour Lieutenant Bardenfleth was second in command), the ship-of-the-line *Holsten*, the blockship *Indfødsretten*, and, furthest north, the frigate *Hjælperen*.

Tucked among these gunships were smaller vessels, some already moored, others in the process of being warped and towed into position. There were the converted cavalry barges *Rendsborg*, *Nyborg* and *Aggershus*, the gun barges *Sværdfisken* and *Søhesten*, the signals frigate *Elven* and Fleet Battery No 1. Bille knew that they were working night and day at Nyholm dockyard to make ready the *Hajen*, the last artillery barge.

Trekroner Fort and its lines of tents, the only quarters for the men of the Fort, were still just a grey smudge, as were the two blockships *Elefanten* and *Mars* in the mouth of the Kronløbet Channel. But further up the channel, Lieutenant Bille could make out the armed flotilla comprising the ships-of-the-line *Danmark* and *Trekroner*, and the frigate *Iris*, under the command of his namesake Lieutenant Captain Steen Bille. They were to have transported artillery pieces and military stores up to Norway and brought back desperately needed Norwegian sailors to the Copenhagen defence force.

Friend and foe

For the hundredth time that week Michael Bille trained his telescope to the south. Would the allies come to Denmark's assistance? And would they arrive in time? He knew only too well that the ice at the eastern end of the Gulf of Finland would not break up until the beginning of May. So looking for the Russian squadron from Kronstadt was a pointless exercise. But what about the Reval squadron? The ice there thawed earlier and winter in the Baltic *had* been unusually mild that year. Rumours were already rife about the Swedish squadron. Bille knew that the Swedish Minister of the Navy, Admiral Cronstedt, had visited the Crown Prince as the King of Sweden's Liaison Officer. He knew, too, that Cronstedt had promised that the Swedish Skerries Fleet would be despatched from Stockholm to join the force defending the Sound. What Bille was looking so hopefully for was the squadron of seven ships-of-the-line and three frigates that lay fully equipped in Karlskrona, ready to join the combined squadron that, in June, was to display the might of the League of Armed Neutrality to the belligerent nations. But would the Swedes come? Bille knew that pilots had been gathered in the fishing village of Dragør to the south, ready to take the Swedish vessels up the channel through Drogden Shallows. Like every soul gently bobbing on the Copenhagen Roads that morning, Bille was hoping against hope. And he was not the only one to nurture nagging doubts about Sweden and the Swedes.

If and when it came, help would come from the south – and danger from the north. Shortly before Lieutenant Captain Bille's force was to have weighed anchor for Norway a British fleet of more than fifty ships had rounded the Skaw and entered the Kattegat. Nobody in Copenhagen had ever heard of the admiral commanding the fleet, but his second in command was known to all – Vice Admiral Lord Nelson. Three years earlier he had crushed Bonaparte's fleet at the Battle of the Nile. And the Royal Navy was now at anchor off the entrance to the Sound. The commandant of Kronborg Castle had sent dispatch riders at full speed to Crown Prince Frederik; and the optical telegraph system had been sending messages regularly from Kronborg down the chain of signal stations along the coast at Nivaa, Høje Sandbjerg and Fortunen to the signals mast at Nyholm, with updates on the movements of the British fleet. The latest stated that its admiral had demanded safe passage past Kronborg. The two fast brigs *Sarpen* and *Nidelven* had been ordered north to observe and report any indications that the Fleet was about to weigh anchor.

Appointment

When Michael Bille had come up on deck everything had been quiet – the first hour of the morning watch was always as quiet as the grave – and his thoughts had wandered back to that Monday afternoon exactly a week ago. He had been teaching navigation to the cadets at the Naval Academy, which was also his home. He lived in the north-easterly of the four palaces of Amalienborg, the old Brockdorff Palace on the other side of the square from the other palaces, the residences of Crown Prince Frederik, the mad King Christian VII and the king's brother, also called Prince Frederik. Most of his officer friends had already been given appointments and he was anxious at having been left out. Three years earlier he had married seventeen-year-old Marie Friedlieb, daughter of a vicar, and their first and only child, Christian, was just eighteen months old. Michael Bille was hardly eager to leave his wife and son and die for king and country, and he was honest enough to admit it to himself. But he was resentful and bitter over Britain's behaviour towards Denmark. And he was not unaware of what others might be thinking of his not being given an appointment. He had, in fact, applied for one and it came as something of a relief when, late in the afternoon of 23 March, he received orders to report on board the blockship *Prøvestenen*.

He had just an hour to pack his things, an hour of hectic activity in the old rococo palace that was his service residence. Family and friends turned up to make their farewells; Kristine, the maid, busied herself making tea and sandwiches; and Marie flitted between pouring tea, weeping and packing. When the time came to kiss his infant son goodbye, he too had to bite his lip to keep back the tears. And then he was off, up Amaliegade to Toldboden, the Customs Quay, to look for a ferry boat that could row him out to his ship. As busy as he had been, he had had the presence of mind to pick up a fur-lined coat, warm clothes and a hammock, and, to the later delight of his messmates, bread, cheese, sausage and aquavit.

Bille already knew something of the *Prøvestenen*'s problems – not enough officers, the crew was grumbling, she was still not on her station and she was leaking – but as he stood on the upper deck after sunset that day he realized things were much worse than he had expected. An angry man, who turned out to be the young Contract Lieutenant Rosenkilde, was striding up and down the deck bemoaning his bad luck at having been appointed second in command of this damned ship; another was standing on the bulwarks cursing that no one would help him get sacks of provisions aboard and the crew were bellowing like cattle for something to drink. What he had been told of conditions on board since his arrival was anything but encouraging. The captain, one Commander Runge, had proved completely incompetent. He had spent most of his time sitting in his cabin complaining that the ship had not been properly fitted out in Holmen Dockyard and there was a leak in the deckhead above his cot; he had made a mountain out of a molehill about this problem and his peevishness had put every man on board against him. Instead of answering questions, he had told people to go to hell, punched them on the nose or kicked them, depending on their rank. Bille had the feeling he had taken to the bottle and that the crew had no intention of remaining on board with *him* in command.

He and the newly designated second in command, Lieutenant Commander Ravn, got immediately to work in sorting things out and stamping their own identity on the ship. They started by knocking the bung out of a barrel of beer. The next day

5

Commander Runge disappeared, officially to take up the post of second in command of a ship-of-the-line then being fitted out in the naval dockyard, and the new captain, Commander Lassen, made a new ship out of the *Prøvestenen*. The leaks were caulked, the ship was warped into station in the King's Deep and moored to four heavy anchors and gunnery drills were started. One thing Bille could not complain about was lack of will among the national servicemen, the volunteers, the pressed men or the soldiers. But with so many men never having set foot before on the deck of a warship, the first few days were a complete shambles. He was bombarded from all sides with questions on anything and everything under the sun – a brewer demanded to know where he was to sleep, a smith wanted to know where he could urinate, a coach driver was curious as to where one of his boots had got to, a printer wanted to know if it was all right for him to write his watch bill number in red chalk on his bunk. The list was endless.

Bille had concentrated on organizing the ship with a watch and quarter bill; then men had pulled hard to warp the heavy hull south against wind and tide and get her moored on the station Commodore Fischer had allocated. The *Prøvestenen* had received her fair share of scathing signals from Fischer to get her in position and ready for action. One day he had come aboard unannounced to carry out an inspection and, in his usual belligerent manner, given the unfortunate officer of the day, Contract Lieutenant Koefoed, a blistering tirade for not paying him ceremonial honours as he came across the brow amidst all the hustle and bustle.

But as soon as the *Prøvestenen* was snugly at her moorings, gunnery drills had begun and the men had been exercised in getting to their guns and preparing them as quickly as possible when the drums beat to quarters. The Commodore's impatience was not entirely unjustified. When Bille was on board the *Dannebrog* one day during roll call Olfert Fischer himself had explained to him that the *Prøvestenen* was a crucial element in the defence structure because of her heavy guns.

The British are coming

When Bille came up on deck that morning everything had been quiet. But he sensed immediately that it would not last long. During the night the wind had moved round to the north – just what the British had been waiting for to pass Kronborg and sail down towards Copenhagen.

And Bille could see that Commodore Fischer was also on deck. As early as 0500, when it was barely light enough to see, the *Dannebrog* had signalled the *Elefanten* to keep a good lookout. Almost immediately afterwards, another signal was sent to Commodore Bille on board the ship-of-the-line *Danmark* to send an officer across to the *Dannebrog*. And as the sun crept over the horizon the general signal fluttered to the *Dannebrog*'s masthead for the squadron to clear for action.

Olfert Fischer's vigilance was well-founded. At precisely 0700 a peal of muffled thunder was heard from Kronborg. The signal came from the *Dannebrog* to open fire as soon as the enemy was in range. The gunfire lasted an hour. And then everything was still. And the brig *Nidelven* could be seen through the telescopes tearing down from the north under full sail, flying the signal from her mainmast that the enemy was approaching.

When the gunfire had started everyone on board the *Prøvestenen* knew what it meant. Every pair of eyes was peering north, despite the fact that there was nothing to be seen. And deep inside himself, Bille had to admit to a clutch at his heart. Shortly after the initial gunnery exchange, a ferryman had come aboard with a note from Marie in which she wrote: "Can now hear what is happening at Kronborg. God have mercy on me in my despair." She was up and about when he arrived, said the ferryman, and weeping, and he had seen the infant Christian. Bille scribbled a few words for him to take back, thanking her for her note and reassuring her he was in good spirits; Commander Lassen sent a similar missive ashore to his wife.

So far the enemy had been beyond visible range. But slowly the British topsails began to appear over the horizon. One by one in relentless succession. Every telescope was trained on the fleet that seemed to have no end. Sail after sail appeared. Bille studied them with concern through his telescope. The cannon at Kronborg had fired non-stop for an hour, but not a single stay had been parted, not a single sail holed. Bille sensed the same worry among his men – how had the British warships managed to get past Kronborg totally unscathed? It was a fear which must not be allowed to spread. So, with false cheerfulness, Bille asked whether there were enough enemy ships for their liking or whether they would prefer a few more. The ensuing laughter broke the anxious moment and the crew turned their full attention to the gunnery drills they knew would all too soon be put to the test.

Why fight?

Denmark had not been at war for 80 years. Now a defensive force, hastily put together and inadequately manned, would have to face an enemy with crushing military superiority. On board the *Prøvestenen* that morning of 30 March there must have been many asking themselves why. For most the answer, or at least part of it, would have been because they had to. This would undoubtedly have been the answer of the ship's officers and petty officers, and of the drafted soldiers and sailors, and, although with a different irony, of the pressed men. But what about the countless volunteers? Quite how voluntary their service may have been is a moot point but many were certainly there that day either after hearing the Crown Prince's rhetoric on 'protecting our beloved country' or for the reward of 15 rigsdaler, that is two to three months' wages.

But Michael Bille was not alone in his love of country, nor in his bitterness at the arrogance shown by the greatest naval power in the world in the eight years the war had now lasted, in its treatment of ships flying the neutral Danish flag. In the patrician drawing rooms of Copenhagen, patriotic fervour was at boiling point; in the gentlemen's clubs and coffee houses, the poets were unanimous – the men out on Copenhagen Roads were fighting 'for country, freedom and honour'. These were words that may well have had some sort of meaning for the many souls on board the *Prøvestenen* that grey morning in March. But the real reason Denmark and Britain were at war in those hours was known to very few. The Tsar of Russia and his closest advisers in St. Petersburg knew it. The First Consul of France, General Bonaparte, and his Foreign Minister, Talleyrand, knew it. And the Cabinet in Downing Street and the Admiralty in Whitehall knew it.

In Copenhagen, the real reason was known only by Crown Prince Frederik and the Ministers of the Privy Council.

The battle about to be waged in the King's Deep was really not Denmark's fight at all. It was a fight about something else entirely – the struggle among the major powers for supremacy in Europe.

Chapter 2

Denmark and High Politics

The blessings of neutrality

It is one of the ironies of history that the battle about to be fought was the result of more than 80 years of peace and neutrality in Denmark.

When Frederik IV signed the peace treaty in 1720 after the Great Northern War, he also signed away any plans Denmark might have had for regaining the Danish and Norwegian provinces Christian IV and Frederik III had conceded to Sweden.

Frederik IV ruled over a kingdom that stretched from North Cape to the Elbe, the equivalent of Copenhagen to Carthage. But in terms of European politics, Denmark was small fry and the 1720 peace had been arranged by the major powers behind the backs of the Danish and Swedish negotiating teams. In the middle of the eighteenth century Denmark could still exert a certain influence on northern European politics, but around 1800 nations such as Denmark and Sweden had effectively lost control of their own political destiny. Their lack of political influence was reflected in their military power, which had stagnated, whilst the armies and navies of the major powers had grown fast. Throughout the eighteenth century the Danish fleet comprised a score or so of sea-worthy ships-of-the-line. At the beginning of the same century Britain had more than 125 ships-of-the-line; in 1750, 150 and in 1801, 190. Around 1800 countries such as Denmark and Sweden were client states in the European political arena, and pawns in the alliance system of the major powers.

Denmark had had no territorial aspirations since 1720. Its political objectives lay exclusively in maintaining what territories it had left. But even the pursuit of this policy of peace was beyond Denmark's abilities.

It was no accident of history that in 1718 King Karl XII of Sweden was killed in battle in Norway in an attempt to gain territorial compensation for the provinces the country had lost in Finland, the Baltic States and North Germany. And since 1772 conquest of Norway had been the thread running through Swedish foreign policy. It is a fact that this threat to Denmark was lifted in 1792, for a time at least, when Gustav III was assassinated. But when the young Gustav IV Adolf came to power, he re-introduced his father's Norwegian policy.

The Danish government knew of the Swedish plan and its naval strategy was accordingly directed against the threat from its neighbour. The objectives of this strategy were two-fold: to ensure enough power at sea to prevent Sweden taking control of the Sound and overrunning Copenhagen; and to prevent Sweden from breaking lines of communication between Denmark and Norway. But real security for the Danish monarchy lay in an alliance with Russia. Russia feared, not without justification, that Sweden would try to regain the Finnish provinces it had lost after the Great Northern War, and, with the signing of the 1773 Alliance, Denmark and Russia had committed themselves to come to each others aid in the event of Swedish aggression.

But it was not an alliance between equals. Russia was a major power, Denmark a client state; and Denmark needed Russia more than Russia needed Denmark. In St. Petersburg they knew this and acted accordingly; in Copenhagen they knew this too, and also acted accordingly. The price of Norway's remaining within the Danish monarchy was dependence on Russia and Russian foreign policy. This does not imply that Denmark was completely robbed of any political manoeuverability, but it *was* limited – to what, in terms of overall security policy, Russia could and would accept.

Political balancing act

Throughout the eighteenth century, when war and peace were in the realm only of the major powers, Denmark enjoyed the longest period of peace in its history. And successive Danish governments worked single-mindedly to use this peace to promote trade and shipping under the Danish flag. They pursued this policy when the major powers were at peace and when they were at war. And they pursued it when everyone was suddenly crying out for tonnage under a neutral flag.

In the eighteenth century Europe was undergoing explosive growth. The population almost doubled, production expanded even more and demands for goods and transport grew correspondingly. And commodities from overseas, such as sugar, spices, coffee, tea, porcelain, cotton and silk were no longer luxury articles affordable by the elite few; they had become everyday consumer items for the growing populations of Europe.

This powerful boom in economic growth also brought with it increased dependence on being able to export, import and maintain links between the home country and her overseas colonies. Developments in global economy made individual nations more vulnerable than they had ever been before. Economic warfare was not invented in the eighteenth century – it is as old as war itself. But it did assume increasing importance and grew to a global scale, culminating in Napoleon's blockade of continental Europe in 1806. War at sea was no longer merely a question of fleet operations and engagements. In military terms, it was just as important to impose blockades on the enemy's ports and coastlines, to take enemy merchantmen, to occupy the enemy's overseas colonies and to prevent economic warfare being nullified by the enemy blatantly continuing his commercial activities under the protection of a neutral flag.

It was inevitable, therefore, that tension and conflicts would arise between countries at war and those who were neutral. And with Britain's dominance at sea, in practice this meant tension and conflicts between Britain and neutral seafaring nations like Denmark.

The conflict of interests was clear, and recognized by both parties. Britain's position as a major power was based on her navy and its superiority at sea. This was a position that could not be maintained if neutral countries undermined the economic warfare being waged by the navy and British privateers. Faced with this fact, a neutral seafaring nation like Denmark had to proclaim its right as an independent state to trade with whom it liked, with what it liked and where it liked. Britain's war belonged to Britain, not to Danish merchants and shipping companies.

In reality, however, relations between belligerent Britain and neutral Denmark were much more complex and much more convoluted. No two wars were alike. Relations between Britain and

Denmark had never been an isolated affair that could be determined solely by military might. It was determined by the current situation in high politics.

No, wars were different. And Britain had not been equally strong in all its wars. During the Seven Years War (1756–63) she had been in a very strong military position. She had thus been able to set very restrictive limits on how Danish merchants and ship owners could make the most of what was then highly profitable international trade, and there was nothing the Danish government could do about it. During the American War of Independence (1775–83), however, Britain had been stretched to the limit, both in America and at sea. Denmark had been able to press Britain into making concessions, and trade and shipping under the Danish flag, the Dannebrog, experienced a boom such as had never been seen before. When Britain entered the Revolutionary Wars in 1793 it was a new kind of war. Republican France used revolutionary ideology as a weapon against the conservative alliances of the major powers, who were blockading ports to starve the French into restoring the Bourbons to the throne. Economic warfare was being waged with a determination that was unparalleled. Trade and shipping under the Danish flag was carried out at great risk, but also with huge profits. During this deafening sabre-rattling between the major powers, the Danish government kept a very low profile.

On the other hand, British–Danish relations were never an either-or affair; never a question of either ultimatums or total self-destruction. Denmark had a card up her sleeve to win British acceptance of a degree of freedom that would allow her to exploit trade opportunities – her position in the international system. The governments of both countries knew that Britain had no interest in pushing Denmark so far that she would ally herself with France or join forces with other neutral states in a league of neutrality directed against Britain. Relations between Britain and Denmark were a political balancing act, with adjustments in the point of gravity being made constantly with political and military developments, and with the continual reassessment of each others possible reactions.

Profiteers
The most obvious bone of contention between the two countries was the issue of the principles of neutrality, of the rights and obligations of the neutral and warring parties.

There were, of course, as many opinions on this issue as there were states, and they were all in perfect accord with the current economic and political interests of those states. There were no generally accepted rights and no international courts to adjudicate in international differences of opinion. As far as Britain and Denmark were concerned, their only recourse was the 1670 treaty between the two countries; however, it was not only old but ambiguous. So what happened in practice was that cases involving Danish ships were tried by British courts, which passed judgement according to political directives, and the only court of appeal in Britain was political in its composition.

In principle the neutral powers claimed the right to deal with whom they wanted, with what they wanted and when they wanted. That meant that neutrals could trade with countries at war *and* their colonies; that they might transport goods belonging to belligerents – in slogan form, free ship free goods; that war contraband should be defined solely as war materials; that neutral convoys were not to be visited and searched on the high seas; and finally that the neutrals were prepared to recognize only effective blockade of coasts and harbours, not mere paper blockades.

On these issues Britain naturally took an extremely restrictive point of view and Denmark, equally naturally, applied a highly liberal interpretation. For Britain they were matters of crucial political and military importance. For Denmark it was only a question of money, but undeniably huge sums of money.

The war between the major powers created an explosive demand for neutral tonnage and Danish merchants and ship owners had made fortunes from trade and freight transport in European waters and the Mediterranean, in the transport of slaves from Africa, in trade with the West Indies and in overseas trade with China, India, Java and Mauritius. The sums involved were astronomical. Between 1772 and 1807, in one branch of trade alone – the Asiatic – cargoes were discharged in Denmark to the value of 135 million rigsdaler; at that time the income of the Kingdom of Denmark varied from six million in 1772 to nine million in 1800.

But just how Danish was this trade and seafaring under the neutral Dannebrog? Both the British and Danish governments knew full well that most of it was carried out by Danish ships and for Danish consignees. But they also knew that the Dannebrog served, to some degree at least, as a flag of convenience. Many Danish ships carried cargoes that according to the bills of lading were destined for Denmark, but which in reality were consignments for warring nations. And many ships sailing under the Danish flag were in reality owned by one or other of the nations at war. There were many cases of individual Danish merchants, trading companies and captains (and the occasional front man) making quick profits. But there were others that were nothing less than the blatant systematic abuse of neutrality. The largest transaction during the Revolutionary Wars, at least the largest recorded transaction, was the contract between the wealthy Copenhagen merchant Frédéric de Coninck and, with the silent approval of Minister of Finance Ernst Schimmelmann, the Dutch East India Company. It involved twenty large ships sent to Java to sneak in Dutch colonial products to the markets of Europe via Copenhagen under the very noses of British men-of-war and privateers.

Everyone took part in neutrality abuse, even, during the American War of Independence, ministers and senior civil servants. But this was of little concern to the Danish government. It was single-minded in its determination to reach its objective – to make as much money as possible. So it accepted with no undue difficulty the means to the end, that the Dannebrog be used as camouflage for the activities of the warring nations. What worried the Danish government was how far it was politically advisable to defend abuse of neutrality against Britain and when it would be wisest to wash their hands of the whole business and allow the merchants and shipowners and their foreign business connections to start running the risks themselves.

The pivotal question in Danish neutrality politics was how could the Danish government avoid getting into so difficult a position with Britain that it would be forced to choose between military conflict and political defeat? Hence, during both the Seven Years War and the American War of Independence there had been a common thread running through the weft of Danish policy in every conflict between Denmark and Britain – Denmark pursued a policy of *defensive* neutrality.

Defensive neutrality
This principle of defensive neutrality had been implemented by Denmark consistently adopting the most liberal of interpretations of the contentious principles of neutrality – only, equally consistently, to cave in every time Britain made a move to reach a solution in principle or enter into debate on the subject. At the core of this

defensive neutrality policy was the double-barrelled tactic of formally avoiding the abandonment of the disputed principle and, at the same time, to shelve it until better times. As a result the Danish government trod carefully in any question of the principle while covertly supporting the multifarious forms of neutrality abuse that were so rife under the protection of the Danish flag. The government was not blind to the possibilities presented by neutral alliances against Britain but it realized that the neutral states were also prone to in-fighting and that it would be easy for Britain to play one off against the other. Even in 1780, when Russia was the most vociferous in advocating a League of Armed Neutrality embracing every principle Denmark had claimed against the British, she elected to stick to her policy of defensive neutrality. Denmark's dependence on Russia in terms of national security necessitated her joining the League, but the Danish government discreetly let it be known to Britain that it had no intention of making use of its membership. The interests of Danish merchants and ship owners were best served by a policy of defensive neutrality, with the Danish government, as it was so cleverly worded in 1781, limiting itself to "speaking for our own case and easing our way through as best we can".

During the American War of Independence the economic results of the policy of defensive neutrality had exceeded even the most daring of expectations. When Britain went to war with France in February 1793 tradition and experience both spoke for maintaining the defensive strategy. Foreign Minister A.P. Bernstorff discreetly passed on the message to the king's merchants and ship owners that they could expect no help from the government if they were caught transporting war contraband or goods belonging to nations at war, or if they called at ports under blockade.

And he took just as defensive a view of convoys. During previous wars Denmark had provided a naval escort for Danish merchant ships, though she had never had any illusions that Danish warships would be capable of providing any effective global protection of activities pursued under the Danish flag, nor that it would be able to withstand the demands of British warships to visit and search Danish convoys. The Danish convoy tactic had been a game of political roulette. Denmark knew Britain would never recognize the principle of inviolability, but the Danish government had consciously played on the fact that Britain, in a period of tension, would stop short of violating the flag of the king of Denmark, which a search at gunpoint would involve, for fear of driving the Danes into the arms of the French. During the American War of Independence the convoy system had been a political success. But Bernstorff knew that the only reason it had worked was that Britain had found herself in such an unusually pressured military situation.

But in 1793 she did not. Which was the reason for his sarcasm when Danish merchants and shippers asked him for convoys: "So you want war? I can get you that tomorrow. But I can't get us out of it again."

Bernstorff was resolute in his decision to continue the policy of defensive neutrality. This did not prevent Denmark signing a Convention of Neutrality with Sweden in 1794, a treaty which would act as an outward expression of the common will to maintain neutrality. Nor did it prevent the government from going to great lengths in supporting trade and seafaring by granting Danish citizenship to foreign captains, by issuing ship's papers which it knew full well would be used to camouflage foreign ships and cargoes, and by appointing completely unknown skippers as lieutenants in the Danish navy when they were to continue their passage under the bargain basement Danish flag of convenience. But despite heated diplomatic arguments over the increasingly frequent and aggressive actions against ships flying the Danish flag, and despite pressure from the Danes, who wanted to see even more support for trade and shipping and a firmer attitude towards the warring parties, Denmark maintained her policy of defensive neutrality.

But in June 1797, just as the war at sea was entering a crucial phase, the old statesman died. His death heralded not just an important reshuffle of the Danish government, but a change in policy.

OFFENSIVE POLICY

With A.P. Bernstorff's death, political leadership reverted to Crown Prince Frederik. He had grown up an orphan. He had not seen his mother, the English-born Queen Caroline Matilda (sister of George III), since he was three years old and had never had any real human contact with his father, the mad King Christian VII. In the

16

period when the cabinet was under the control of the dowager Queen Juliane Marie, he had been neglected. He got his revenge by taking power with a coup in the Privy Council at the age of sixteen. He had no desire, though, to dispel the myth that an absolute monarch himself managed his kingdoms and lands – so for the rest of his pitiful life, his father had daily to attend the Privy Council and put his signature -'Approved. Christian Rex' – to thousands and thousands of documents of whose content and significance he understood not a word.

Thus the political reality was that until the king's death in 1808 Frederik acted as Regent. His first act had been to recall former Foreign Minister Count A.P. Bernstorff from his political exile. He enjoyed not only the respect of the Crown Prince but his affection, and until his death he functioned as de facto political leader.

But in 1797 Crown Prince Frederik was twenty-nine years old. He had taken an active part in the work of government during the extensive agricultural reforms; as president of the Board of Admiralty, he had functioned, to all intents and purposes, as Minister of the Navy since 1792; and he had a highly developed sense of honour when it came to the prestige of the country and the flag. And now he wanted to rule himself. His choice of Foreign Minister was a signal of how he intended to do so. He appointed Bernstorff's eldest son, the twenty-eight-year-old diplomat Christian Bernstorff, to the post but gave him no seat on the Privy Council. The two young men worked together reasonably well. The Crown Prince had confidence in his Foreign Minister, who, for his part, understood the Crown Prince's intentions and was willing to submit to his will. But their collaboration took place outside the Privy Council, whose work thus seldom involved matters of foreign policy, giving them little influence in this area.

So 1797 saw a change not just in the dramatis personae in the political arena but also in the way politics was conducted. Danish foreign policy took a new tack. The policy of defensive neutrality changed to one of offensive neutrality – Denmark introduced the convoy system.

In 1797 Danish convoys were a political gamble, just as they had always been. A change in political leadership was not in itself enough to explain the adoption of an offensive policy and the war at sea escalated. It gave impetus to those who had already been advocating convoys for some time – interest groups such as merchants and ship owners, who had a powerful spokesman in Minister of Finance Ernst Schimmelmann, and, to a certain extent, to the Crown Prince and the Navy, who felt insulted by the increasing number of actions against ships flying the Danish flag and who believed that taking a firm stand would be politically effective.

Barely a month was to pass after his taking up his appointment before the young Foreign Minister was put to his first test – pressure for a convoy escort of the richly laden ships that were on their way home from the East Indies. At first he managed to withstand that pressure, but the convoy lobby stepped up their campaign considerably. Reports of actions against Danish ships by French privateers were arriving daily. And shortly after the new year the convoy supporters moved into action.

The man behind it all was Frédéric de Coninck. He had promised his Dutch business connections that, through his friend and neighbour Minister of Finance Schimmelmann, he would be able to arrange a convoy for the Dutch shipments from Java that were to be brought to Europe under the Danish flag of convenience. On 24 January 1798 Schimmelmann brought the convoy issue up at a meeting of the Privy Council. He explained to the Crown Prince and the ministers that in 1798 there were forty East Indiamen under the Danish flag on passage for Copenhagen. He was wise enough not to try and conceal the fact that some of them had once belonged to the French and their Dutch allies and that they contained "cargoes for French and Dutch accounts", but, in the best interests of Denmark's economy, he strongly recommended providing convoy escort.

Despite the concerns of the Foreign Minister, the merchants and ship owners got what they wanted. The convoy camp wasted no time in putting their victory to good use. In the spring of 1798 convoy protection was extended to include the Mediterranean and passage to and from the West Indies. By the summer of that year the convoy victory was complete – convoys were to be implemented on the routes where the risk was greatest by far, between Denmark and the Mediterranean.

Collision course
The convoy policy meant that, wherever they sailed, in however small a ship, Danish naval officers were to refuse any demand to visit and search, if necessary by force. The convoy supporters knew

full well that any show of force against the Danish ensign could have unimaginable political consequences. In the spring of 1798 they could justify their views, to some extent at least, by the fact that Britain had gone on the defensive, that the British fleet had withdrawn from the Mediterranean and that the prime purpose of the convoys was to provide protection against French privateers. But they knew equally well that the day Britain reclaimed her supremacy in and control of the Mediterranean, Danish convoys would be an affront to Britain and a thorn in the side of British warfare at sea.

A few months later that was exactly what happened. The British fleet returned to the Mediterranean. Nelson decimated Bonaparte's fleet at Aboukir Bay and British warships stopped an entire Swedish convoy on its way down the English Channel.

Christian Bernstorff knew immediately what that meant. In August 1798 he advised the Crown Prince that the political situation had changed dramatically and that Britain would not surrender what she regarded as her right to visit and search neutral convoys. He also offered a plan for how this collision course could be avoided – the Danish navy could be given permission to permit such searches in the event that they were outgunned by the British. The Board of Admiralty, with the Crown Prince at its head, rejected the plan and stuck to the unwavering refusal to allow boarding.

In the long term the decision the Crown Prince made was crucial. He knew that at that time, convoys were of little economic significance, with the exception of trade in the Mediterranean. But he also knew that, thus far, superior British forces had given way to the resistance of Danish escort commanders to allow their ships to be boarded. At that momentous meeting in the Admiralty building on Gammelholm he approved yet another inflexible order for convoy commodores: papers were being written for the small naval brig *Nidelven* to escort twenty-one merchantmen through the English Channel.

The Crown Prince acted in accordance with his strong convictions of the need to uphold the prestige of Danish sovereignty and respect for its flag, and in the belief that he would win his political poker game. A conflict with British warships was only a question of time.

The first took place on 2 December 1798 off Gibraltar, where the Danish frigate *Triton* had retaken a merchant ship extracted from her convoy by two British privateers. The British Commander-in-Chief in the Mediterranean was Admiral Lord St. Vincent; the commander of the Danish squadron in the same waters was Commodore Steen Bille. They took diametrically opposed standpoints on the actions of the Danish convoy commodore, but both recognized the fact that the issue was political dynamite and wisely left it to be sorted out by their governments.

In London the government and its legal advisers had not a moment's doubt that Britain, as a nation at war, had the inalienable right to search neutral convoys. In Copenhagen the British envoy Lord Fitzgerald was therefore instructed to deliver a sharply worded protest. Christian Bernstorff's initial reaction was even harsher – Denmark would never, as long as it possessed any sense of honour, budge an inch in the principle of the inviolability of its convoys. And although Britain underlined her determination by allowing the Admiralty courts to declare the entire Swedish convoy as prizes – and by justifying that decision as a consequence of the refusal to allow it to be searched – the final Danish response was one of unswaying refusal to allow boarding of her convoys and insistance on their immunity.

The convoy conflict

Britain's initial reaction was to do nothing. But on 24 December 1799 a new and more serious incident took place. That Christmas Eve morning the frigate *Havfruen* entered the Straits of Gibraltar with a convoy of twelve ships. The commodore, Commander van Dockum, came from Malaga and his orders from the Squadron Commander were to escort the convoy of merchantmen through the Straits and out into the safety of the Atlantic. During the passage he was hailed by a British squadron of three ships with demands to stop and receive boarders. Van Dockum refused and informed them of his clear and unambiguous orders to do so. When the British put a boat in the water anyway, he fired on it and two seamen were wounded. Despite their overwhelming superiority, the British did not return fire; when van Dockum later in the day entered Gibraltar, where the entire Mediterranean fleet was riding at anchor, even Lord Keith, its Commander-in-Chief, did not retaliate. Not because of the *Havfruen* and her forty guns, but because using force against the Danish frigate could unleash undesirable political reactions in a situation that was already complicated in the extreme. And just like St. Vincent, Keith limited his actions to reporting the affair to his superiors.

This time London decided to act. The Admiralty issued strict instructions to every commanding officer in the fleet to stop and search neutral convoys; if they were met with resistance, they were to capture the convoy and its warship escort and conduct them to an English harbour. Thereafter, Lord Grenville, the Foreign Minister, sent instructions to the envoy in Copenhagen, Anthony Merry, Lord Fitzgerald's successor, to inform Bernstorff that Britain now demanded that Denmark drop her claims of immunity for neutral convoys.

On the evening of 7 April 1800 Merry called on the Danish Foreign Minister to present Britain's demands for Denmark to abandon her policy of offensive neutrality. He was met with a point blank refusal.

By this time Denmark had intensified its offensive policy even more, in the utmost secrecy. When news of the *Havfruen* incident reached Copenhagen in January 1800 the Danish government had reacted by requesting the support of a major power in the struggle with Britain that seemed inevitable. By the autumn of 1799 the coalition forged between Russia, Austria and Britain the previous year was already falling apart, a fact known to both Bernstorff and Merry. They also knew that Tsar Paul was working on putting together a block of neutral states with Russia at the head and that a League of Armed Neutrality similar to that formed by Catherine the Great in 1780 might well be the outcome. What Merry did not know, however, was that in the past few months Bernstorff had sent signals to St. Petersburg of Denmark's interest in a neutral alliance. And although he had not yet received acceptance from the Russians by the meeting of 7 April, he acted towards the envoy as if he had, and persuaded Merry to relax his demands and ask for new orders from London before he went further with matters at his end.

So the outcome of the *Havfruen* incident was yet another Danish rejection of the British claims in the convoy issue. All the British government got out of it was a vitriolic note of reply from Bernstorff, obviously written with the eyes of St. Petersburg in mind, and the information from Merry that yet another convoy was preparing to set sail for the Mediterranean.

The *Freya* affair

The Danish government adhered firmly to its policy of offensive neutrality. Even before he delivered his scathing note to Merry, Bernstorff had received the approbation of the Crown Prince and the Privy Council to appeal directly to the Tsar for help. One of the most skilful diplomats in the Danish foreign service was Niels Rosenkrantz. Then envoy in Berlin, he was sent to St. Petersburg to plead Russia's support in the convoy conflict. His speedy departure from Berlin was the talking point of the capitals of Europe. Both Lord Grenville in Britain and Talleyrand in France were informed of his mission and put the same interpretation on it – the formation of a neutral alliance. The response in St. Petersburg was positive, but Russia wanted to play a waiting game. Every government in Europe spent the summer of 1800 waiting anxiously for the outcome of the battle in north Italy between the French and the Austrians, the result of which would have a decisive influence on the international political situation.

Meanwhile, the Danish convoys continued as if nothing had happened and the Danish Admiralty continued to receive regular reports that British warships had backed down against the convoy commodores' refusal to be searched. So for Bernstorff it was routine paperwork when, on 19 June, he was reading through yet another set of convoy orders for Commander Krabbe of the frigate *Freya*, who was to escort a convoy from Christiansand to the Mediterranean. The route would take them through the English Channel and Krabbe was ordered to resist any demands to board "with every means at his disposal".

The *Freya* sailed from Flekkerø on 21 July with six merchant ships under her protection. Their passage through the North Sea was uneventful and in the afternoon of 25 July they were at the mouth of the English Channel.

Twelve miles north-east of Ostend that afternoon a British squadron of four frigates and a lugger was on station. The names of the ships that met that day contained their own ironic symbolism. Freya was the goddess of fertility and fruitfulness – and the neutral trade the frigate was escorting was undeniably fruitful. But Captain Baker's frigate bore the ominous name of *Nemesis*. And both captains had been issued with orders on which there could be no compromise. Commander Krabbe was to repel any search with force and Captain Baker was to implement it with force.

At 1430 the British sighted the convoy. Captain Baker gave orders to start the chase and Captain Gage of the frigate *Terpsichore*, who lay closest to the convoy, received a signal to board and search. Gage hailed the *Freya* and ordered her to heave to. Krabbe replied that he would resist. Gage made a signal requesting permission to open fire, but was told to wait; the squadron commander wanted to hear for himself the reason for the refusal. It was almost 2000 before Baker got within hailing range of the *Freya*, which at that time was maintaining a position between her escorts and the British ships. He informed Krabbe that he insisted on boarding the convoy and asked if he would indeed resist such an attempt. Krabbe answered that he was under orders to refuse such intervention. Baker shouted back that he was going to put a boat in the water and board the Danish ship and that he would regard it as a hostile act if Krabbe opened fire on it. He launched his boat from the *Nemesis* and Krabbe opened fire with a single shot that did not find its mark. The *Nemesis* immediately directed a broadside against the *Freya*. And the *Freya* returned fire.

At that point in time the British warships had encircled the *Freya* at very close quarters. Against Krabbe's paltry 40 guns, they had more than a convincing superiority. The *Nemesis* had 38 guns, *Prévoyante* 36, *Terpsichore* 32 and *Arrow* 30. What is more, *Prévoyante* and *Arrow* had taken up a position from which they could send their shot down the length of the *Freya*'s hull.

The outcome was inevitable. After half an hour, with one man dead and five injured aboard the *Freya* and four dead and four wounded in the British ships, Krabbe struck his colours. The British took the badly damaged frigate and conducted her and the convoy to the roads off Deal. From here Commander Krabbe immediately sent a message to his envoy in London and Captain Baker's report was sent by optical telegraph to the Admiralty in Whitehall. The two captains had acted according to their orders and showed commendable coolness. The *Freya* affair was now a political issue. And, as it turned out, high politics.

The last warning
In London the Danish envoy, Count Wedel Jarlsberg, did what he could to prevent the *Freya* affair developing into an open conflict between Britain and Denmark. But the decision was not his; it lay entirely in the hands of the British government.

To them it could hardly have come at a worse moment. At the

end of July 1800 Britain was close to becoming politically isolated. On 14 June Bonaparte had defeated the Austrians at the Battle of Marengo and William Pitt's cabinet had to face the fact that their Austrian allies would make peace with France. Russia was adopting an increasingly hostile position towards Britain, culminating in the Tsar breaking diplomatic relations. The threatening spectre of a League of Armed Neutrality was looming on the horizon.

The Cabinet was therefore divided on the question of how Britain should react to the *Freya* affair. The First Sea Lord, Lord Spencer, was concerned at the stretched resources of the Fleet and spoke for avoiding conflict with the neutral countries by tipping the wink to commanding officers not to be too enthusiastic in seeking out neutral convoys. Lord Grenville, on the other hand, wanted to use the *Freya* affair to solve the convoy conflict with Denmark once and for all. The meeting in Downing Street ended with Pitt taking Grenville's hard line against Denmark.

The cabinet reached two decisions. The prominent diplomat, Lord Whitworth, who had just returned from St. Petersburg as ambassador, was to be sent to Copenhagen. And a Royal Navy squadron of strength was to sail into Danish waters to support his mission.

Whitworth was on his way to Copenhagen on 4 August on board the frigate *Andromeda*. Lord Grenville had empowered him to issue two threats: the first was that the squadron would be used against Denmark if his demands were refused; the second was that Britain would capture the Danish colonies and seize all Danish merchantmen if Denmark entered a League of Armed Neutrality. But Lord Grenville really wanted to avoid open conflict and had authorized Whitworth to let the Danes make a choice: they could rescind the orders to the convoy commodores to resist boarding and allow the British to visit and search, or they could suspend all convoys until the two governments had come to a negotiated understanding on the principles of neutral convoys. If Denmark accepted just one of these options Britain would release the *Freya* and her convoy immediately.

The orders sent to Vice Admiral Dickson at the same time show that Britain *hoped* that Denmark would yield to the show of military power and that the conflict could be isolated. But the Cabinet also realized that if Russia and Sweden entered the conflict on Denmark's side, Britain must be prepared to take them on too.

Britain's demands in the question of convoys were no less than an ultimatum.

In Denmark things were peaceful, with no threats looming on the horizon. Throughout the summer the Elsinore Roads were chock-a-block with ships on their way in and out of the Sound. On 2 August a convoy arrived from Hull, escorted by the naval sloop *Favourite*. But the following day a Royal Navy cutter came hurtling down from the north under every scrap of sail she could carry. She was bearing despatches to the convoy commodore. An hour later every British ship in the Elsinore Roads had weighed anchor and was sailing northwards under the protective wing of the *Favourite*.

The interpretation considered most likely in Copenhagen was that relations between Britain and Russia had deteriorated even further. But on 6 August rumours started flying that a Danish convoy had been engaged by British warships. The next afternoon Wedel Jarlsberg's courier arrived with reports on the *Freya* affair and Lord Whitworth's mission, but not mentioning that his mission was to be supported by a powerful British squadron.

The convoy conflict with Britain had thus become a reality. The Danish government reacted immediately, and the decision Crown Prince Frederik and his closest advisers made on the morning of 8 August showed clearly that Denmark had no intention of abandoning its policy of offensive neutrality.

Six Danish ships-of-the-line, two 80s, two 74s and two 64s, were immediately ordered to clear for action. Seamen were called up across the kingdom. Danish merchant seamen aboard ships making passage through the Sound were pressed into naval duty. The squadron of four ships-of-the-line already at sea was ordered to assemble with all haste south of Elsinore. And the naval brig *Sarpen* was sent to the Skaw to serve as the eyes of the fleet.

Such military preparations could not be hidden from sight. Nor, indeed, should they be; they were a demonstration of Denmark's decisiveness. But the political decisions reached that same morning, and which were to have a crucial effect on later developments, were kept very secret. In the Privy Council Crown Prince Frederik obtained the signature of the King on an order to the envoy in St. Petersburg. Niels Rosenkrantz was to reassure the Tsar that Denmark would defend the principle of the inviolability of neutral convoys but that it would need Russia's help in so doing. He was also to request the Tsar to accept the leadership of a League of Armed Neutrality.

The order was sent by courier on 9 August via Stockholm and by the fast naval cutter *Svanen*, which had been placed at Rosenkrantz's disposal as despatch vessel.

The Danish government had consciously burned their bridges behind them. Now they awaited the arrival of Lord Whitworth and news of whether the Tsar was willing to place the military might of Russia firmly behind the Danish policy of offensive neutrality.

Chapter 3

DRESS REHEARSAL FOR WAR

Late on the afternoon of 11 August 1800 the *Andromeda* dropped anchor off Hellebœk. Whitworth went ashore and arrived in Copenhagen the same evening, when he was briefed by Anthony Merry on the Danish preparations of the fleet and on the despatch of the courier to St. Petersburg. Whitworth saw immediately the tactics he had to adopt. He knew that an answer from the Tsar could not be expected before the first week of September at the earliest and he knew that Count Bernstorff would therefore do everything in his power to drag negotiations out as long as possible. Whitworth's job was to press the Danes into accepting Britain's demands before a positive answer from Russia could encourage their resistance and strengthen their position at the negotiating table.

Whitworth's opening arguments at his first meeting at the Danish Foreign Minister's country residence outside Copenhagen were blunt and candid. After the usual introductory pleasantnesses, and after the two had spelled out their legal positions on the convoy conflict, Whitworth told Bernstorff that a British fleet was on its way to the Sound. He also informed him that he was considering presenting the Danish government with an ultimatum.

This put Bernstorff in the position of having to fight on two fronts. On the one side he had to draw things out, with a negotiator who had already showed that he knew time was of critical importance. And on the other he had to persuade Crown Prince Frederik to agree to the concessions, because, although Bernstorff had, on several occasions, been grateful to make good use of the Crown Prince's renowned intransigence in diplomatic negotiations, his greatest problem at the moment was that same intransigence towards the convoy conflict. In the midst of the hectic preparations on 9 August the Crown Prince had taken the time to write a personal letter of commendation to Commander Krabbe, expressing his great approval of his action: "You behaved like a true Dane".

The Crown Prince had reacted strongly to Britain's overt display of military superiority in the convoy conflict. He expressed his indignation to one of his closest advisers towards "that pompous British ministry". He was aware of the danger to Danish ships on the oceans of the world but was confident Denmark could disrupt Britain's trade in the Baltic. "If Pitt and Grenville think I can be easily scared, they're wrong. I have right on my side and I'm the leader of the Danish people. I will defy them in everything." Such statements proved to be more than brief tantrums. When he was later told of the arrival of the Royal Navy, he declared that he would sooner see Copenhagen in flames than surrender his independence.

The Crown Prince's intransigence was a political reality. His patriotic fervour for Denmark's prestige was well known but it did not make matters any easier for the Danish Foreign Minister. Whitworth, though, had let the Foreign Minister know from the start that he would not tolerate any delaying tactics and that the Crown Prince was Bernstorff's problem, not his. Whitworth was waiting only for the arrival of the squadron before he presented his ultimatum. And the moment he heard that Vice Admiral Dickson and his ships were off Kullen, a spit of land on the Swedish coast just north of Elsinore, he played his trump card.

Copenhagen threatened with bombardment
Dickson's squadron comprised nine ships-of-the-line, five gun brigs and four bomb ships. On 20 August it passed Kronborg, with a courteous exchange of gun salutes, and anchored south of Elsinore – and south of the four ships-of-the-line under Captain Lütken, thus cutting them off from Copenhagen. One of the large British ships continued further south down the Sound, anchoring off Sophienberg, some 25 km north of Copenhagen. She was the ship-of-the-line *Romney*. On 21 August Whitworth boarded HMS *Romney* to plan, in conference with Vice Admiral Dickson and the *Romney*'s captain, Sir Home Popham, the show of power intended to break Bernstorff's and the Crown Prince's resistance.

Their plan was to leave the eight ships-of-the-line up at Elsinore but in a position where they could prevent the Danish squadron from making a dash for Copenhagen. The *Romney* was to anchor in Copenhagen Roads and between the two, the bomb ships and gun brigs would be stationed to act as a signals line. The bomb ships were deliberately designated as the southernmost vessels, closest to Copenhagen, as a clear warning of what Denmark could expect if it ignored the British ultimatum. Whitworth had left that on the table the same morning he drove up to Sophienberg; if Britain's demands were not met within eight days, Whitworth and the entire British mission would leave Copenhagen.

Diplomatic etiquette prevented him from specifying what would happen in that case, but the implication was obvious. And the immediate reaction from the Danes was to reorganize their military strategy from one of offensive political display of naval power to defensive measures in the capital against a British bombardment.

Up to that time all military activity had been concentrated on preparing a squadron of battleships to demonstrate Denmark's resoluteness, both to Britain and to the neutral countries. When news of the *Freya* affair reached Copenhagen the commander of the naval dockyard Holmen had been ordered to make ready six of the best and most powerful ships-of-the-line in the fleet – the *Neptunus* and *Valdemar* with 80 guns, the two 74s *Odin* and *Justitia*, and the two 64s *Ditmarsken* and *Prinsesse Louise Augusta*. On the arrival of Dickson's squadron off Kullen, he received further orders to prepare seven more – the 74s *Kronprinsesse Marie*, *Trekroner*, *Indfødsretten*, *Fyn* and *Sjælland*, and the two 60s, *Dannebrog* and *Holsten*.

At that time defence of Copenhagen had a lower priority. But on 14 August Captain Lützow was put in charge of the King's Deep defences; three days later a plan was presented by the permanent Defence Board. The original plan from 1784 for three sea forts was not realized due to shortage of funds. All there was in August 1800 was a single, half-built fort, Trekroner, on the northern tip of the Refshale Shoal. So the Defence Plan of 17 August was very much a hasty improvization. Trekroner was to be manned by 200 soldiers with tents and digging tools. Defence of the entrance to the Kronløbet Channel was delegated to Trekroner Fort, two block-ships and a Fleet Battery to be moored in the location of the planned Stubben Fort. Where Prøvesten Fort should have been at the southern entrance to the King's Deep, two converted cavalry barges were moored.

It was this defence of the capital that assumed first priority after the delivery of the British ultimatum on the morning of 21 August.

But it was a hopeless race against time. On the same day captains were appointed for the blockships *Jylland* and *Mars* and for the converted cavalry barges *Rendsborg* and *Nyborg*; the third, *Aggershus*, was not under command until 25 August. Fleet Batteries 1, with 20 guns, and 2 and 3, both with 8, were ordered to be moved to Trekroner Fort harbour. And the Chief of Police of Copenhagen was ordered to press 1,400 men.

Whilst carpenters and craftsmen at Holmen worked day and night on the ships needed to defend the capital, further north in Elsinore a war of nerves was being waged between Vice Admiral Dickson and Captain Lütken. Twice the Danish squadron had weighed anchor to move to a position between the British and Copenhagen. And twice the British ships had followed suit and anchored south of Lütken's men-of-war, with full naval courtesy being observed and gun salutes given as they passed each other. On the afternoon of 25 August Lieutenant Roepstorff went aboard the *Prinsesse Sophie Frederikke* with orders for Lütken to sail down to Copenhagen and join the defences. He weighed anchor immediately and this time the British did nothing to stop him. That same afternoon the Danish battle squadron dropped anchor on the Copenhagen Roads, where there was not a defending ship to be seen.

Whitworth's ultimatum expired on 28 August. The day before, Lützow had to report that the guns on Trekroner Fort were in such a dangerous condition that they would probably kill their crews if fired. Not until the evening of that day, 27 August, were the first ships of the defence line – the blockship *Mars* and the converted cavalry barge *Rendsborg* – warped out through the boom. The next day they were joined by the blockship *Jylland* and the converted cavalry barge *Nyborg*, picking up their detachment of soldiers on the way at Toldboden, the Customs Quay. And not until 29 August was the last cavalry barge, *Aggershus*, ready to be moved out of the dockyard.

So when the British ultimatum reached its deadline not one of the Danish defence ships was on station and on 28 August Copenhagen was totally defenceless. When Sir Home Popham assured the First Lord of the Admiralty that the British bomb vessels would be capable of burning and destroying Copenhagen and the Danish fleet, his claims were therefore hardly wild exaggeration. At around the same time, Lützow and the Danish Government arrived at the same assessment – the capital, the dockyard and the fleet were utterly defenceless against bombardment. At least at such short notice.

The Bernstorff finesse

When Whitworth met with Foreign Minister Bernstorff again, after the presentation of the British ultimatum and after the demonstration of British sea power, it was obvious that Bernstorff was now more pliable. It was also obvious that he was more amenable towards the British solution of suspending all Danish convoys. In other words, he fell back on the tactic of the policy of defensive neutrality – of preserving its principles at the same time as waiting for more favourable circumstances. But it was also clear that the Crown Prince was not yet prepared to capitulate and the Foreign Minister needed a little leeway. When it came to making concessions in matters of prestige Whitworth was forthcoming; but on questions of real significance, such as Denmark's right to lead convoys through the Mediterranean, he was uncompromising. It was not until the evening of 26 August that the two could arrive at a mutually acceptable solution – a provisional convention, whose principle issues were to be drafted at a later stage and by which Denmark undertook to suspend all convoys until the two governments had reached agreement on those principles.

This was precisely the model Lord Grenville preferred himself. With this in mind, Whitworth willingly gave his consent for the Danish Foreign Minister to draft the text of the convention and for it to be signed *after* the expiry of the ultimatum. On the morning of 29 August the two negotiators were ready to meet and sign, seal and deliver the provisional treaty. It had already been approved by the Danish government and on arrival in London was quickly ratified by the British, who had thus got what they wanted in the first place.

Or had they? Lords Whitworth and Grenville thought so. But the truth of the matter is that they had walked right into the Danish Foreign Minister's trap. During the long and difficult negotiations Whitworth had specified that Danish convoys should be suspended until Britain and Denmark, *after the war*, could reach agreement on the principle issue. In the actual text of the treaty, Bernstorff had changed *after the war* to read *after later negotiations*. Such an amendment did not escape the eagle eye of an experienced diplomat like Whitworth, but he saw it as a change in Britain's favour, allowing them, in terms of diplomacy, to postpone such negotiations indefinitely. And both Whitworth and Grenville were convinced that such wording had put one of the most powerful players in a League of Armed Neutrality out of the game.

Bernstorff, however, had known just what he was doing. He was expecting a positive reaction from Russia to Denmark's proposal for the formation of such a League and, as soon as that was a reality, Denmark could demand, with the full support of the League, that Britain begin negotiations on the convoy principle immediately.

With the provisional treaty of 29 August 1800 Denmark had stuck to its policy of offensive neutrality. Bernstorff considered Britain to be in the political wilderness and hard pressed in military terms. He thus predicted that Britain would have to give in to the purely political pressure from the League and, at the same time, recognize once and for all the contentious principles of neutrality, including the immunity of neutral convoys.

THE LEAGUE OF ARMED NEUTRALITY

The Danish reaction to the *Freya* affair, then, was to request the Tsar to establish a League of Armed Neutrality. The proposal arrived in St. Peterburg at a particularly auspicious time, on the heels, in fact, of the bad news that the two former enemies, France and Austria, had made peace, an event which markedly tipped the balance of European power in their favour. Tsar Paul now *needed* the support of the neutral countries. As head of a bloc of neutral states, he would be in the best position to promote Russia's interests in the eyes of France, Austria and Britain.

On 4 September a courier arrived in Copenhagen with a formal invitation from the Tsar to join forces and establish a League of Armed Neutrality. There was also news from Rosenkrantz that the Tsar fully approved of the strategy of renegotiation with Britain of the convoy principle as soon as possible and that the Tsar would give such talks his every support.

Thus far the policy of offensive neutrality had been a success for the Danes. But on 10 October the Tsar made a decision that changed everything – and that was to seal Denmark's fate. The Russian despot made secret political advances to the French First Consul. The objective in terms of major politics was to form an alliance between the Tsar and Bonaparte that would allow them together to dictate their will on the rest of the continent of Europe.

And Denmark and Sweden, in such a constellation, would become buffer states, Russia's first line of defence against Britain.

The Danish and Swedish governments were informed of the Tsar's approach to France, but not of his long-term objectives. They could hardly fail to notice how enthusiastic the Tsar's ministers had suddenly become to finalize negotiations of the formation of the League of Armed Neutrality, nor that they were showing unusual interest in its military strength.

The draft presented by the Russian Foreign Minister on 14 October reiterated the principles of free ship, free goods and of respecting only effective blockades. Nonetheless, it represented a greater challenge to Britain than in 1780 by containing a much more restrictive definition of contraband and the principle of the inviolability of neutral convoys. Most interesting of all, however, was the Russian draft of a number of secret clauses in the League's articles. They concerned the battleships and frigates the members were to put at its disposal. Denmark and Sweden were allowed to fill in the *numbers* themselves, but the Russians left them in no doubt as to the approximate figure acceptable. By the spring of 1801 Russia was to have ready for action fifteen ships-of the line and five frigates, Denmark eight battleships and two frigates and Sweden seven battleships and three frigates. Rosenkrantz interjected that a squadron of thirty battleships looked more like a precursor for war than neutrality. And his fears were confirmed when the Russians asked directly whether the Danes themselves would be able to block the Sound to the British fleet, or whether they would need the help of Russia and Sweden.

This militarization of the League of Armed Neutrality was diametrically opposed to Denmark's wishes and interests. On the other hand, it generated little concern in Copenhagen, where the Crown Prince obtained the King's approval on 4 November for Rosenkrantz formally to finalize Denmark's membership of the League of Armed Neutrality, secret clauses and all.

On that very day things went wild in St. Petersburg. The Tsar placed an embargo on all British ships in Russian ports.

Chained to Russia

Tsar Paul was Grand Master of the Order of St John and the Knights of Malta and it was his belief that the British had given their word that, when the island was won back from the French, Russian troops were to be part of the occupying force. On 5 September the

French garrison in Valletta surrendered to the British, who thereupon occupied Malta alone. This incensed the Tsar enough to order the embargo and to report to Lord Grenville that Britain's standpoint on the Malta issue would have serious consequences for relations between the two countries.

Denmark and Sweden were quickly involved in the diplomatic crisis. On 9 November the Tsar 'invited' – the word order was not used – the King of Sweden to St. Petersburg to discuss matters of mutual defence interest. The following day he formally requested Denmark, with subtly veiled threats, to make ready for an attack by the British in the spring of 1801 and to deny its fleet passage into the Baltic.

The embargo and the military demands were cause for grave concern in the Danish government, which now had to face up to the likelihood of war with Britain. But the view was also unanimous that it could hardly say no. Denmark was Russia's ally in the 1773 Alliance and Russia was still the only power that could, and would, come to Denmark's assistance against Sweden and that could, and would, provide a guarantee that Norway would remain within the Danish monarchy. In any conflict between Russia and Britain – in which Russia wanted access to the Baltic neatly corked up, and in which Britain would try and force passage through the Sound and the Great Belt – Denmark could not simply declare herself neutral. If she were to meet her long-term security political objectives, Denmark had no option but to go along with the Russian terms. In that concrete situation, she had to put her complete loyalty behind the League of Armed Neutrality, an organization whose formation Denmark herself had proposed.

And all this despite the fact that the Danish government at that time viewed the League with growing scepticism.

Prussia was forced to accept the Tsar's 'invitation'. And once Prussia had bowed to the Tsar's demands to confiscate the huge British warehouse stocks in Hamburg and occupy Hanover, the ancestral home of George III, it would be operating in areas at the southern border of the Danish kingdom, areas in which Berlin and Copenhagen had a clear conflict of interests. To make the Danish government's Gordian knot complete, it knew that the Prussians were doing whatever they could in St. Petersburg to sow seeds of doubt as to Denmark's political credibility as a member of the League of Armed Neutrality.

Denmark's relations with Sweden became even more tense. The

Swedish government, too, was energetic in its efforts to discredit Denmark in the eyes of the Tsar. They also did what they possibly could to increase the Tsar's interest in the defence of the Danish passages into the Baltic; they wanted not only to restore the duty-free privilege in the Sound that they had lost in 1720 but also to get a share of the Sound toll themselves. What was much more serious, during his visit to St. Petersburg, the Swedish king had suggested to the Tsar that Sweden should be given Norway, with Denmark being compensated with a small area of northern Germany. It was not the Swedish king's proposal in itself that came as such a shock to the Danish government (it really expected little better); it was the Tsar's hesitation in rejecting such a proposal until his advisers had pointed out the dangers inherent in supporting a country that was Russia's traditional enemy.

Relations with Russia were also a problem for Denmark. It was now apparent to the Danish government that Russia was using Denmark as a pawn on the chessboard of its own conflict with Britain and in its struggle for power on the continent of Europe. It also became apparent that, to the Tsar, the defence of the League of Armed Neutrality was synonymous with the defence of the Baltic and Russia. The Tsar himself had laconically drawn Rosenkrantz's attention to the fact that the ice thawed last in Russian naval dockyards, so Denmark would be on its own if the British chose to attack in April 1801. On 16 December, when Rosenkrantz signed the Treaty of Neutrality with Russia in the Mikhailovsk Palace, and a month later, when King Christian VII of Denmark ratified it, the Danish government had many excellent reasons to take a gloomy view of the future of the League of Armed Neutrality, and of Denmark herself. Theoretically Denmark was an equal member of the League, whose four members had committed themselves to defending the principles of neutrality that Denmark had been campaigning for over the last century and more. In practice the League was something else entirely. Three small nations with clear conflicts of interests had committed themselves to supporting the Tsar in his conflict with Britain over the Malta affair and in his guardianship of Russian interests throughout the continent of Europe. At that time any well-educated person was familiar with Voltaire's ironic words about the Holy Roman Empire – it was neither Holy, Roman nor an Empire. When the pages of the calendar turned from 1800 to 1801 little political vision was needed to see that the League of Armed Neutrality was neither a league, armed nor neutral.

Of all the members of the so-called League, Denmark was by far the most vulnerable. The planned formidable naval squadron of the League could not put to sea until May or June of 1801 at the very earliest. But Britain had let it be known at the beginning of the year that it would respond to this blatant challenge to its superiority at sea with war and that it would carry out a preemptive strike before the League's members could organize their united forces. And the nearest target for a British fleet action in the early spring of 1801 was known to all – Copenhagen.

BRITAIN STRIKES

On 29 August, when Count Bernstorff signed his name to the provisional convoy convention, the British government and the new envoy in Copenhagen, William Drummond, felt secure against a League of Armed Neutrality, at least a league with Denmark among its members.

But Drummond had not been in Copenhagen for more than a few days before he heard through the grapevine that not only was such a League being formed but that Denmark was a prospective member. He went post-haste to the Foreign Minister. And Bernstorff, for the first and last time, made use of the League to threaten Britain. He confirmed the envoy's supposition and tried to make Drummond understand the difficulty in refusing to support the Tsar in this matter.

Drummond reported this intelligence immediately to London. But Foreign Minister Grenville reacted not at all, either to the envoy or to Denmark. In the autumn of 1800 the overall situation of major politics was phenomenally complex, and Grenville knew that any reaction would be perceived as a sign of weakness that would be exploited politically by Britain's opponents.

Lord Grenville could afford to ignore Denmark with impunity, but he could not ignore Russia's provocation. He had no option other than to react to the Tsar's embargo. And that reaction revealed that it was the League of Armed Neutrality, and not the paltry Malta hiccup, that was the central issue. The decision to prepare for war was taken in London in the first few days of December and the Admiralty planned a major fleet operation for the spring of 1801. Lord Grenville refused any further negotiation with the Tsar until the embargo was lifted and diplomatic relations re-established. And the Cabinet planned its strategy against the League of Armed Neutrality – Denmark and Sweden should be threatened seriously enough to make them withdraw, whereafter the Prussians would probably pull out of their own accord. And the arch enemy, Russia, would stand alone.

On 16 December the self-same day the League of Armed Neutrality became a reality in St. Petersburg, Britain struck. Lord Grenville presented Denmark and Sweden with an ultimatum, and he did it in such a way that it was impossible for the two governments to contact each other before the deadline had passed. On the same day the Swedish envoy in London received the ultimatum at the same time that a courier left Downing Street for Copenhagen with an identical ultimatum.

He arrived in Copenhagen late in the afternoon of 27 December. Drummond was to demand a clear declaration of Denmark's relationship with the League of Armed Neutrality and give Denmark the choice of war or peace. And he was to inform Count Bernstorff that the courier would leave Copenhagen within seventy-two hours, whether he had received an answer or not.

On the evening of 27 December, therefore, the envoy contacted the Danish Foreign Minister and presented him with the option of remaining in or leaving the League of Armed Neutrality. The answer was in undiplomatic plain language. The Foreign Minister emphasized that the League was not directed against Britain and that Denmark's intentions were entirely peaceful, but that Denmark was, and intended to remain, a member of the League of Armed Neutrality.

Bernstorff knew exactly what he was doing and was fully aware of the consequences of his actions. As Drummond left through one door Bernstorff left through another and went straight to Crown Prince Frederik, who went to the Admiralty later that evening to sign the orders to prepare Copenhagen's defences against an attack in the spring of 1801.

Danish intransigence

Immediate action was taken in London as well. Lord Grenville had fully expected the Danes to collapse under threat, but if they did not, then war was inevitable. And on 13 January it became a reality, on that day the courier returned from Copenhagen. Grenville received the information that the Tsar was preparing for war and the Cabinet issued definitive orders. It placed embargoes on every Danish, Swedish and Russian vessel in British ports; it issued orders to apprehend merchantmen and men-of-war at sea belonging to those countries; it ordered Denmark's and Sweden's colonies to be occupied and it decided to take no action against Prussia in order to give them the opportunity voluntarily to withdraw from the League of Armed Neutrality. On 13 January the Cabinet decided that further diplomatic talks would be to no avail and that the country's most effective negotiators were now Admirals Parker and Nelson.

William Pitt's Cabinet had reacted decisively to the serious threat the League posed to Britain's position in high politics. Shortly afterwards, however, that same Cabinet was forced to resign over the issue of the political rights of Irish Catholics. The Danish Cabinet held their breath for a short while in the hope that the new Cabinet formed by Henry Addington would follow a more peaceful policy, but is was composed of Pitt's political cronies and the decision to meet the League of Armed Neutrality with force was upheld. This should not be misunderstood as meaning that Britain would reject a negotiated solution to the problem, but such talks would not be allowed to delay military preparations, nor spoil Britain's chances of taking on the members of the League one by one.

And Britain *did* make two attempts to reach a political solution with Denmark before the battleships did the talking. One was the result of an anonymous letter Lord Grenville received in mid-February. The clumsily worded letter implied that Crown Prince Frederik looked favourably upon a compromise on the principles of neutrality and that he wished to negotiate with a British envoy for an alliance and for urgent military assistance against Russia.

The British government was convinced the letter was from the Crown Prince's father-in-law, Prince Karl of Hesse, who was known to have tried his hand before at private foreign policy in a similarly unhelpful manner. As one of its last deeds, Pitt's Cabinet decided to send a spokesman. The choice fell on the 34-year-old Member of Parliament Nicholas Vansittart, who had enough political prestige to be received in Copenhagen and little enough that Britain would not lose face if his mission failed.

Vansittart left immediately to visit Prince Karl in Slesvig, only to discover that the Prince denied any knowledge of the letter and urged the British envoy to request an audience with the Crown

Prince in Copenhagen. Vansittart decided to follow his advice, and met an icy reception in Copenhagen. His request for an audience was rejected out of hand and all he achieved was a conversation with Count Bernstorff on 14 March. During this talk the Danish Foreign Minister adopted a demonstratively unyielding position. He refused to recognize Vansittart as an official representative before Britain had lifted the embargo on Denmark's ships and those of her allies; he refused to turn his back on Russia and he refused to discuss principles of neutrality without involving the other members of the League. And when Vansittart dropped the bombshell that a powerful British fleet was already on its way to Denmark, Bernstorff dismissed it out of hand. Which brought that conversation, and Vansittart's mission, to an end.

The second British attempt to defuse the situation was made a week later. On 20 March it was known in Copenhagen that the Fleet had reached the Kattegat. That day a Royal Navy frigate arrived in Elsinore under a flag of truce and that evening Lieutenant McCulloch delivered an ultimatum from the new Foreign Minister, Lord Hawkesbury, to the British envoy. Drummond was once again to demand an agreement with Denmark on the principles of neutrality and free passage for the Fleet through the Danish straits. If the Danes were amenable to those demands Britain was willing to enter a defence alliance with Denmark, and twenty British ships-of-the-line would patrol the Baltic alongside ten Danish ships for as long as the conflict with Russia lasted. Denmark was given forty-eight hours to give an answer and they were told a refusal would mean war.

On the evening of 20 March Drummond sent Lord Hawkesbury's note to Count Bernstorff and informed him that, if the demands were rejected, he would have respectfully to request his passports the very next day.

In many respects the situation that day was similar to that of August the previous year. Then, too, a superior British fleet had been in Danish waters; then, too, the Danish government had given in. In 1801 the Fleet was more than twice as strong, but this time the Danish government did *not* give in. And on the morning of 21 March Drummond received the answer from the Danes. It was a blank refusal. Included in the note were his passports.

With this development the last political card had been played. The same day Drummond, Vansittart and the British mission left the Danish capital and boarded the Fleet anchored off Kullen.

Vansittart informed Admiral Sir Hyde Parker that he could regard the Danish refusal as a declaration of war. Crown Prince Frederik made the same declaration to his generals. Denmark was now at war with Great Britain.

The Danish government had not only rejected all Britain's demands and proposals, it had done so with unprecedented inflexibility and single-mindedness. This behaviour was not due to any continuing obligations to the League of Armed Neutrality and its principles, nor out of any feelings of loyalty towards Russia, Sweden or Prussia, nor was it out of any falsely optimistic hopes of the outcome of a military confrontation. It had simply chosen the lesser of two evils: one was war with Britain, a war Denmark knew it would lose; the other was the disintegration of the state. In March 1801 Denmark was gripped tight in the jaws of major politics, with these two options alone to choose between – and the lesser of the two evils was war with Britain.

THE IRON GRIP OF MAJOR POLITICS

The fear that the Danish monarchy as an independent state would disappear from the map of the world was no panic reaction. In March 1801 it was a very real threat.

Nobody had forced Denmark to introduce a policy of offensive neutrality in 1798. During its confrontation with Britain it had had more than one opportunity to change its offensive course, but stuck to its guns. The most recent and most noteworthy was the decision Denmark made in the *Freya* affair. Denmark got the League of Armed Neutrality it had begged for. And despite the fact that the Danish government had felt very uncomfortable with the Tsar's militarization of the League, and despite the fact that it had been extremely concerned about the prospect of an armed conflict with Britain, it had still remained an active member. When the King ratified the Treaty of Neutrality with Russia in the Privy Council on 16 January the government had been unanimous in its belief that the country's dependence on Russia gave them no alternative. If Denmark were to break with the Tsar at that point they ran the risk of his giving Sweden a free hand in the contentious issue of Norway.

But in January 1801 the prospect of war with Britain became a certainty. And in March, when Drummond and Vansittart offered political and military alliance, Denmark was forced to review its policy of offensive neutrality. But they still said no. And kept on saying no.

They did so because the very existence of the Danish monarchy was at stake. The political overtures between Russia and France made in the autumn of 1800 had borne fruit in January 1801.

On 3 December Austria had been soundly thrashed by the French at Hohenlinden; General Moreau's cavalry had pushed forward to within 60 km of Vienna and Austria had been forced into making peace with France, at the price of surrendering its status as a major power, both political and military. Thus only two major players remained in the political arena of the continent of Europe – Russia and France. And in the first few months of 1801 a tremor of fear passed over the capitals of Europe at seeing the Russian despot and the French First Consul forging a political alliance similar to the one later made at Tilsit in 1807 between Napoleon and Alexander I. Both rulers needed an alliance that would allow them, in unison, to dictate their wills across Europe, and both plotted to give as little as possible and take as much as possible. Around New Year their couriers crossed on the slush-covered roads between St. Petersburg and Paris. And the governments of Europe adjusted to a conflict with Britain, which was the only item on their agenda the two rulers were actually able to agree on.

On the same day that the Tsar's courier arrived in Paris with the final papers of acceptance of a political alliance the French Foreign Minister had been engaged in serious talks with the Danish envoy. Talleyrand informed him that a political agreement between France and Russia was imminent, and he issued an unambiguous warning: if Denmark were to enter any negotiations with Britain, she would cease to exist, but if, on the other hand, she took up the fight, it would result in honour and advantage to Denmark. A few days later Bonaparte himself gave the same message to the envoy, also informing him that he intended to force Prussia and Portugal to take an active part in the war against Britain on the side of Russia and France.

So it was a very worried Foreign Minister who informed the Privy Council at Amalienborg Palace on 6 February not only of the French-Russian development but also of its consequences for the Danish monarchy. The government agreed that Denmark had to take sides and indeed agreed on which side they should take. War with Britain would bring disastrous financial losses. But if Denmark patched up its differences with Britain and withdrew from the League of Armed Neutrality the monarchy would cease to exist as an independent state. With Russia's help, Sweden would take Norway, and France and Russia would push Prussia into occupying Holstein, Slesvig and Jutland. So the government reached the logical and unanimous conclusion that Denmark must choose war with Britain, and hope for their due reward when their allies proved victorious.

Three days later Austria signed an unconditional armistice drafted by the French. This put Prussia under immediate pressure from France and Russia to turn their backs on Britain. And in March 1801 every port on the continent, from Archangel to the Adriatic, was either closed to British shipping or about to be.

Neither Christian Bernstorff nor his counterparts in the capitals of Europe expected the understanding between Bonaparte and the Tsar to last for ever; there were simply too many conflicts of interest between them. But, as long as it did last, their will was law throughout the continent. And no country could refuse to take part in their joint war against Britain.

The Danish government had all the information it needed and there was full and complete agreement between Crown Prince Frederik, his Foreign Minister and the Ministers of the Privy Council on what Denmark should do in that immediate situation. In March 1801 Denmark had run out of options; it would have to join the war against Britain and demonstrate its undying loyalty to the Tsar and Bonaparte. The Crown Prince's dismissal of Vansittart's request for an audience, Bernstorff's complete rejection of the British envoy's demands and threats, and his point blank refusal on 20 March to negotiate any further with him, even with the Fleet waiting impatiently in the Kattegat, were thus well-considered and politically consistent acts.

Not a shot had yet been fired. But war was now a brutal reality.

Chapter 4

Britain attacks

Strategy and tactics

When Britain made the decision in December 1800 to go to war with the member states of the League of Armed Neutrality, the cabinet had no strategy of how to do so. The picture of the League, and thus also the military situation on the continent, was still too vague.

The first military plans were to send a fleet to the Baltic against Russia. The last time a British fleet had been in action in the Baltic was in 1726, when Sir Richard Wager, in company with a Danish squadron, had blocked the Gulf of Finland. So, for the Royal Navy, the Baltic Sea was more or less uncharted waters. The first step the First Lord took, therefore, was to gather information from men who had specialist knowledge of the Russian fleet and the passage through the Great Belt. On hearing this, the Commander-in-Chief of the Channel Fleet, Lord St. Vincent, warmly recommended his second in command, Vice Admiral Sir Hyde Parker. During the Ochakov crisis in 1791 he had been part of the team to plan the action against Russia and the passage through the Great Belt, and was therefore, in this respect, the most knowledgeable officer in the Royal Navy.

In his consultations with Lord Spencer, Parker proved to be a shrewd and far-sighted strategist. Any action against Russia, he stressed, would encounter two problems – the navigation and the need for special vessels. The waters were shallow and difficult to navigate, and the enemy would douse the lights ashore and remove the buoys. The Navy would require experienced pilots, which meant small vessels for surveying and marking shoals and rocks. The enemy would also employ countless small ships – gunboats, galleys and fireships. The British would need the same variety of vessels – four to six bomb vessels, six fireships and a handful of converted coal barges with a draft of between eleven and thirteen feet and a freeboard of four feet, that could be fitted with eighteen to twenty 24-pounders to protect the smaller ships and carry out raids on low-lying batteries and ships hiding behind moles. The Fleet was also to carry special anchors and anchor cables.

After the new year the Cabinet had a much clearer picture of the League of Armed Neutrality and the relations between its members. It began to look as if a major fleet action against Russia would not be necessary after all; perhaps the League would simply fall apart if one of its members were to be at the receiving end of a fast and overwhelming attack. And the sights were shifted from Russia to Denmark.

The idea for a short, sharp and ruthless raid was not the First Lord's. Lord Spencer was concerned, as he had been during the *Freya* affair, about over-stretching British naval resources more than they were already. The idea came from Prime Minister William Pitt's dynamic Minister of War, Henry Dundas.

He briefed his ministerial colleagues on the global significance of the League of Armed Neutrality and put it into overall political perspective. He acknowledged that the Navy was stretched to the limit: the blockade of French, Spanish and Dutch naval ports was tying down a large share of its ships and Britain still needed a considerable fleet to repel any attempt to invade the British Isles, as well as resisting surprise attacks in the Mediterranean, the West Indies and at the Cape of Good Hope. He was firmly convinced that the military turning point in the war between Britain and France would come in the summer of 1801. If Britain did not send a large fleet to the Baltic as soon as the weather allowed and demolish the League of Armed Neutrality, by capturing or destroying the Danish fleet, then they would lose the war they had been fighting for eight years. He conceded that to follow this plan would mean reducing British fleet strengths across the board, weakening the Channel Fleet and the blockade of Brest, and indeed putting ships to sea that did not fully meet the exacting requirements of the Admiralty. But the Baltic Fleet *must* be given first priority and it must be made so powerful that victory was a certainty. Dundas ended his persuasive argument by stating that he himself was confident that it was more than feasible for Britain to have a fleet in Danish waters as soon as early March, a fleet, furthermore, that would be more than capable of capturing or destroying the Danish navy and thereby activating the detonator that would blow up the League of Armed Neutrality.

OPERATION COPENHAGEN

The Minister of War convinced his colleagues that Britain could win the Revolutionary Wars at Copenhagen. The Cabinet reached three decisive conclusions at its meeting on 13 January: an embargo on all Danish, Swedish and Russian merchantmen in British ports; the apprehension at sea of their merchantmen and men-of-war; and the occupation of colonies belonging to Denmark and Sweden – Tranquebar and Serampore in India, and the Danish and Swedish islands in the West Indies. Another burning question was resolved – who was to command the operation. Commander-in-Chief of the Baltic Fleet would be Admiral Sir Hyde Parker; his second would be Vice Admiral Lord Nelson.

The combination was well considered. Parker would make a politically reliable Commander-in-Chief and Nelson would ensure the victory. But these two naval officers were as different in background and temperament as chalk and cheese, and the friction between them was to have a decisive influence on the operations of the Baltic Fleet.

Sixty-one-year-old Sir Hyde Parker came from an old and influential naval family. He had recently returned home from the West Indies, where as admiral of the station, the prize money he had collected had made him a wealthy man. The day before Christmas Eve he had married the eighteen-year-old daughter of a fellow admiral. As Commander-in-Chief West Indies Station, and as second-in-command of the Channel Fleet, he had acquired a reputation of being fussy and finicky. His opinions and behaviour were typical of someone brought up in the pre-Revolutionary era.

Nelson had served most of his career during the wars against France. At that time, he was 42, and in the previous three years had won more admiration and envy than most people in an entire lifetime. This skinny son of a Norfolk parson, now blind in one eye and minus his right arm, had made his reputation in the battle with the Spanish fleet at Cape St. Vincent, and after his victory at the Nile against Bonaparte's Mediterranean fleet he was the darling of the nation. But in the Admiralty, and among his fellow admirals, there was concern about his cavalier attitude to orders. And his private life was public scandal. His relationship with Lady Hamilton, whom he had met during his long period of duty with the court of Naples, was common knowledge. On 30 January 1801 Emma Hamilton gave birth to his daughter Horatia and on 4 March, just before the Baltic Fleet set sail, Nelson separated from his wife permanently.

Many knew Nelson, but few saw the same man. His ambition knew no limit; he was a hopeless hypochondriac and yet as tough as nails when he needed to be; he was impossibly impatient and had difficulty concealing it; he switched, in the blink of an eye, from suspicion to blind faith, from hostility to friendliness. He had an intuitive understanding of the human condition and a unique ability to generate confidence and inspire not only his officers but the ordinary Jack Tar, who idolized the little naval hero for his great sense of effect and drama. But even in such a cadre of naval officers as cliquish and riddled with political intrigue as the Royal Navy was at that time, his disloyalty to his superiors was legendary. Before he even met his new commanding officer, his opinion of Hyde Parker was critical to the point of hysteria.

On 27 January the British public read that Sir Hyde Parker had been appointed as Commander-in-Chief, with Nelson as his second-in-command, of a squadron intended, as it was enigmatically expressed, for 'a particular service'. The Admiralty immediately set to work in pruning the Channel Fleet, and thereby easing the British blockade of the French and Spanish fleets in Brest. The Channel Fleet had to give up two three-deckers and nine two-deckers to the embryo fleet destined for the Danish capital.

In mid-February the strategy was complete. A month earlier both Lords Spencer and St. Vincent had been thinking in terms of a massive amphibious operation against the Danish fleet's home dockyard at Nyholm, involving no fewer than 10,000 men. And even in early February St. Vincent believed that Parker would need 20,000 elite troops under the command of a skilful general if they were to have any chance of success, and that bomb ships could simply not be used against Copenhagen. But such thoughts of a grand invasion were dropped when the Minister of War drafted the final orders on 23 February.

Parker's orders were clear and very detailed. A fleet of at least twenty ships-of-the-line, accompanied by frigates and minor vessels, was to be despatched to Copenhagen immediately. As soon as the fleet had rounded the Skaw Parker was instructed to detach a ship with instructions from the British Foreign Minister to the envoy in Copenhagen and inform him the fleet was on its way. The envoy was then to give the Danes a deadline of 48 hours to accede to Britain's demands. Parker had been given a copy of these instructions and was ordered to position his forces in such a way as to facilitate his military objectives.

If the Danish government rejected the ultimatum he was to take or destroy the Danish fleet and as much as possible of the stores and supplies in its shore establishments, and to seize any ship flying the Danish, Swedish or Russian flags. As the British government was anxious to spare Copenhagen the consequences of bombardment of military targets, Parker was given leave, after the outbreak of hostilities, to inform the Danish military commanders, and if at all possible the civilian population, that he was willing to show mercy; on one condition – that the Danish fleet and its entire arsenal were handed over to the British.

Having done this, he was to wait in the Sound with his fleet for further operation orders in the Baltic then still being planned.

So the prime objective of the expedition was to take or destroy the Danish fleet. The means by which it would be achieved was bombardment, or threat of bombardment, of the capital. The soldiers being transported by the Fleet were not intended for use in amphibious operations as such, but to storm forts such as Trekroner.

The Fleet puts to sea

On 25 February Parker received instructions from the Admiralty to convey himself to the assembly point for the Baltic Fleet, the Norfolk port of Great Yarmouth, and there hoist his flag and make preparations to get the Fleet under way. He complied immediately. He sent orders to Nelson, who was then in Portsmouth, to get the Baltic Fleet's two three-deckers, eleven two-deckers and sundry minor vessels to Yarmouth and pick up the thirteen shallow-draft special operations vessels, at anchor off the Downs, on the way. On 26 February Parker left London with his young bride and two days later arrived at Yarmouth, where they installed themselves in the Wrestler's Arms inn. Parker's flagship, HMS *London*, was still in Portsmouth and he hoisted his flag on the two-decker *Ardent*.

So the admiral had arrived – but not his fleet.

Time was a critical factor in the British strategy. The naval dockyards at Portsmouth, Chatham and Sheerness were therefore working round the clock to make the ships ready. And the dockyard workers' attempts to exploit the urgency of the situation by labour disputes for a pay rise were nipped in the bud. St. Vincent, who had recently succeeded Lord Spencer as First Lord, summarily dismissed dockyard representatives and cracked the whip even harder. In Portsmouth, Nelson worked incessantly to get his squadron to sea. At last, on the morning of 28 February, the troops could be embarked – 780 men from the 49th Regiment of Foot and 114 men from the Corps of Riflemen under the command of Lieutenant Colonel the Hon. William Stewart, who was quartered on board Nelson's flagship, the *St. George*. As their preparations were completed, the ships set sail, singly or in groups, and made their way up the Channel.

When Parker hoisted his flag from the mainmast of the *Ardent* on 28 February there were very few of the ships of the Baltic Fleet off Yarmouth, but on 1 March they began to arrive, in dribs and drabs, from the various ports and naval dockyards – line-of-battle ships, frigates, brigs, bombships and bomb tenders. On the evening of 6 March the *St. George* arrived in company with five of the two-deckers from Portsmouth; three days later the *London* dropped anchor. The following morning the Commander-in-Chief of the Baltic Fleet's flag was transferred to his flagship. Later the same day Parker received orders to put to sea with what ships he had and not wait for late-comers. The general signal was made for all commanding officers to report on board the flagship and to prepare their ships for immediate passage. Meanwhile, Parker put the finishing touches to his orders for Rear Admirals Totty and Graves to follow the main fleet and join the Commander-in-Chief wherever they might find him – off the Skaw, in the Kattegat or the Sound.

He himself, however, remained ensconced ashore and his second-in-command was close to a nervous breakdown from sheer impatience.

Almost as soon as the anchor had dropped in the Yarmouth Roads on the morning of 7 March Nelson had gone ashore to report to his commanding officer. At 0800 precisely he marched through the front door of the Wrestler's Arms, together with Captain Thomas Masterman Hardy, his flag captain, and Colonel Stewart. Nelson had done nothing to conceal his disapproval of Parker's remaining ashore. When Nelson eventually met Parker and his Captain of the Fleet, William Domett, he was afire with the desire to get the Baltic Fleet to sea. He returned to his ship deeply frustrated over the fact that Parker had not shown him the confidence of informing him of the Fleet's destination or mission. As soon as he was back on board the *St. George*, he vented his feelings by writing to the Admiralty and informing them of his fears that Parker would delay departure for another two weeks.

It was this letter that lay behind the Admiralty's order to Parker to put to sea as soon as he had a favourable wind. On 10 March Parker had even ordered all his officers to remain aboard their ships, but stayed ashore himself. And there were rumours, which reached the ears of the Admiralty, that Lady Parker intended to give a ball on 13 March.

Lord St. Vincent reacted with fury. As First Lord he regarded the time factor as crucial. Yet all he got from Parker was a constant stream of paper – critical reports on the ships and their condition; reports that left the impression of a Commander-in-Chief who was dilatory, and who put regulations and safety before efficiency and urgency. These reports had irritated St. Vincent greatly and his patience was now at an end. In his usual direct fashion, he wrote a private and blistering letter to Parker; he had heard, he wrote, that the admiral was considering postponing departure until 13 March. He wanted to make it crystal clear that everything depended upon Parker carrying out his orders quickly and efficiently, that there was not a moment to spare and that just one hour's delay of the Fleet's departure, once the wind was in his favour, would have disastrous consequences for Parker's career.

St. Vincent wrote his broadside letter at 1430 on 11 March. The Admiralty courier rode as he had never ridden before and covered the 200 km from London to Yarmouth in just under seven hours. At about ten that evening Nelson could triumph in the fact that Sir Hyde Parker had finally gone aboard the *London* in a fit of pique, and that a general signal was given to shorten anchor at midnight and weigh at dawn.

With sunrise at 0530, the signal to weigh anchor was hoisted. One by one, the ships got under way. And at 0730 on 12 March, with the ships clear of the bar, Parker sent the signal to take up formation on the flagship.

The British *had* succeeded in putting together a powerful fleet. And they *had* succeeded in getting it to sea fast enough for them to seize the initiative and take on the members of the League of Armed Neutrality one by one.

The size of the fleet reflected the political and military importance the Cabinet attached to the League; it was one of the biggest battle fleets Britain had formed since Admiral Howe had defeated the French in the Atlantic on 1 June 1794. When Sir John Jervis had beaten the Spanish fleet off Cape St. Vincent in February 1797, he did it with just fifteen battleships; when Admiral Duncan vanquished the Dutch fleet off Camperdown in October 1797, he had seventeen; and when Nelson annihilated the French fleet at Aboukir Bay in 1798, he had fourteen.

The fleet that left the Yarmouth Roads on the morning of 12 March 1801 comprised seventeen battleships, four frigates, three brigs, nine gun brigs, three sloops, seven bombships and their tenders, two luggers, a fireship and a cutter. When it had rounded the Skaw and the last stragglers had caught up, Sir Hyde Parker commanded a fleet of twenty ships-of-the-line and almost twice that many smaller vessels.

The wind was out of the south-west. Course was set north-north-east. The destination was no longer a secret – they were heading for Copenhagen.

Destination Denmark

March was no month for conducting fleet operations in northern waters. It was dark. In the twelve hours of daylight the Fleet saw the sun only in sporadic glimpses behind the cloud cover; the ships were unable to make a noon sun sight and their position had to be estimated by dead reckoning. And it was bitterly cold. Snow fell almost every day; ice made ropes and canvas stiff and unmanageable; and it jammed the hundreds of blocks and tackles essential to the safe handling of the ship. The men who, until recently, had been serving in the Mediterranean were chilled to the marrow of their bones; those who had come from the Brest blockade begged to be back in the November storms of the Atlantic. Wherever their station, they were all used to the continual cacophony of noises aboard a ship – the incessant groaning of the hull and the shrill howl of wind in the rigging. But there was now a new sound the men of the Baltic Fleet would never forget – the constant bark of coughing, from the captain down to the youngest powder monkey.

The Commander-in-Chief had issued orders for the battleships to sail in three divisions, with the support vessels to their leeward. But it was one thing issuing orders and another following them in the storms that split the Fleet time and time again. A barrage of signals was sent from the *London* for the ships to keep their stations. But despite keeping a careful lookout and despite the almost continual shriek of bosun's calls piping the men on deck and sending them aloft to set or take in sails, it proved an impossible task to keep the Fleet together in the formation ordered. One day, indeed, Parker could see only half the ships in his command.

Parker fumbled his fleet forward with extreme caution. The cloud cover that was virtually unbroken from the first day made it impossible to fix their position accurately. On board the *London*, therefore, soundings were taken every half hour to determine the depth of water and nature of the seabed, so as to get a reasonable idea, by comparison with the chart, of where they were. Nelson was in a rage aboard the *St. George* at his superior's slowness and caution. As things turned out, Parker had every reason to proceed with care. Five days after leaving Yarmouth the Baltic Fleet was only hours away from becoming the worst naval disaster since the Spanish Armada.

On the evening of 17 March the window panes in the small fishing village of Hansted trembled to the sound of heavy guns rolling through the fog of the North Sea, barely three miles offshore. It was the signal shot from Parker to his fleet to wear ship and alter course from north-north-east to north-west. During the morning he had sent the brig *Cruizer* to the east to reconnoitre. Shortly after noon Captain Brisbane returned with the alarming news that he had sighted the summit of Bovbjerg High south-east by east, at a distance of only twelve miles. According to the navigation plan, the Baltic Fleet should by then have been well off Jammer Bay, on a safe course for the Skaw. But its actual position was some fifty miles to the south of that position, frighteningly close to the coast of Jutland. It was at the eleventh hour, therefore, that a new course was set, out to the safety of the open sea.

None of the fishermen of Hansted actually saw the British fleet. They heard only the phantom-like thud of their guns. Two days later, however, the people of the village of Hirtshals *did* see it, far out in Jammer Bay, heading for the Skaw.

As mentioned, Parker had received orders to get to sea immediately without waiting for stragglers at the Yarmouth Roads rendezvous point. During the passage, therefore, new ships caught up with them. A few hours after leaving Yarmouth the ship-of-the-line *Edgar* arrived and, later the same day, the two fireships *Alecto* and *Otter*. On 18 March Rear Admiral Graves arrived in the battle-ship *Defiance*, and some hours later, the battleship *Elephant*. The frigate *Amazon* joined the fleet at the Skaw and on 24 March the last two ships appeared over the horizon – the frigate *Jamaica* and the fireship *Zephyr*.

But one ship never made it – in contradiction to her name the ship-of-the-line *Invincible*. When she turned towards Yarmouth to pick up Parker's orders, she went aground on a sandbank and sank with the loss of the more than 400 on board – almost 150 more than the British casualties on 2 April.

Two of the smallest vessels had to leave the fleet. On the after-noon of 15 August the fireship *Alecto* sent the signal that she had sprung a leak. After the *London*'s carpenter had made the hazardous crossing to inspect the damage, Parker detached the lugger *Rover* to escort *Alecto* to the nearest harbour and then rejoin the force.

The fleet battled through foul weather for the whole of the first week. When it rounded the Skaw and turned down the Kattegat, it moderated somewhat, but only for a short while. A new gale whistled out of the west and the passage down the Swedish coast was laborious. During the passage the strong westerly gale blew the gun brig *Blazer* within range of Varberg Fort and Lieutenant Tiller was powerless to do anything other than surrender himself and his ship to the Swedes.

It was not until the evening of 22 March that the Fleet could anchor some 6 or 7 miles north-west of the Kullen peninsula on the coast of Sweden.

Turbot diplomacy

Bitter cold and frequent loss of contact were the hallmarks of the Baltic Fleet's passage. Much the same could be said of the relation-ship between the Commander-in-Chief and his second in command.

In such a close-knit community, the opinion of the second in command of his commanding officer could not remain a secret for long, and certainly not when the second in command was Nelson. And Parker had not let it pass. He had made their first meeting that morning of 7 March in the Wrestler's Arms a curt, formal affair. As Commander-in-Chief he had no obligation to confide his orders to his second in command, nor even to discuss them with him. But that is certainly what would have been *expected* and what *should* have happened. Although Nelson, with his sad lack of discretion and tact, had no one to blame for the frosty atmosphere but himself he had every reason, as second senior officer afloat, to feel offended at Parker's unwillingness to share information. But he was far too professional a naval officer, and far too excited about the forth-coming action, to let it affect his judgement and behaviour. If Parker would not open up to him, he would have to open up to Parker. Nelson sent a mediator across to Parker – a turbot.

On board the *St. George*, Lieutenant Layman had spoken of the fine turbot to be caught on the Dogger Bank. Nelson had eagerly enquired as to when the fleet would be in that position and towards the evening of 14 March he had a net put out. In the catch was one large turbot, which he immediately had sent to Parker. When his officers pointed out that nightfall was approaching and that the weather was still foul, he just repeated his order, adding, "I know the Chief is fond of good living and he shall have the turbot."

A boat shoved off from the *St. George* with the turbot, and a note from Nelson. His ruse worked. The boat returned with a polite note from Parker, in which he thanked Nelson for his kind gesture. And although he wrote that Nelson was, under no circumstances, to inconvenience himself by paying a courtesy call to the flagship, he did lift the veil from his plans. His orders were to deliver instruc-tions to the envoy in Copenhagen and give the Danes forty-eight hours to reply to an ultimatum. It was therefore his intention to anchor the fleet close to the entrance of the Sound. And not until that time had he considered issuing orders to prepare for battle.

Nelson had got the information he wanted, but he did not much like it. The plan Parker was hinting at was far from the decisive strategy William Pitt had told Nelson he expected. In Nelson's opinion, the Danes would feel very secure with the British fleet lying to anchor in the Kattegat. If it were looming large in the Copenhagen Roads when the Danish Foreign Minister had to deliver the reply of his government, he would think twice about giving an answer that would mean the Danish fleet and capital would go up in flames. What Nelson wanted was for the fleet to pass Kronborg with all haste, whether the Danes opened fire or not, and drop anchor off Copenhagen. It would have an enormous psychological effect and prevent the Danes using those 48 hours to strengthen their fortifications any further.

When the fleet passed the Skaw, in fair weather, Nelson paid his unbidden courtesy call on board the *London*. He was met with anything but openness, but certainly with clarity of opinion. That same afternoon the frigate *Blanche* was to be sent to deliver despatches to the envoy in Copenhagen. And Nelson was relieved to hear that Parker had changed his mind and intended to pass Kronborg immediately and anchor off Copenhagen to underline the seriousness of the British demands. Nelson was convinced this was all it would take to make the Danes see sense. He changed the course of the conversation, therefore, to the remainder of the fleet's operations. He recommended that it should then proceed immediately to Reval, before the ice broke up and the Russian squadron stationed there could withdraw safely to Kronstadt. On this point Parker had to disappoint his second in command. The Fleet would remain in the Sound until new orders arrived from Britain.

THE SOUND OR THE BELT?

Parker wanted to head directly for Copenhagen. That was the decision he had made and that was what he had told Nelson. But would he stick to that decision? No. For an entire week, a very critical week, he demonstrated such extraordinary insecurity and indecision that it later cost him his command and his career.

On the afternoon of 19 March the frigate *Blanche* had left the Fleet with Lord Hawkesbury's ultimatum to the Danish government. Late in the evening of 22 March, almost as the Fleet let go their anchors off Kullen, Captain Hammond returned. With him he brought two eyewitnesses from Copenhagen – diplomat William Drummond and MP Nicholas Vansittart.

Parker then received the letter from Vansittart stating that he could regard Denmark's rejection of Britain's demands as a declaration of war and move on to the execution of the Admiralty's orders. Also that evening, Drummond went aboard the flagship. What he had to relate about the strength and position of Copenhagen's fortifications did not sound particularly encouraging to Parker's ears and he started fretting that he would not be able to unleash his battleships against them in such shallow waters. But he did not change his plans. At midnight on 22 March his intentions were still to go straight for Copenhagen.

The next morning he had changed his mind. Shortly after dawn Vansittart had boarded the flagship. He, too, gave Hyde Parker a thumbnail sketch of the very strong defence ships moored in shallow water, and therefore even more dangerous to attack. He also brought disturbing rumours: the Swedes had promised to send a flotilla of gunboats and five of the Karlskrona squadron's ships-of-the-line to reinforce Copenhagen's defences; the Russians were making every attempt to get their fleet to sea and they were currently engaged in actually *sawing* the Reval squadron's twelve or fourteen battleships free of the ice.

This intelligence report, and concerns for Kronborg's cannon, made the Commander-in-Chief waver. He sent for Nelson.

When Nelson received the order to report on board he believed it was because the fleet was about to go into action and Parker wanted to discuss tactics with him. As he stood opposite the Admiral and the diplomat, he was told that Parker had changed his mind. He had now decided to let his fleet lie at anchor in the Kattegat.

Nelson was stunned. He wanted to go for the enemy's jugular there and then and force him to his knees. And to him the Tsar was the most dangerous of Britain's enemies in the League of Armed Neutrality and, therefore, the one to be crushed first.

But Nelson was not in command of the Baltic Fleet – Parker was. So Nelson's most pressing problem was to convince his superior to act – and to act now. He subjected the British diplomat to nothing less than a detailed interrogation on the strength and location of the Danish defence forces. He then analysed this intelligence, defined the Baltic Fleet's options and made it quite clear which he preferred.

Nelson based his argument on the fact that day by day, hour by hour, the enemy was strengthening his position and that there was not a moment to be wasted. The problem was thus not whether an attack should be launched, but how.

As Nelson saw it, they had a choice between passing through the Sound or through the Great Belt.

If Parker chose the Sound, Nelson was sure that Kronborg's cannon would inflict only minor damage on the fleet. Once at Copenhagen, there were two possible gambits. Parker could attack from the north, engaging Trekroner Fort and the ships in the Kronløbet Channel, the only entrance to the port of Copenhagen. This was the strongest sector and it would be "taking the bull by the horns". But it would mean taking the heaviest of losses and, furthermore, they would be incapable of preventing the Swedish and Russian fleets from joining up with the Danes. So Nelson's recommendation was to pass through the Hollander Deep further offshore and attack the Danish line from the south, at its Achilles heel. This would allow them to bombard the city at the same time as keeping the Swedes and Russians at bay.

Passage through the Great Belt, which Nelson preferred because it presented the opportunity of a lightning attack on Russia, would take, optimistically, four or five days. From the Baltic, Parker could enter the Sound from the south, attack Copenhagen and still prevent the League from reinforcing the Danes. But if the wind in the Baltic were favourable Nelson recommended sending half the fleet to Reval to destroy the squadron there, whilst the other half sailed for Copenhagen.

In short, Nelson was encouraging his commanding officer to countermand the clear and inflexible orders from the Admiralty. Nelson knew that this was a very bold operation, but, he believed, the bolder the operation the safer it was. And in their situation a decisively executed attack and a clear victory were of greatest importance for Britain.

Nelson won. Parker yielded to his second in command and opened up to him. The tangible aloofness Nelson had earlier felt from his superior was now replaced by openness and trust. And shortly afterwards Parker informed the Admiralty that he had decided to deviate from his orders. He now intended to take the Baltic Fleet through the Great Belt and thereafter let the wind decide whether the next step would be Reval and destruction of the squadron there or the Sound and bombardment of Copenhagen.

To do – or not to do?

In the late afternoon of 23 March Nelson returned to the *St. George* confident that Parker had made his decision and would stick to it. But the next day was to be one full of surprises.

That morning the fleet weighed anchor and left Kullen on a southerly course. The wind was from the west but veered during the morning to west-north-west. The pilots had been asked what wind the fleet would need to pass the Sound; a north-westerly, they replied. At two in the afternoon the wind veered from west-north-west to north and there it remained for the next four or five hours. When the pilots were consulted again, they agreed that the wind was favourable and the fleet would be able to pass Kronborg whilst it was still light.

At that point numerous telescopes were trained on the flagship. Why did the Commander-in-Chief not make the signal to weigh and head south under the favourable wind? Kronborg, the scene of another bout of indecision that is equally famous, was only twelve miles to the south and, with that fresh northerly wind, the fleet could pass the fortress and anchor between Hven and Nivaa before nightfall. They waited and waited, but still no signal flew. And in the evening the wind shifted to the south. Their chance for a swift dash past Kronborg and an attack on an incomplete and ill-prepared Danish defence line was lost.

The fault was Nelson's. Parker had once more wavered and Nelson had cajoled him into sticking to the Great Belt plan.

Early in the morning of 24 March Hyde Parker had written to Nelson. He had again reviewed their plan of a Great Belt passage and had found many good reasons that spoke against it.

When Nelson received the letter and request to go over to the flagship it was 1000. He had just finished writing a narrative of everything he had told Parker and Vansittart the day before. He took this draft letter with him to the *London* and in Parker's great cabin read it aloud to him. Formally, he was just giving his superior a briefing on the advice he had offered the day before. But both knew exactly what that letter – which Nelson did *not* hand over to Parker – actually was. It was documentary evidence of Nelson's activity and decisiveness, and Parker's passivity and indecision. And it did the trick. Parker reverted to his decision to go through the Great Belt.

Nelson had blatantly pressured his commanding officer. In Parker's defence, though, is the fact that before Nelson returned to the *St. George* at around 1300, supplementary orders had arrived from the Admiralty.

Two hours earlier the frigate *Jamaica* had joined the fleet. Captain Rose had left Yarmouth four days before and dashed across the North Sea, bringing despatches sent from the Ministry of War on 14 March to the Admiralty and then speedily forwarded to the Baltic Fleet.

The British government had been working on a strategy that

embraced Denmark, Russia *and* Sweden. But the orders Parker had received just prior to his departure covered only the action against Denmark. That accomplished, he was to wait in the Sound for further orders. Meanwhile, the British government had grown concerned about the mild winter in the Baltic. The League's fleet might be able to leave earlier than reckoned with, so the government decided to expedite the operations against Russia and Sweden.

The Cabinet, like Nelson, regarded Russia as the main opponent. And Parker's new instructions ordered him, as soon as he had accomplished his task in Denmark, to continue into the Baltic without a moment's delay and proceed to Reval. There he was to carry out an immediate attack with the objectives of destroying the naval establishment and taking or destroying the Reval squadron. Having done that, he was to proceed to Kronstadt and mete out the same punishment to the Russians.

Orders concerning Sweden were a little more subtle. On his way back from Reval and Kronstadt, Parker was to proceed to Karlskrona. If Sweden adopted a hostile posture, he was to engage them, as he had done the Russians. If, on the other hand, they indicated they would accept peace with Britain on the same conditions as those offered to the Danes, then Parker should extend them every assistance in defending them against Russia.

These supplementary orders emphasized strongly the necessity of speedy and decisive action against Russia and may have supported Parker in his decision to follow Nelson's advice after all and take the Great Belt option. At any rate, when the fleet anchored on the evening of 24 March between Kullen and Kronborg he was firmly resolved to pass through the Great Belt.

Onwards to Copenhagen
On 25 March, an hour and a half before sunrise, the Baltic Fleet weighed anchor and the fifty ships took up a course of west-north-west up the Kattegat. At around 1000, with the Fleet six miles or so north-east of the tiny island of Hesselø, a boat from the flagship came alongside the *St. George*. Aboard was Captain Otway of the *London* with a request from Parker to attend him. Once more the Admiral was in doubt as to whether he should take the Fleet through the Great Belt.

He had originally based his decision on the discussions with Vansittart and Nelson but he had continued his deliberations with Domett, his Captain of the Fleet, and with Otway, his Flag Captain. And they were both opposed to the plan.

One of Domett's objections was that the navigation in the Great Belt was much more difficult than in the Sound, and that only one of the battleship commanders, Captain Murray of the *Edgar*, had ever sailed through it. Parker's Flag Captain also pointed out his concern for the difficulty of attacking Copenhagen coming up the Sound from the south. The largest of their battleships would not be able to cross the Drogden Shallows and even the smaller 64s would be hard pushed. This would mean only the minor vessels of the fleet would be able to engage the line of ships in the King's Deep and if they ran into trouble they would be able to expect no help from the battleships. Furthermore, if the Danes had installed batteries at Dragør, on the southern tip of the island of Amager, Parker would have to pass even closer under their guns than he would at Kronborg.

Domett therefore urged his Commander-in-Chief to take the Sound route. His option was shared by Otway, who was summarily sent to collect Nelson.

Nelson was furious that Parker had changed his mind yet again, as with the wind. When Otway broke the news Nelson exploded and cursed that he did not care which passage they took so long as they engaged the Danes in battle. In the heaving, choppy seas, the one-armed admiral was hoisted over the side into Otway's boat and rowed back to the flagship. By this time it was almost 1100 and Parker was given a sharp reminder of the navigational problems of the uncharted route through the Great Belt. One of the small bombship tenders hoisted a signal that she had run aground off Hesselø, which stirred Parker's doubts even more. When Nelson arrived aboard the flagship, therefore, Parker informed him of his fears of grounding in the Great Belt and that he had decided, after all, to transit the Sound. That was his third change of mind in the space of four days. Nelson made no comment.

So shortly after eleven the Fleet tacked and set course for the Sound. At sunset it dropped anchor off Hornbæk. From there Parker detached the frigate *Hyena* and the sloop *Pylades*, with orders to patrol off Kullen and inform the ships still racing to join the Fleet that he had sailed for Copenhagen Roads.

The definitive, final decision had been made. But how long would it be before Parker got that northerly wind he needed, the one he had not taken advantage of two days before?

When Parker made that decision, it was also agreed that the attack on the Danish defence line should be led by Nelson, with Rear Admiral Graves as his second-in-command. As the fleet lay off Kronborg, impatiently waiting for the change in wind, the time was put to valuable use. Without having yet seen what they were up against, they decided how they would tackle it. The passage under the cannon of Kronborg Castle was planned and Parker ensured that it would be Denmark who would bear the responsibility for the first shot.

The next day the fleet was still off Hornbæk. And on that day the tactics of the attack on the defences of Copenhagen Roads were finalized.

That morning Nelson received orders from Hyde Parker to take a division of the Baltic fleet under his command. It comprised the five 74s *Elephant, Defiance, Russell, Bellona* and *Monarch,* the three 64s *Agamemnon, Ardent* and *Polyphemus, Glatton* with 56 guns, *Isis* with 50 and most of the minor vessels.

Nelson used the day on the detailed planning of the attack and briefing his Divisional commanders.

Nelson's division would pass Kronborg first and anchor north of the Middle Ground Shoal off Copenhagen. Parker's division was to follow and anchor north of Nelson. After reconnoitring the defence line, Nelson would then pass through the Hollander Deep and engage the ships in the King's Deep from the south. Three of his lightest ships-of-the-line, *Ardent, Glatton* and *Isis,* were to sail past the two most southerly blockships, firing as they went, drop anchor and engage the fourth and fifth ships opposite. The *Arrow* and *Dart,* together with the gun brigs, were to take on the two first blockships. The two fireships were to be sent against the two block-ships in the Kronløbet Channel. And finally, under the cover of the smoke of battle, a quick attack was to be made on Trekroner Fort and Lynetten battery. This amphibious operation would involve the twenty-five shallow-draught oar-propelled vessels, each with a 24-pounder on board, and 1,250 seamen and soldiers under the command of Captain Fremantle and the commander of the British troops, Lieutenant Colonel Stewart.

Nelson was optimistic, as were most of the men in the Baltic Fleet. They were well aware that the Danes had been working fran-tically to strengthen their defences, and indeed were still doing so.

But they took comfort in the fact that they were not about to face an enemy used to the rage and roar of battle, but a people who had been living in peace for eighty years.

At 1900 Parker ordered Nelson to shift his flag from the *St. George* to the *Elephant*. At 2000 Nelson joined his old friend and comrade-in-arms from the Nile, Captain Thomas Foley, and Nelson's flag was hoisted to the top of the foremast. All he, and the fleet, were waiting for now was for the wind to change to the north.

But on 27 March there was no change in the weather – near calm and a breeze from the south. During the morning Parker came aboard the *Elephant* to discuss plans with Nelson. And the day was used to exercise the crew. The shallow-draught vessels and launches, armed with a carronade and equipped with a heavy anchor cable, carried out rowing manoeuvres and the rest of the men in the fleet were put to gun drills and small arms practice. In the afternoon two of the bombships took up their station, under the protection of the frigate *Blanche*, from where they would be able to bombard Kronborg if the fortress opened fire on the Fleet.

Towards evening Parker opened his diplomatic offensive. A letter was sent by the brig *Cruizer* to the commandant of Kronborg. In it Parker demanded to know, as Denmark had expelled the British envoy, whether the commandant had orders to fire on the British Fleet when they passed under his guns. He also made it clear that the first shot fired by the Danes would be regarded as a declaration of war.

Colonel Stricker received the letter on the morning of 28 March. So it was not until noon that Parker received his reply. Stricker had sent a dispatch rider to Copenhagen for instructions and as soon as they arrived he would inform Parker.

The Danes were playing for time. From the deck of his flagship at six minutes past ten Parker had been able to see the optical telegraph on Kronborg's main tower sending a message to Copenhagen. The British used the time to prepare their contingency plans for passing Kronborg. Parker told Nelson to move his bombships closer to the fortress but with strict orders not to open fire unless fired upon. And, with the approach of the evening, the seven bombships and the ship-of-the-line *Edgar* were snugly at anchor some five or six miles north-west of Kronborg. But the day passed, and the evening, and there was still no message from the commandant. Nelson was among those who expected the worst. Colonel Stricker may well have said that he had no orders to fire but Nelson was sceptical – "The Devil trust them, I will not."

Not until shortly before midnight did Captain Brisbane board the *London* with a Danish officer bearing a letter from the commandant. The handwriting was Colonel Stricker's but the message was from Crown Prince Frederik. Stricker wrote that the British envoy had not been expelled but had himself asked for his passports; and he requested Parker to submit any political proposals, if he had brought any. But his answer to Parker's question was clear – he could not allow a fleet whose intentions were unknown to him to approach the guns of Kronborg.

Parker's reaction was instant. At 0200 the Danish officer left the flagship with Parker's reply: he was prepared to receive a Danish proposal at any time but had to state that Denmark's behaviour towards Britain was hostile. He regarded the commandant's reply as a declaration of war.

Even Parker's prodigious patience was about to run out and he was sorely tempted, he confided to Nelson, to begin the bombardment of Kronborg immediately. But he kept his anger in check and used 29 March to finalize details of the passage of the Sound. At around noon the entire fleet weighed anchor and set course for the south. In the early evening they anchored again off Hammermøllen, only three or four miles from the mouth of the Sound. At the same hour the *Edgar* and her clutch of seven bombships up-anchored and crept into a position just over a mile from Kronborg, with springs on their anchor cables to allow them to train their mortars and be at instant readiness to begin bombarding.

Fear has wide eyes

Since they left Yarmouth the spectre of Kronborg had haunted the British naval officers. Parker had registered the reinforcement of the fortification's seaward batteries with concern; he had been worried about exposing his ships to the fire from Kronborg and from Helsingborg, on the Swedish coast, just two miles from Elsinore; Nelson, too, had admitted that masts and yards would be damaged.

Their fears of the cannon of Kronborg were really only in the mind: as an old Russian proverb has it, fear has wide eyes. The fact of the matter was that no one in the British fleet had made the slightest effort to confirm whether any batteries had been set up at all on the Swedish coast. And despite the fact that they *knew* the Sound was 4,000 metres across at its narrowest point and that even heavy 36-pounders had an effective range of only 1,600 metres, no one had reached the elementary conclusion that there was an 800-metre corridor in mid-channel that was out of effective range of the guns of both sides, down which the fleet could pass with impunity.

So the expectation was that they would be fired upon and return fire. On the evening of 29 March all was ready for the fateful passage. On board the *Monarch*, the ship-of-the-line designated to be the first to run the gauntlet, seventeen-year-old midshipman William Millard stole a few minutes to admire the scenery. The evening was calm and clear; behind the fortress the sun had painted the heavens a flaming red and from the deck of the *Monarch* it appeared as if Kronborg was emerging from the waves, halfway across the Sound between Denmark and Sweden.

During the night the wind changed, at last, to west-north-west.

At 0500, as soon as it was light enough to read signals, flags were hoisted aboard the *London*. Nelson and Parker ordered their divisions to set sail, take up a formation of line ahead and proceed down the Sound. The *Edgar* and the bombships were told to clear for action and be ready to lay down the bombardment that would act as covering fire for the fleet as it passed the mouths of the guns at Kronborg.

On board the *Monarch*, Captain Mosse had made all his preparations hours ago; the crew had been roused before dawn, the anchor weighed and catted well before the Commander-in-Chief's signal fluttered up the halyards. The crew was poised for action and, before the signal was executed by being hauled down at the rush, the *Monarch*'s jib was set and she was under way, surging forward to the head of Nelson's division.

The line of ships formed a sweeping arc down the Sound, with the minor vessels tucked away in the middle, under the protection of the battleships. As the *Monarch* came abeam of Kronborg Captain Mosse ordered the colours to be hoisted.

That was apparently just what the troops in the fortress had been waiting for. Before *Monarch*'s colours were at half-mast the first shot from Kronborg was fired. It fell short, but not by much, the spray from the ball hitting the water splashed through the open ports of the lower gundeck. The *Monarch* replied instantly with a broadside.

In the same instant Parker signalled the *Edgar*, and the bombships began hurling their projectiles at Kronborg and Elsinore. The barrage continued as Nelson's and Parker's divisions passed the fortress and whilst the *Edgar* and the bombships withdrew, in the rear of the fleet, and headed down the Sound. But the damage caused was negligible compared to the powder and shot used up and there were only one casualty and two slightly wounded in the garrison. Kronborg's guns also proved to be totally ineffective. When the ships following in the *Edgar*'s wake realized that they were out of range of the Danish guns and that there were no batteries at all on the Swedish side they ceased firing and saved their ammunition for Copenhagen. The Baltic Fleet passed the imposing fortress without being hit by a single ball and they were a valuable piece of military intelligence the richer – Kronborg was indeed a piece of theatrical scenery.

By around 0900 both divisions had passed Kronborg and the Commander-in-Chief instructed the *Edgar* and her charges to tuck in behind. Parker's division anchored in a line between Hven and Vedbæk, whilst Nelson continued south and dropped anchor in battle formation at about 1000 off Taarbæk.

Eighteen days had passed since the fleet had left Yarmouth and now it was in the Sound. To port and starboard there were vistas of winter-grey fields and forests. From the deck of the leading ship, the *Monarch*, there was still nothing to be seen to the south other than an unbroken expanse of leaden-grey water. But slowly the spires and towers of the Danish capital began to emerge on the horizon and, as the Fleet closed the distance, the defences waiting to greet it took on more detail. When the *Monarch* anchored off Taarbæk the panorama was one of a wall of ships, minor vessels and forts. To the young Midshipman Millard the Danish fortifications looked formidable.

Chapter 5

COPENHAGEN'S FORTIFICATIONS

THE CALM BEFORE THE STORM

Copenhagen was calm once more after the crisis between Denmark and Britain passed with the signing of the provisional convention on 29 August 1800. From the Danish point of view it had been a political triumph – and a military fiasco. The ships-of-the-line the Danish admiralty had ordered to be made ready for action had not been and the crisis had shown with embarrassing clarity that Copenhagen was defenceless against unexpected attack.

In military terms the all-clear was sounded when Count Bernstorff and Lord Whitworth signed the convention. The Admiralty, therefore, cancelled the preparations of the fortifications of Copenhagen Roads and in the first days of September orders were issued to return the two blockships, the three converted cavalry barges and the three floating batteries to the dockyard and disarm them.

By that time the refitting of the battle squadron was so close to completion that the government decided to let it continue. And on 16 September Rear Admiral Wleugel hoisted his flag on the 80-gun *Neptunus* as squadron commander of nine ships-of-the-line and, over the next four weeks, he carried out work-up exercises in the Sound until he was ordered to return to Copenhagen on 13 October. He was to disarm, unrig and decommission the squadron as quickly as possible. The squadron's military objective had been to train the officers and men in naval tactics. The political objective, however, had been to demonstrate to friend and foe alike that Denmark was resolute about its policy of offensive neutrality.

That it had achieved but winter was creeping on and at that time the Danish government saw nothing on the horizon that could be perceived as a threat to peace. When two frigates returned home from overseas convoy duty in mid-September they too were ordered to be laid up in the dockyard, 'as in time of peace'. At the same time the Admiralty sent one of the newest battleships, the *Sejeren*, to the Mediterranean. And as late as 21 November a frigate of the most powerful class in the Danish navy, the 40-gun *Thetis*, followed her.

But refitting warships takes time. It also took time to mobilize national servicemen from the recruiting officers in Denmark, Slesvig and Norway. This was why preparations for each year's fleet commitments began in November. And in November 1800 the Danish government knew exactly how many ships it required for 1801. On 14 November it had committed itself to providing eight ships-of-the-line and two frigates to the League of Armed Neutrality, above and beyond what it needed for its own use. On 21 November, therefore, Rear Admiral Wleugel, after talks with Crown Prince Frederik, laid the plans for 1801 before the Admiralty – ten battleships and five frigates were to be made ready for sea, along with sundry minor vessels. They were to be crewed to 'middle-manning standards', that is for active service but not for war. To achieve this, 4,733 seamen had to be signed up from the three provinces of the kingdom, Denmark, Slesvig and Norway. Those coming from Denmark and Slesvig were to muster in Copenhagen in late March, those from the southern districts of Norway in early April. Not until the end of April were the men from Bergen and Trondheim to arrive. The orders to the recruiting officers were sent off, orders which showed that the government believed 1801 would be yet another year of peace for Denmark.

The clouds gather

But almost immediately clouds began to gather on the horizon. Shortly afterwards came the alarming news that the Tsar had placed an embargo on all British ships in Russian ports. And on 2 December the Danish Government received the Tsar's ominous note that he foresaw a British attack on the League of Armed Neutrality in the spring of 1801 and that he expected active military participation by the Danes.

Now the Danish Government had to consider the very real possibility of an armed conflict between the League and Britain. It did not, however, overreact. Certainly it expedited the work already begun on getting the 1801 quota of ships ready for active service. The commandant of Holmen Dockyard was ordered immediately to start loading ballast in seven battleships and was further authorized to requisition every master carpenter in Copenhagen to swell the ranks of Holmen's craftsmen in order to speed up the work. But the government ordered no more ships to be made ready than they were already committed to. Nor did it extend the call-up of national servicemen, except in the Zealand area, where the recruiting officer was told to get hold of every man he could get his hands on.

Precisely because preparing and manning the ships of the fleet was such a time-consuming business, the Admiralty's orders for the coming year functioned as a very reliable political barometer. In December, the government was still regarding the future with equanimity. As late as two days before Christmas the commander of the Danish Mediterranean squadron received instructions not to send his ships – the ship-of-the-line *Sejeren*, the frigates *Najaden*, *Havfruen* and *Freya* and the brig *Nidelven* – home until the conflict with the states of North Africa over their impeding the free passage of ships flying the Danish flag had been resolved. And it would be his decision, when the time came, as to whether the ships were to take a route up the English Channel or round the top of Scotland. It was a fact that Denmark was a member of the League of Armed Neutrality, but, despite the Tsar's militarization of the League, the Danish government felt reasonably secure. They had, of course, considered what might happen in 1801, but one eventuality was not part of their deliberations – war with Britain.

THE DEFENCE PLAN

Two days before Christmas war with Britain was still not an item on the Government's agenda. Two days after Christmas the Government issued its first war orders.

When Bernstorff had assured the British envoy on 27 December that Denmark had no intention of withdrawing from the League of Armed Neutrality he knew the consequences of such steadfastness – military conflict with Britain. As soon as the British envoy was out of the door Bernstorff went to the Crown Prince to brief him on the conversation. The Crown Prince, with equal haste, went to the Admiralty, from where, on the same evening, the first batch of war orders was issued. The permanent Defence Commission was told to have a plan for the defence of Copenhagen ready for the spring. The Fleet Naval Architect, Lieutenant Commander Hohlenberg, was ordered to join the Commission and specifically instructed to make proposals for "the defence afloat".

Four months earlier, in August, the Government had been faced with exactly the same problem. At that time it had proved impossible to defend Copenhagen against bombardment, at least at such short notice. Meanwhile, the Government had done nothing whatsoever to remedy the situation. It had still not issued the orders for the construction of more floating battery rafts, armed with twenty guns, than Fleet Battery No 1, the prototype from 1787 that the Navy already had. And Trekroner Fort was no nearer completion in December than it had been in August. It could take sixty-six 24-pounders, but there were no gun carriages, merely the temporary low wooden beds adequate for their trials in 1789. Neither did the Fort have any buildings to house men and materiel. And the fortifications on the ten-foot ramparts, supposed to provide protection to the gun crews, were still makeshift affairs of wood and earth, no higher than two feet.

In December 1800, then, Copenhagen's defences were still as big a problem as they had been in August and, if the truth were known, always had been.

There were two reasons underlying the city's amazing vulnerability. One was that there was but a single channel from the port and the naval dockyard out to the Sound; an enemy who succeeded in blocking that channel with wrecks would thus bottle up the navy and paralyse Denmark's military forces. The other was the simple fact that mortars had twice the effective range of guns; enemy bomb vessels could therefore bombard Copenhagen, the Naval Dockyard and the fleet anchorage from the King's Deep with impunity; they were out of effective range of shore batteries.

This was no news to anybody. For more than a hundred years it had been recognized that Copenhagen was the kingdom's weakest point. Several attempts had been made to install fortifications. The most recent had been in 1784, when the Defence Commission had presented its grand plan, with the introductory explanation of why the defence of the capital was so crucial:

"A matter of such import as ensuring the safety and security of Your Majesty's gracious personage, the Royal Family, the most precious possessions of the kingdom, Your Majesty's fleet and its arsenal, drydock and associated buildings, the army's arsenal, the national archives, Your Majesty's civil administration, the public libraries, the property of Danish trading companies, and the wealthiest of citizens, from attack by sea from one of Your Majesty's declared enemies, requires not only the greatest attention and vigilance but is of such urgency and priority that neither time nor cost should deter the initiation of any action which can resolve the situation."

The plans presented by the Commission were realistic in military terms but hugely expensive. Permanent forts on each side of the harbour entrance channel, Kronløbet – one on the Stubben Shoal and another on the northern tongue of Refshale Shoal – were to be constructed to prevent an enemy from blocking it.

Bombardment countermeasures, however, were much more complicated. The Commission proposed that a third fort should be built at the southern entrance to the King's Deep, on the site of the old Prøvesten Fort. The northern end of the Deep would be protected by Trekroner Fort. The central stretch of the Deep, however, would be out of the effective range of the artillery placed on these forts. To fill this chink in the armour against enemy bombships, the Commission proposed the construction of very shallow draft fleet batteries which could be moored on the Refshale Shoal itself.

The King's Deep emergency plan

In 1784 the Defence Plan received royal assent. The following year work actually began. Sixteen years later all that had been accomplished was the half-finished Trekroner Fort. Stubben and Prøvesten Forts had proved unaffordable. And still the only Fleet Battery in existence was the by now very waterlogged and not at all shallow draft prototype, Fleet Battery No 1, built by naval architect Henrik Gerner thirteen years previously.

On 27 December Bernstorff was all too well aware of this. And so was Crown Prince Frederik. Copenhagen simply had no defence. So the plan the Defence Commission was told, that evening, to put together was for little more than hastily improvised fortifications.

The Commission acted quickly and, two days later, a provisional defence plan landed on the desks of the Admiralty.

It made it quite clear in its introductory comments that the principal threat with a spring attack was bombardment from the King's Deep. It fully accepted the harsh realities it was up against: that there was no Prøvesten Fort; that there was only one of the twelve planned Fleet Batteries actually in existence and that it could not include the operational fleet, that is ships-of-the-line and frigates, among the assets at its disposal. The government's dilemma then, as it had been throughout the eighteenth century, was that Denmark could not afford, politically that is, to involve the navy in any conflict that might arise. Because it was the fleet that was the cornerstone of the monarchy's national security against Swedish aggression and of the country's credibility in St. Petersburg. The operational fleet, therefore, was sacrosanct.

As far as the Commission was concerned, therefore, the vital goal was to keep control of the King's Deep. What it proposed was a stationary force to cover the waters around Trekroner and Prøvesten Shoal and a mobile force to cover the stretch of the Deep in between that was out of range of the forts' guns. The mobile force would consist of the navy's three converted cavalry barges and the frigate *Hjælperen*; they were much more manoeuvrable than Gerner's Fleet Battery. For the same reason the Commission recommended the inclusion of gunboats in the defences.

The provisional plan was approved and work on preparing the vessels began immediately. And the Commission itself, of which Commodore Olfert Fischer became a member on 5 January, got on with preparing the final defence plan.

Presented on 21 January, it was an elaboration of the basic ideas of the provisional plan, but with much beefed-up forces.

The immobile defence was indeed to consist of Trekroner Fort at the northern end of the King's Deep and an improvised fort at the southern end. Improvised, perhaps, but ingenious nevertheless. Close to the site of the old Prøvesten Fort three decommissioned battleships due for the breaker's yard, the *Christian VII* (later renamed the *Prøvestenen*), *Jylland* and *Wagrien*, were to be fitted with two additional keels and put aground to form an arc-shaped fort. This immobile force was to be reinforced by positioning mortars on Trekroner Fort, at the shore battery Quintus on the northern line of ramparts on the mainland, and at what was known as Stricker's Battery, whose construction on the island of Amager, opposite the innovative fort on Prøvesten Shoal, had been ordered on 12 January.

The mobile defences were to be deployed between Trekroner and Prøvesten Forts – twelve vessels to be moored in parallel outer and inner lines. The outer line would be formed by the largest ships with the heaviest guns – the blockships *Dannebrog* and *Indfødsretten*, the frigate *Hjælperen*, the converted cavalry barges, *Aggershus*, *Nyborg* and *Rendsborg*, and two vessels due for scrapping that were now to be refitted as blockships, the East India Company's old China ship *Charlotte Amalie* and the frigate *Kronborg*. Of these only *Hjælperen* and the cavalry barges were to carry sail.

The inner line would consist of Fleet Battery No 1 and three artillery barges, large prams usually used for transporting guns but which would now be fitted with a gun deck and put into action. The Commission also proposed deploying twelve light gunboats, highly manoeuvrable under sail, as the mobile force. The final unit designated was the light frigate *Elven*, also under sail, to act as the defence line's signals vessel.

Defence of the harbour entrance channel was allocated to Trekroner Fort and two blockships, the obsolete battleships *Elefanten* and *Mars*, in place of Stubben Fort, which had never got further than the drawing board.

This plan, presented on 21 January, received the approval of both the Crown Prince and the Admiralty. It was little more than an improvisation of the grand defence plan of sixteen years earlier in 1784, but the experiences of August 1800 had shown that building up a defence structure along *those* lines took time. The burning question in 1801, therefore, was whether this time the navy would be able to reach its goals before the British arrived.

RACE AGAINST TIME

After the New Year of 1801 the Danish Government was in a race against time – a race to build up their defences before the British came knocking at the door and a race to solve the problems of spreading its limited resources most effectively.

Copenhagen was not Denmark and Denmark was not the entire monarchy. The Government was faced with the task of defending territory in Norway, Denmark and the duchies. Their problem was that they did not have the officers and soldiers, artillery and weapons to do the job. And that the navy did not possess the men or naval stores necessary to exert the monarchy's authority in its territorial waters. As early in the crisis as December the Crown Prince made it perfectly clear that he would not hear of any plans that did not maintain the navy and army as coherent units and that they were not to be made available for local defence commitments. That would have to be built up locally and rely almost entirely on local resources.

The Government was realistic enough from the beginning to abandon any hopes of defending the country's extensive coastline. Instead, the local authorities in Denmark, Norway and the duchies concentrated their efforts in defending strategically important fjords and ports with earthworks and ramparts, and anchored vessels. In Oslo Fjord and off the coast of Christiansand these were supplemented with armed merchant ships commanded by Contract Lieutenants, whose job it was to deter English privateers. But the tools necessary to get the job done were not available and time was running out. When the British fleet arrived in Danish waters there was no effective defence at all in Denmark, Norway or the duchies.

Nor were there any forces to counter a British attempt at an amphibious invasion. The army's hands were tied to defending Copenhagen and operations on the southern border. So the local defence forces ended up being a mishmash of local militia and newly formed volunteer companies. The government fell back on alternative resources to defend the coasts. In December of the previous year the government had already begun drawing up plans for a home guard of veteran soldiers. When war became an inevitable reality this plan assumed much greater urgency. On 19 January the orders for its formation were promulgated, followed on 13 February by similar orders for the duchies. The morale of the officers and NCOs of this home guard was high. But there was a palpable shortage of officers and equipment, and a catastrophic lack of weapons. As late as 20 March the commanding general in Jutland urged the county authorities to instruct their men to turn up with scythes mounted on wooden shafts – "a fearsome weapon in the hands of a brave Dane". It was an impossible task, given the time available, to train and arm the militia, the volunteers and the home guard regiments.

It was also a bleak military fact that when the British fleet dropped anchor off Copenhagen on 30 March there were no local coastal defences either. At that time the British could have gone ashore at their leisure anywhere in Denmark, Norway and the duchies.

Compared to the defensive fiasco, the offensive operations of the Danish army in northern Germany were a success.

The army in the duchies was set against British naval superiority. At the end of March it had moved towards the southern border under the command of Prince Karl of Hesse. On 29 March the independent German city state of Hamburg accepted the Prince's demands and surrendered the city to him. Danish troops took the city's gates and the city council began half-heartedly confiscating British goods in the warehouses. On April 5 the towns of Lübeck and Travemünde were also taken. But the Prince's plans to seize the Duchy of Lauenburg and thereby push the Danish border down to the Elbe met with fierce resistance from the Prussians and had to be dropped.

In reality this seeming success was another fiasco. The British warehouse stocks had, in the nick of time, been transferred to the ownership of middlemen. And the Lauenburg campaign succeeded only in making the already precarious relationships with Prussia even worse. From the viewpoint of the war with Britain it had no military or political significance whatsoever.

The war would be waged in Copenhagen and both governments knew that.

A considerable part of the army was already assembled in and around Copenhagen. So it was only natural that it was here it would be deployed in the defence of the capital and of the Kronborg fortifications against surprise attack.

Just after the new year there were six infantry regiments in Copenhagen, whose ranks were swelled in the first two months of the year with the recall to the regiment of country soldiers and recruits. These were the Danish Regiment, the Norwegian Regiment, the King's Own Regiment, the Crown Prince's Regiment, Prince Frederik's Regiment and the Zealand Infantry Regiment. The Funen Infantry Regiment and the 1st and 3rd Jutland Regiments were also called up to serve in the fleet and on the Copenhagen defences. This joint service operation was necessary because the Marines Corps had managed to find barely a quarter of the numbers needed and the Copenhagen garrison was unable to release any men to cover the shortfall. Along the coasts of the Sound and North Zealand, platoons of the Rifle Corps Light Infantry and the 1st and 2nd battalions of the Light Infantry were posted. The coast down the Sound was patrolled by companies of the Regiment of Hussars and the Zealand Cavalry Regiment. The artillery at the Citadel, the fortifications in Copenhagen and at Nyholm were manned by the Artillery and Engineer Corps, the

Copenhagen Artillery Company and men from the Naval Artillery Division and Holmen dockyard. The last players in the line-up were the Copenhagen Militia Companies, which had recently grown in numbers, and the university corps, the Crown Prince's Own Volunteer Corps, formed as late as 25 March.

Copenhagen was the pivotal fortification of the monarchy. When war came it was in impeccable shape, both in terms of men and equipment – eventually.

First priority of the Defences

But the expected attack would not be directed at Copenhagen the fortress but against the King's Deep. And the problems arising from that situation were Navy problems.

Until the evening of 27 December the Navy had been assigned one task and only one – to make ready for action the eight battleships and two frigates that were to be Denmark's contribution to the League of Armed Neutrality squadron in the spring of 1801. But that evening the military situation changed radically; the navy now had both to prepare a fighting squadron and establish defences on the Copenhagen Roads.

This placed great demands on manpower and equipment, but not entirely impossible demands. The equipment and naval stores *were* at hand, in the arsenals at Nyholm and Gammelholm, and the ships *were* in the naval dockyard. It would be horrendously expensive but it could be done, provided the Navy was given the time. But time was the very commodity the Admiralty did not have. It knew the Russians would not be able to arrive in time and it counted on receiving no help from the Swedes in defending Copenhagen. This was a purely Danish affair. The Admiralty also knew that the British fleet could be in Danish waters as early as March. It was thus the time factor that made it impossible simultaneously to make a squadron battleworthy and establish defences off Copenhagen. There were just not enough hands to do the job. The Danish government was therefore faced with having to make a very difficult choice, a choice they put off making for as long as possible.

In the last few days of the year the Admiralty believed that once the carpenters from the Copenhagen shipyards were drafted into service for the Navy the manpower problem would be solved and both tasks could be undertaken in parallel. In fact the preparation of the battleships was pushed even harder. On 11 December three ships-of-the-line, the *Kronprinsesse Marie*, *Trekroner* and

Ditmarsken, were ordered to be ballasted. On 30 December Crown Prince Frederik issued similar orders for another five battleships, the *Valdemar, Neptunus, Dannebrog, Prinsesse Sophie Frederikke* and *Skjold*. This completed, the ships were to be fitted out and equipped "as battle-worthy ships of the reserve for time of war". And as late as 19 January the Crown Prince signed orders for yet another five ships to be ballasted, stored and laid up as reserve ships – the *Arveprins Frederik, Odin, Justitia, Prinsesse Louise Augusta* and *Holsten*.

From the end of January, though, the focus was shifted to Copenhagen's defences. It is true that on 26 January the fleet's artillery was divided to meet the requirements of both the battle squadron and the defences. It is also true that the Admiralty, with its requisition of soldiers, was working with manpower from the army earmarked for both the battle squadron and the defences. But the absolute top priority now became the fortification of Copenhagen. The final Defence Plan presented on 21 January called for more vessels and equipment than the provisional plan of 29 December had outlined. On 2 February, therefore, two old ships-of-the-line were designated as further reinforcement of the defences. Now it was a matter of all hands to the pumps to get the defences ready before the British arrived. On the same day the Fleet Naval Architect expected to have all the defence vessels required in all respects ready for action by 1 March. At that time the hulls were fully repaired and inspected, but the ships needed rigging and provisioning. And not until 14 March, when all the defence vessels were ready and actually being moved into position in the Roads, were any command appointments made for the ten ships-of-the-line of the battle squadron. The work that recommenced on the battleships was again interrupted only a week later, however, when the news broke that the British were now in Danish waters. On 2 April, the day of the battle itself, the ten battleships lying in the naval dockyard, not intended for use in the battle but vital to the commitment to the League of Armed Neutrality, were still not rigged, provisioned or manned.

At no point had there ever been any plans for the battle squadron to take part in the defence of Copenhagen. That would have gone directly against the basic principle of Danish foreign and naval policy – to keep the operational naval fleet together as a coherent unit, undamaged and intact. Indeed, it was the fleet itself that was the first asset to be protected from British bombardment. When

Crown Prince Frederik and the Admiralty had given higher priority to the preparation of the defences than the to the fitting out of the battleships there was really no choice to be made at all. The fleet was sacrosanct.

THE PLAN AND THE DESPAIR

The nerve centre of the Copenhagen defences was the Defence Commission. On 27 December an expert in shipbuilding joined its numbers, the Fleet Naval Architect Lieutenant Commander Hohlenberg. And on 5 February the last member appointed, Commodore Olfert Fischer, was placed in overall command of the defences of Copenhagen Roads. The execution of the Commission's plan was put in the hands of an efficient and experienced officer, Captain Ole Kierulff. He was manager of the largest place of work in the monarchy and his strictness was legendary. One story has it that a naval officer once informed a sailor of the appointed time for their ship's departure, adding the customary, "God willing". The sailor retorted, "Whether God is willing or not is neither here nor there. It's what the Captain of Holmen wants that matters!"

The naval dockyard of Holmen was a military establishment run with military discipline, though the intensive work throughout the winter months of 1801 was not completed by harsh discipline alone. There was a carrot as well as a stick. The Holmen Medal for Faithful Service instituted by Christian VII on 29 January, his birthday, and which is still presented to this day, was a tangible mark of incentive and encouragement for the dockyard's highly qualified craftsmen.

The basic principles of the Defence Plan had been drawn up by the Defence Commission in its provisional plan of 29 December – "firstly to ensure, as much as possible, the control of the two crucial areas around Trekroner and Prøvesten Forts; and secondly to be in possession of a suitably manoeuvrable force to deploy between these two elements." These provisional plans were finalized and formally incorporated into the Defence Plan of 21 January.

Trekroner Fort was already there. The six sides of the ten-foot-high ramparts, a double quay structure filled with earth, formed a small harbour. In February a work gang from Nyholm was sent out to the Fort to give it the finishing touches and on 12 March Major Meyer of the Marine Corps was appointed in command. The Fort's ordnance consisted of sixty-six 24-pounders and three mortars, manned by troops from the Marine Corps, the Navy, the Artillery Corps and Prince Frederik's Regiment. There were no quarters for the men and they had to live as in the field, in tents put up on the narrow walls of the Fort. There were no powder magazines either and a barge was to be used as powder ship, the former de Connick & Co.'s East Indiaman, the *Providentia,* which went to the bottom on 2 April. During the battle the men were almost completely unprotected. It was not until it was all over that a temporary defensive wall of sandbags was ordered to be put in place.

But there was at least some kind of fort at the northern end of the King's Deep; at the southern end there was still just open water where the provisional fort should have been.

The task with the fewest problems was to set up an artillery battery on the coast north of the fishing village of Kastrup. On 12 January Major General Peymann was instructed to install a battery "as part of the Defences of the Roads but principally to reinforce the Prøvesten position", and equip it with eight 36-pounders and two mortars. This small battery, now known by the name of its commander, Lieutenant Stricker, son of the commandant of Kronborg, was not quite fully equipped on 2 April, the day of the battle, but with its six 36-pounders and two mortars it was still able to provide the support it was intended to give.

But the temporary fort it was supposed to support was never established.

According to the Defence Plan the three battleships rescued from the breaker's yard, the former three-decker *Christian VII* from 1767, now renamed *Prøvestenen,* the 70-gun *Jylland* from 1760 and the 60-gun *Wagrien* from 1773, were to represent a "fixed defence force". Fitted with two extra keels, they were to be towed into the shallow water over Prøvesten Shoal, arranged as a three-sided fort and filled with rocks until they sank and rested securely on the shoal. Work on fitting the keels was started immediately. When the Defence Commission began supplying the guns for the defences, the heaviest were reserved for this hastily improvised construction. Command was given to one of the very few Danish naval officers with combat experience, Commander F.C. Risbrich, who had fought with the Royal Navy in the American War of Independence.

But towards the end of February doubt began to set in, not about whether such a temporary fort could be built, but whether it could be done before the British were at the door. So, to be on the safe side, the Admiralty decided on 19 February to work to two artillery plans – Plan A if the fort had been established, and Plan B if the three ships were to be moored in the line as orthodox blockships. Apparently it was the very zealous and, in the eyes of certain senior officers, pushy young Fleet Architect Hohlenberg who went behind the backs of the Defence Commission and convinced the Crown Prince and the Admiralty that, because of the ice, it would be impossible to have the makeshift fort finished in time. And before the Commission had issued any statement about the change of plan on this decisive issue, the Admiralty, off their own bat, dropped the idea of a fort at Prøvesten. Instead, the three ships would be moored as blockships. Captains were appointed for all three – Commander Branth for the *Jylland*, Commander Risbrich for the *Wagrien* and Commander Runge for the *Prøvestenen*. At this juncture the Defence Commission washed its hands of the whole affair. But as long as the three vessels were to be moored as blockships in the King's Deep they would need to be fitted with guns on both sides, a consequence the Admiralty accepted, removing guns from the ships of the battle squadron and transferring them to the defence line.

Abandoning the idea of Prøvesten Fort was tantamount to abandoning the basic principles of the Defence Plan. It also meant an immediate weakening of the defences; the southern end of the Deep was now open to raking gunfire from the British ships that attacked from that direction.

Reinforcing the defence line

Paradoxically, the weakening of the defence line also made it stronger. The main reason was the patriotism of the captains of the numerous East Indiamen and West Indies ships that lay in the port of Copenhagen, not daring to put to sea since the British had started apprehending Danish ships. They volunteered themselves and their ships as "privateers or any other purpose the Admiralty may require". They could not really be used in the defence line itself; the members of the Defence Commission were unanimous in their opinion that even the largest of the merchantmen were not sturdy enough. But they were not slow in taking the opportunity to propose to the Admiralty that the floating defences did need reinforcing. They suggested that either "the *Sjælland* and the *Holsten* or the *Fyn* and the *Holsten* be moored, with masts, shrouds and stays". The members of the Board of Admiralty also agreed that it would be an excellent move for "the *Sjælland* and *Holsten* to provide support to the defences". So even before the Admiralty started worrying about whether Prøvesten Fort could be built in time it accepted the need to reinforce the floating defences between the two forts. On 5 February it wasted no time in promulgating orders for the 74-gunner *Sjælland* from 1787 and the 60-gun *Holsten* from 1772 to be armed with 36-pounders and to be included in the defences afloat. Work on the two ships, which the Fleet Architect described as being "ancient and decrepit and fit for service only in the North Sea and the Baltic on summer days", was commenced. On 23 February they were ready to be moved into position, captains were appointed and five days later they were formally placed under the command of Commodore Olfert Fischer.

Defeat a foregone conclusion

The King's Deep defences may not have been ideal but at the end of the day, it had the forces the Defence Commission had proposed on 21 January. But did that still mean it was strong enough to meet the military objective of maintaining Danish control of the Deep and thus preventing a British bombardment? By no means. Denmark would lose the impending battle. The youngest member of the Defence Commission, Commodore Olfert Fischer, and the oldest, newly promoted Vice Admiral Wleugel, were agreed on that salient point.

Very early in February Olfert Fischer had explained to the Defence Commission in no uncertain terms that Denmark did not stand a chance. When he had given his support to the proposal of reinforcing the defence line with the battleships *Sjælland* and *Holsten*, he had done so "to reduce the distances between the ships in the line". His argument was professional and irrefutable: "Any attack on a moored line of defence such as this would be very simple, especially when the distances between the ships is large; the destructive power of the ships would be minimized as the enemy only has to destroy one or more ships in the line and then expose the others to raking fire." Fischer's warning was far from being a purely theoretical analysis. Just before the battle he had the three artillery barges and Fleet Battery No 1 moved into the line between the heavy ships, with the express intention of making it as difficult as possible to break the line. But he had already presented his military evaluation of the forthcoming battle to the Defence

Commission in the first few days of February. With the Defence Plan proposed, and with the forces at their disposal, there was nothing more they could do except "reduce the distances between the ships in the line and, in the event of our being overpowered, fight for as long as possible; but to arrive at any means of avoiding the inevitable is, I believe, beyond human endeavour."

Four months after the battle, at a time when many were trying to make Olfert Fischer a scapegoat, Vice Admiral Wleugel declared himself in complete agreement with that assessment. And he knew what he was talking about. In 1775 he had surveyed the Copenhagen Roads; he had sat on the Defence Commission since it was founded in 1777; from 1804 until 1822 he was Admiral of the Fleet and he was an officer who commanded universal respect. In the summer of 1801, when the Defence Commission analysed the defeat of 2 April in an effort to learn from their mistakes, the Admiral did not conceal the fact that he sided with Fischer: "Our newly acquired experience was not necessary to be able to see that a defence force, however large it may be in numbers, consisting solely of ships, could be overwhelmed by a superior force." He went on, "Even if such defences were supported on their flanks by Trekroner and Prøvesten Forts, making the task more difficult for the enemy, the seabed in that area is such that ships passing these batteries will do so at such a range that an enemy with significantly greater firepower would have only to choose his moment to destroy that section of the defences consisting of ships, which would mean the section they were intended to defend would be exposed."

Forts or no forts, few ships or many, the Defence Plan adopted was doomed to failure. Both Crown Prince Frederik and the Admiralty knew that. But the Crown Prince and his Ministers were also terribly aware of the fact that they had no choice. Denmark had to fight a hopeless battle because of politics.

THE DEFENCE LINE FORMS UP

In January concerted efforts were made on both tasks – to prepare the battle squadron and the defence line. In the race against time, during February the defence line came to assume highest priority. But at the end of that month the Admiralty had to turn its head, for a time at least, and concentrate its efforts on a new commitment – sending help to Norway.

Crown Prince Frederik had been informed in a missive sent by courier of the many local defence measures needed in Norway. On 20 February he had promised to send two warships, the 40-gun frigate *Iris* and the 18-gun brig *Sarpen*, to Norway with provisions and military stores as soon as the ice broke up. This plan was changed, however, towards the end of the month when it was decided to send a full squadron by supplementing the two ships with the two 74s, *Danmark* and *Trekroner*. They were among the first ships to pass through the boom, the combined barrier and pedestrian bridge across the harbour entrance between the naval dockyard and the Customs Quay, and as they moved out into the Kronløbet Channel on 9 March, the squadron commander, Commodore Steen Bille, received his orders. As soon as his ships were ready he was to set sail for Norway with merchantmen full of corn, at anchor and ready to go, under his protection.

As yet he was far from ready. The preparations took time and during the warping through the Kronløbet Channel both battleships went aground. The *Danmark* was stuck so fast she had to lighten ship. At 0200 on 9 March Bille had sent the signal to make one more effort to get her afloat, with the only result that the *Trekroner* parted her heaviest cable. What took most time was what always had to be done when a warship was moved out to the Roads – she had to be stored and provisioned; powder had to be rowed across from the Citadel and, most time-consuming of all, she had to be rigged and her sails bent on. For a ship-of-the-line this involved somewhere between twelve and fifteen kilometres of rope and cordage and two thousand square metres of canvas. The crew worked valiantly, shoulder to shoulder with the men from Holmen. But the squadron was still a few days away from being ready to sail when the British fleet showed up on the evening of 22 March and dropped anchor off Kullen. The Norway squadron never left Copenhagen. On the other hand, with war against Britain so perilously close, the Admiralty now had at its disposal a seaworthy squadron of two battleships, a frigate and two brigs, fully armed and manned by experienced hands.

Kronløbet Channel in March

For a short time the Norway squadron had been the first priority, – but not really at the expense of the preparation and positioning of the defence line. What put the warping of the ships out to the Roads behind schedule was the thick ice in the harbour and channel in most of February.

The most urgent requirement was to get the hulk that was to function as guard ship on the Roads warped into position. And on 5 February Commander von Thun had received orders to take command of the blockship *Elefanten*, warp her out two days later and anchor to Olfert Fischer's instructions. Because of the ice he was unable to comply and it was not until 27 February that the Crown Prince could issue a new set of orders requiring von Thun to warp out on 1 March "and make every endeavour to assume his station with all despatch". And not before 5 March, a whole month after the first set of orders, was the old blockship on her station at the entrance to the Kronløbet Channel. At 2000 she fired the first of many shots as guard ship, daily at 0400 and 2000.

Whilst the Admiralty waited for the ice to break up it turned its attentions to preparing the gunboats that had been proposed by the Defence Commission in its provisional plan. During the last two weeks of February captains had been appointed for the eleven gunboats, which manning regulations stated required sixty-nine hands, and commanders for the two divisions they were organized into. Olfert Fischer drafted signals procedures, exercised the vessels and transferred part of their crews to the vessels in the defence line.

Meanwhile the weather had improved and the ice had broken up. The Admiralty promulgated orders by which two ships a day were to be warped out through the boom and the following morning the soldiers requisitioned from the army were embarked from the Customs Quay.

In the course of the next week half the ships and vessels, now almost fully equipped, had been moved out of the dockyard and into the harbour channel, towed into the Kronløbet Channel and laboriously warped into place. On 4 March the blockships *Sjælland* and *Holsten* were moved; on 5 March the frigate *Iris* and the brig *Sarpen*; on 6 March the blockships *Dannebrog* and *Mars*; on 7 March the blockship *Indfødsretten* and the frigate *Hjælperen*; on 8 March the battleships *Danmark* and *Trekroner*; and finally, on, 10 March the converted cavalry barges *Nyborg* and *Rendsborg*.

As soon as the vessels had passed the boom the command pennant was hoisted and the backbreaking work began. In bitter cold and winter darkness, and constantly fighting wind and tide, the men had to pull on their oars to warp the heavy ships out through the Kronløbet Channel, north about Trekroner Fort and down to their appointed positions in the King's Deep. The crews were shaken early, on most ships at 0400, when the guard ship fired her morning shot. Hammocks were lashed and stowed, breakfast eaten and the daily routine of life on board a ship of the navy began. On some of the vessels, the *Hjælperen* and the three converted cavalry barges, the first job was rigging and bending on sails. But common to them all was the work of hoisting aboard the never-ending stream of stores and provisions from the shore – and the dreaded warping.

Heavy kedge anchors were loaded into the ships' largest launches and rowed a hundred metres or so ahead of the ship, where they let go the anchor. On board the ship the crew manned the capstan, first to raise their own anchor and then to haul in on the kedge anchor's cable until the ship had crept forward that distance, and then let its own anchor go again. The kedge anchor was recovered, lowered into the launch again and the whole process repeated. Row forward, drop the kedge, raise the ships's anchor, pull the ship forward, drop anchor and transfer the kedge. Time and time again, with the ship moving at snail's pace into position.

It was exhausting work and it was an agonisingly slow affair. Most of the vessels had to be warped in this way for three or four miles. In foul weather warping was impossible and even when it was calm it was a cold and crippling job, which a humane captain could at least make bearable by issuing an extra tot of aquavit. Once the ship had arrived at its station the manual labour did not end. The heavy mooring anchors had to be laid. Most of the ships in the King's Deep were moored to four such anchors. Two thick anchor cables were flaked down the length of the ship, taken through the ports aft and led back forrard outboard of both sides of the ship to the anchor cats, where they were each spliced onto a mooring anchor. With the ship in her appointed position, each mooring anchor was then lowered onto a launch or barge, rowed away from the ship and dropped overboard. When all four anchors had been laid, by heaving in on one anchor cable and slacking off on another, the ship would be manoeuvred until it was equidistant from all four anchors. Only then could training begin in earnest to work up the crew, to prepare for action and man the guns.

On the morning of 11 March, when Commander Braun had warped the *Dannebrog* out beyond Trekroner Fort, Olfert Fischer hoisted his broad pennant as Commander-in-Chief of the defences of Copenhagen Roads. The next day he sent his first report to the Admiralty. He could inform them that the *Elefanten* was moored to her four anchors, that the *Mars* would be in the course of the day and that the remaining ships, the *Sjælland, Holsten, Indfødsretten, Hjælperen* and the three converted cavalry barges, were also just off Trekroner Fort and would be moored as soon as wind and tide permitted.

On the same day the Admiralty had issued orders for another series of ship movements. On 14 March it began, with the assistance of the numerous merchant ships in the port of Copenhagen. The brig *Nidelven* and the blockships *Wagrien* and *Jylland* passed the boom; ten of the gunboats followed in the course of that day and the next; on 15 March the blockships *Charlotte Amalie* and *Kronborg* were moved and on 16 March, as tail-end-Charlie in the defence line, the *Prøvestenen*.

The second wave of movements encountered even greater difficulties than the first. On 15 March the wind freshened considerably and during the night reached gale force. Some of the ships already moored dragged their anchors and, with the passing of the storm, the crew had days of hard work ahead of them in re-positioning their ships and re-laying the four mooring anchors once again. Many ships' boats were destroyed during the gale, which delayed the process of storing ship, and the *Prøvestenen* sprang a leak nine inches under the waterline aft. To lift the leak above the water Captain Runge moved several of the guns forrard to trim the ship's nose down. That did indeed achieve its purpose but at the expense of making warping even more laborious.

By mid-March the craftsmen and dockyard workers from Holmen had completed the preparations of the major ships in the defence line and could turn their attentions to the smaller vessels that were still in the dockyard. On 21 March the signals frigate *Elven* and the last gunboat, the *Viborg*, were moved out. When the report of the appearance of the British fleet reached Copenhagen almost immediately afterwards, the Admiralty was suddenly very busy indeed. It had always been the personal responsibility of each commanding officer to ensure his ship was properly provisioned before she left harbour. With everything buzzing about their ears, the Admiralty saw fit to relax this time-honoured regulation. On 23 March Lieutenant Commander Holsten was told "with all speed to see that the vessel placed under your command, the frigate *Elven*, takes up position in the King's Deep. With every confidence in your eagerness and zeal to comply with these orders, you are relieved of responsibility for any shortcomings there may be in the state of your command."

Things moved even faster for the last vessels of the defence line. On 21 March captains were appointed for the artillery barges *Søhesten* and *Sværdfisken* and the seventeen-year-old Sub-Lieutenant Peter Willemoes was put in command of Fleet Battery No 1. The Admiralty pressured the Dockyard Captain to ensure the movement of these ships "as speedily as is humanly possible". Four days later the *Søhesten* and Fleet Battery No. 1 were moved, followed the next day by the *Sværdfisken*. As late as the evening of 30 March Sub-Lieutenant Müller, serving aboard the frigate *Frederiksværn*, received orders to take command of the artillery barge *Hajen*. He worked through the night to get his first command ready at Nyholm Quay and early the next morning his crew arrived – 170 men, soldiers and volunteers from Holmen's staff of workers. And, as the very last ship, almost at the very last moment, the *Hajen* was moved on 31 March with the British fleet in sight.

The miracle of the King's Deep

All the ships of the defence line were past the boom. But were they fully equipped? And were they in position when the Royal Navy arrived?

None of the vessels had all their stores and provisions when they were moored in the King's Deep, but in most cases what was lacking was unimportant. Between the shore and the ships a veritable armada of boats large and small plied back and forth with stores and equipment. In fact, there was only one shortage, albeit serious. Although the Naval Artillery Division had all the guns it needed – in some cases they would have preferred larger calibre pieces than those supplied – they did not have enough carriages for them. And a gun carriage, which had to take the three-ton weight of its gun barrel and withstand the enormous force of the recoil when it was fired, was a highly specialized item of war material that took time and skill to produce. When the last major vessels, that is the *Prøvestenen*, the *Wagrien*, the *Jylland*, the *Charlotte Amalie* and the *Kronborg*, were moved out of the dockyard there were, embarrassingly, not enough gun carriages to go round. To avoid any delay in positioning these units of the defence line, they were told to move anyway, even though there were operational guns on one side alone. The other guns were merely lashed to the deck, awaiting the arrival of their carriages as and when they were constructed.

But by the time Nelson attacked there were still some ships frantically awaiting their gun carriages. On board the *Wagrien* the most powerful guns were chocked up on the city side of the lower gundeck, about as useful as a cargo of scrap iron.

And when the British did arrive the ships of the defence line were still not in place.

The Fleet arrived off Kullen on the evening of 22 March. Two days later Sir Hyde Parker got the northerly wind he needed to pass Kronborg and make the passage down to Copenhagen. At that time only seven of the eighteen vessels of the King's Deep defence line were in position and moored correctly – the *Dannebrog*, *Sjælland*, *Holsten*, *Hjælperen*, *Aggershus*, *Nyborg* and *Rendsborg*. In place perhaps, but with disastrously large intervals between them. The others – the *Elven*, *Prøvestenen*, *Wagrien*, *Jylland*, *Indfødsretten*, *Charlotte Amalie* and *Kronborg* – were in various stages of warping themselves out to their stations. But the three artillery barges and Fleet Battery No 1 were still in the dockyard and were not moved until the next day. What is more, the defence line was still short of a third of its manpower and on only a very few of the vessels had gun drills even begun.

If Sir Hyde Parker had followed his clear and unambiguous orders and pounced on Copenhagen with the first favourable wind he would have met an enemy that was totally disorganized and utterly unprepared. It would have been like letting a pack of wolves loose in a sheep pen. But he did not. The prayers of the Crown Prince's brother-in-law and member of the Privy Council, Duke Frederik Christian of Augustenborg – "Let us hope that our Lord has a miracle up his sleeve for Denmark" – had been answered.

The miracle for the defence line of the King's Deep was ten more days' respite.

Chapter 6

DRAMATIS PERSONAE

THE MANNING OF THE DEFENCES

When the British attacked on the morning of 2 April the ships the Defence Commission had recommended were all in their correct positions. But were they manned to the level the Commission had recommended? And if so, were the crews experienced enough to take on such a professional, well-seasoned opponent?

One thing had been clear from the start: the crews allocated to the ships moored in the line of defence bore no resemblance to those of the Navy's battle squadrons, either in numbers or expertise. Such ships required crews large enough both to sail and fight them, and these well-trained crews had been reserved for the Norway squadron. But the ships in the defence line would not have to manoeuvre, merely stand and fight. On 21 March, therefore, when Olfert Fischer requested a list from each of his commanding officers detailing their manning state – men on board and shortage of hands – he concluded by writing, "It need not include level of experience, merely the number of people".

The men of the defence line were of a mixed bunch: professional naval officers, monthly-contract officers, regular petty officers and ratings, national servicemen, soldiers, marines, volunteers and pressed men. Together they formed the force of more than 5,000 men who stood on the decks of the eighteen King's Deep defence vessels that morning ready to take on the Royal Navy. But the size of each category of sailor was very varied, as were their professional qualifications.

Commanding officers and their wardrooms
The first to be appointed to any man-of-war was her commanding officer. As soon as the Captain of Holmen released a ship from his

charge, fitted with ballast and masts, her captain was appointed. He then took over responsibility for her further preparation. The officers, petty officers and regulars were drafted as the work required; and the largest part of the crew, the seamen and marines, arrived only when the ship was ready to leave the dockyard.

On 5 February, the day Olfert Fischer was appointed Commander-in-Chief of the Defence Line, a captain was appointed to the guard ship *Elefanten* and the frigate *Hjælperen*, which were in all respects ready for action. On 16 February command appointments were made for the *Dannebrog*, *Mars*, *Indfødsretten*, *Charlotte Amalie*, *Kronborg*, *Aggershus*, *Nyborg*, *Rendsborg* and *Elven*. The remainder were posted as the ships were made ready: on 23 February the *Sjælland* and *Holsten*; on 26 February *Prøvestenen*, *Wagrien* and *Jylland*; and on 21 March *Sværdfisken*, *Søhesten* and Fleet Battery No 1. The very last appointment, on 30 March, was the *Hajen*.

The vessels deployed in the King's Deep were there to defend the indispensable fleet of warships and were themselves highly dispensable. With this in mind, it might not have been entirely unrealistic for the Admiralty to appoint captains and officers to man them who were also dispensable.

The Admiralty never justified its command appointments. It had to appoint officers from a cadre of limited size, many of whom were already at sea at that time, not only for the defence of the capital but also for the Norway squadron and the battle squadron which, in a few months' time, would leave to join forces with the Russian and Swedish squadrons.

And there were captains who had their command taken from them before the battle. Commander Runge of the *Prøvestenen* was removed for incompetence and later discharged from the service. Lieutenant Captain Brøer was relieved of command of the *Sjælland* after he had severely injured his knee whilst boarding *Dannebrog*. And though no reason was ever given for Commander Braun's departure from the *Charlotte Amalie*, there is nothing in his later career which indicates any displeasure of the Admiralty. There is one command appointment, however, which has always been a source of amazement, that of seventeen-year-old newly promoted Sub-Lieutenant Peter Willemoes to Fleet Battery No 1. But the Admiralty was highly satisfied with his deportment during the battle. When the forces were reorganized on 4 April he was left in command of his battery.

Of course it is possible that a hand was held over certain naval officers regarded as showing special promise or with particularly good connections. On the other hand, there is nothing to indicate that those appointed to command dispensable vessels were dispensable officers sacrificed to a battle the Admiralty knew they could not win. The commanding officers of the eighteen ships in the King's Deep had the full confidence of the Admiralty and the Crown Prince, and none of them disappointed on 2 April.

But commanding officers are not enough to run a warship. And Olfert Fischer touched a raw nerve when he reported, as late as the morning of 23 March, that "most of the line of defence ships have but two regular officers". In fact, in six of the seven vessels moored in the King's Deep that morning there was only one regular officer – the captain himself. Lieutenant Lillienskjold of the *Hjælperen* had a sub-lieutenant as his second-in-command; the officers aboard the other six ships were newly appointed contract lieutenants.

The Admiralty reacted promptly. On the same day three lieutenant commanders, four lieutenants and a sub-lieutenant were ordered to report to Commodore Fischer. More arrived the next day. On that morning, 23 March, the total complement of officers of the seven defence vessels numbered thirteen, one regular officer and twelve contract lieutenants. On 2 April there were sixty-two officers, eighteen regulars and forty-four contract lieutenants, in the King's Deep.

Mates from the merchant navy
The Admiralty had made an attempt to boost the professional level of the defence line's officers, but on 2 April most of them were still contract officers, not regulars.

But then there was nothing unusual in that. The corps of Danish naval officers was not, and was never intended to be, large enough to man the fleet for war. They were intended to form the cadre of professionals who would command temporary officers, the contract lieutenants, with the lowest rank in the naval hierarchy with a status below that of sub-lieutenant. They were all experienced mates from the largest ships in the merchant fleet, qualified and obliged to serve in the Navy on monthly contracts in time of tension or war, and most of them had served in the very East Indies traffic that had triggered the policy of offensive neutrality and the convoy conflict with Britain.

As soon as the Admiralty became aware of the need for officers to man the ships to battle standards they sent orders to the recruiting officers in Denmark, Norway and Slesvig, and the captain of the naval base in Glückstadt to make a register of mates in the merchant navy who were eligible to serve. Over the next few months almost two hundred found themselves in the King's Navy – seventy-five in Norway, sixty-five in the duchies. A few from the Danish contingent were drafted to harbour defence in Jutland, but most of them, fifty-four in number, were sent to Copenhagen. On 2 and 19 February the first twenty-six received their appointments – ten of them had served in August the previous year as monthly contract officers in the Copenhagen defences – with the twenty-eight remaining officers receiving their orders in batches up to 26 March. They were supplemented by a dozen or so of the most senior midshipmen in the navy, temporarily promoted to acting sub-lieutenants before returning to their courses at the Naval Academy.

In 1801 many of the merchant mates were on overseas passages, but the recruiting officers experienced little difficulty in finding qualified candidates, so the Admiralty could afford to be choosy. Indeed, on 23 March they rejected one Ole Thomsen Dahl on the grounds of his "not being competent to serve as an officer, and lacking the moral character to discharge the duties of such". Of the fifty-four mates selected in Copenhagen, forty or so came from Denmark, the rest from Slesvig. The oldest was forty-six, the youngest nineteen and the average age thirty. On 2 April the East India mates were to pay the price of the Danish exploitation of neutrality – six were killed and eleven wounded.

Regulars and national servicemen
The leadership of good officers was essential for the impending battle, but they were few and far between. By far the largest group on the vessels in the King's Deep on 2 April – 2,739 out of a total of 5,234 – were what the Admiralty classified as "senior rates, carpenters and seamen". There were, in fact, two groups of professionals: one was the personnel from the ranks of the Navy's seamen, gunners and craftsmen; the other were recruited national servicemen and the newly formed naval reserve. The hard core of regular personnel in these groups represented a mere 300 men. The remaining 2,500 or so sent by the recruiting officers were seamen with experience ranging from moderate to high and men from the supplementary reserves, not all of whom had any sea time.

The recruitment of these national servicemen was a barometer of the climate of crisis and war.

The first wave of recruitment took place in November, when there was still peace and no threat of danger. From the recruiting districts of Denmark, Norway and Slesvig 3,733 men were called up; 290 from Stavanger and Trondheim were already in Copenhagen, having been enrolled in the August crisis and retained for the winter. In addition, 1,000 naval reservists were called up. After war became inevitable on 27 December 1800, recruiting officers in Denmark and Slesvig were urged to find another 600 men. And when reports of the British embargo reached Copenhagen recruiting assumed even higher priority. On 29 January the Crown Prince wrote to every recruiting officer in Denmark, Norway and Slesvig ordering them to "call into service every available seaman" and "as many reservists as can be found", and that men from Denmark and Slesvig should be sent to Copenhagen with all despatch. It was a clear warning of the impending war that, on 16 February, the King issued "a moratorium and general pardon" appealing to any seamen who were abroad without leave of absence to return home and sign up to serve their country in its hour of need. If they responded their sins would be forgiven.

The weakness of the Danish navy was not only shortage of men but also shortage of time to gather them together and overcome the logistics challenge of getting them to the capital. Thus had it always been. The lengthiest process was tracking down and rounding up the largest group of national servicemen, seamen from the recruiting districts of Norway. Transporting them to Copenhagen in the middle of winter, when sea traffic was at its lowest ebb, exacerbated the problem even further.

This was a problem the Admiralty had taken steps to solve in early January. If they were unable to find their way to Copenhagen by sea, then they would have to travel by land through Sweden.

For once Denmark and Sweden were allies and the Swedish government reacted promptly and positively to the Danish Foreign Minister's request for free passage through Sweden.

The original plan was for 1,200 men from the southern districts of Norway. But at the end of January, with recruitment then so urgent, the Admiralty desired passage for seamen from Bergen and Trondheim as well. This request, too, was met willingly by the Swedes, as was the plea to allow the march to take place in groups of 80–100 men instead of 50–60.

The journey though Sweden was a success. The route started at the mobilization point at Frederikshald, went through Bohuslen and Halland to Helsingborg. It was divided into nine stages of some forty km, with a rest day every third day. Before they left, every man was given a free pair of new shoes; they were given a daily morning ration of warm beer and food on the journey in the form of bread, butter, cheese and snaps, and, on their rest days, fresh meat. On 20 February the first group of sixty men came under the command of Lieutenant Hvidtfeldt of the Norwegian Army at the Swedish border. For the next fourteen days, the transport system worked like clockwork, with sixty men and a lieutenant arriving every day. After a break in mid-March, the process was started up again with the same precision as before, but now stepped up to eighty men a day. The crossing to Denmark was made from Helsingborg, with the exception of the few days between 25 and 29 March, when the presence of the British fleet necessitated sailing from Landskrona. The last batch arrived on 31 March, just two days before the battle. The Admiralty had succeeded in acquiring a total of 1,561 men fit for battle along the Swedish route to Copenhagen, where they would be divided between the Defence Line and Steen Bille's squadron.

Soldiers at sea

There was one very special group of men aboard the ships of the fleet, the small Marine Corps, which, despite its name, was part of the army. In early February the total number of troops needed by the Admiralty for the battle squadron, the defence line and the four frigates came to 48 officers, 146 petty officers, 39 drummers and 2,501 soldiers, above and beyond the 600 men to man Trekroner Fort and a smaller force for Stricker's Battery. And the Crown Prince gave his approval for the soldiers of the 1st and 3rd Jutland Infantry Regiments, at that time on the march towards Copenhagen, to be taken on board as they arrived. In the hectic days when the ships were warped out to their positions in the defence line the requisitioned platoons mustered very early at the Customs Quay, where they were picked up and rowed out to the vessels in which they were to serve. The troops aboard seventeen of the ships in the King's Deep – the signals frigate *Elven* had none – comprised twelve officers and 958 sergeants, drummers and private soldiers. They came from the Danish and Norwegian Regiments, the King's Own Regiment, the Crown Prince's Regiment, Prince Frederik's Regiment, the Funen Infantry Regiment, the 1st and 3rd

Jutland Infantry Regiments and the Marine Corps. On the larger vessels they were under the command of officers – a major, a first lieutenant, a second lieutenant or subaltern – and on the smaller a sergeant or corporal.

The volunteers

The Admiralty had expedited the recruitment of men eligible for national service, it had adopted unorthodox measures to get the Norwegian contingent to Copenhagen and it had recruited a considerable force of troops. But it was still not adequate to man the Copenhagen defences fully. On 20 March Olfert Fischer was still short of 2,054 men – half the manpower the defences needed according to the Admiralty's manning regulations.

Confronted with this situation, the Admiralty had two courses of action open to it – it could appeal for volunteers, and it could put press gangs on the streets.

Initially, they chose the first option and on 18 March the Crown Prince had broadsheets posted around the capital – "In that all the seamen now present in Copenhagen are required to man our warships, there is thus an urgent need for men, sound of limb, to complete work not requiring any acquaintance with seamanship on other defence structures for the protection and safeguarding of the realm. The magistrates of Copenhagen and authorities in other towns of the kingdom are hereby authorized in the King's name to appeal to every man under their jurisdiction with a skilled trade and under no other obligations to the Crown or in no useful and indispensable occupation that they are duty bound to volunteer for such service within four days."

In addition to pay and free medical treatment, like national serviceman, all volunteers would receive fifteen rigsdaler, a sum of money representing two or three months' wages, on signing up. In his patriarchal appeal, however, the Crown Prince left no one in doubt as to the consequences of not enough volunteers being found: "The zeal of the Royal officials, together with the courage and willingness of my subjects to defend our beloved country, leads the King to trust that this appeal will suffice in the achievement of our objectives so that he will not need to avail himself of the unpleasantness of the use of force and the press to bring the requisite number of men into the service of his Royal person and the nation."

In other words, if you don't want to you have to!

Almost 2,000 men volunteered, most of them in Copenhagen – 1,272 in all, though 59 did not turn up and 33 were rejected. On 23 March the first volunteers from the provinces began to arrive, the first batch, not unnaturally, coming from the capital island of Zealand. Four days later the first men from Funen arrived and the last seven volunteers turned up at Gammelholm dockyard on 1 April, from where they were taken to the converted cavalry barge *Nyborg*, where three of them were to die the following day. In all, 200 men from Zealand and Funen were at their battle stations on the day, and between 4 and 20 April, that is in the fortnight following the action, another 431 men arrived from Jutland and the islands of Funen and Lolland-Falster. One of the exceptions, perhaps, to the adage of better late than never – although with the battle over, there was still great uncertainty about what would happen next.

It was a motley crew that turned up, if ever there was one. Nonetheless, they were all social equals. With society as it was then, it was perfectly understood that the appeal for volunteers did not apply to the upper echelons of society. The burgers of the capital were already organized into citizens' militia companies and the Citizens' Artillery Company. The city's students were organized into the Crown Prince's Own Voluntary Corps, and the remainder of the middle classes, office workers in the flourishing trading houses of Copenhagen and other non-academics, took the initiative to form the King's Voluntary Light Infantry. Patriotism and willingness to serve were just as divided by class and geography as the rest of society. Normal national service was only introduced in the Constitution of 5 June 1849, with the demise of the absolute monarchy.

For this very good reason most of the volunteers were inevitably craftsmen and labourers, and for some the word volunteer was open to discussion; each guild master received word from the local police chief to provide journeymen and apprentices, the number depending on the size of the Guild. Other employers, too, applied patriotic pressure to their staff. The owners and directors of the major sugar refineries made the offer of sixty-two of their work force, at no charge, to meet the needs of the Navy. And the Admiralty duly acknowledged the offer with "approbation and recognition for the generosity and patriotism with which the offer was made", adding that they would rather that volunteers reported to their local police chief under their own steam.

The sixty-one seamen and one ship's boy who volunteered were welcomed with open arms. Almost a quarter of the volunteers were unskilled or casual labourers. Many of this group came from the capital's breweries and distilleries and noticeably few of them from the ranks of the patricians' servants and coachmen. The largest single group were journeymen and apprentices from the capital's fifty or so trade guilds. The largest guilds were the best represented – the shoemakers, smiths, coopers, bricklayers, tailors and ropemakers. Together they made up about a third of the volunteer force. Bakers, however, were highly conspicuous by their absence; and there were very few carpenters, presumably because most of their number had already been called into service at the navy's dockyards. Certain guilds, however, were represented with just a single volunteer member; there was a pewterer, a wigmaker, a paver, a clockmaker and an apprentice chimney sweep. Other trades were similarly represented: there was a single cork cutter, a solitary horse dealer and a French umbrella maker. The volunteers not only came from a variety of trades, but also from a variety of countries.

By far the majority had volunteered in Copenhagen, but only about a third actually came from the city. Another third came from the country and provincial towns, most of them from Jutland. Surprisingly few, only about twelve per cent, came from the rest of the monarchy – Norway, Iceland, Holstein and the colonies. The largest group of foreigners was the Swedes, who made up seventeen per cent of the entire volunteer force. Most of the others came from Germany, but there were two Russians, two Italians, a Spaniard, the aforementioned French umbrella maker, M. Pierre Felgine, and even one volunteer from as far away as the Cape of Good Hope.

Some volunteers attracted more attention than others – the resident Swedes, for example, who as arch enemies of Denmark had nonetheless volunteered to defend the League of Armed Neutrality and its principles. It was also difficult for the citizens of Copenhagen to conceal their astonishment at the fact that seven of the city's Jews had volunteered to fight for their country. Not much notice was taken, however, of the score of lascars from Tranquebar who served under their two serangs on board the *Prøvestenen*. Nor was much attention paid to the black slaves who fought on 2 April. The owner of one of them, a Danish-West Indian merchant, had volunteered the man himself. But the two slaves from St. Croix, in the Danish Virgin Islands, Hans Jonathan and

David Tams, had truly volunteered, which act of gallantry was still not enough for a Danish court to grant them their freedom. The mother country may have been in danger on 2 April, but the rights of property were not.

The volunteers mustered at Gammelholm dockyard, from where they were taken by boat and deposited among the vessels of the defence line. And Olfert Fischer issued orders to the effect that "the honourable gentlemen in command will please me by giving the necessary orders in their ships that the people who may be sent on board the defence vessels, whether they be volunteers or pressed men, will be treated in the best and most decent fashion in order to encourage in them the greatest will to defend their country."

The pressed men

But, and it is a big but, not enough volunteers signed up, or at least not quickly enough. So the Admiralty had to adopt other, more forceful means. On 23 March the official responsible for recruiting on Zealand was ordered "to locate and recruit all non-Danish seamen" who were in Copenhagen at that time. Two days later the King resorted to the threat he had made a week before of pressing men into service.

To begin with, the navy got precious little from the press campaign, possibly because, if the rumours were correct, the Copenhagen chief of police did what he could to avoid recruiting servants and coachmen, in an effort to ingratiate himself with the higher echelons of Copenhagen society. Whatever truth the rumours may have contained, it is a fact that Copenhagen provided only a hundred and thirty-five men for the defences. On 28 March pressed men began to arrive from the provincial towns of Zealand and two days later from Funen. With the arrival of the four men from the town of Middelfart on 1 April the number of pressed men rose to eighty-four.

On 31 March, with the Royal Navy lying off Copenhagen, the Crown Prince screwed the press even tighter: "Every available seaman is to be apprehended. Neither fisherman nor any other man is to be spared in this hour of need. Recruiting officers, as well as the local civil and military authorities, will be held responsible for all men capable of serving in the navy being found and delivered."

On 20 March the defences were short of 2,054 men, almost half of what was needed. The Admiralty had accordingly taken every measure within its power to make up the shortfall of men. And they were successful in their venture. By 21 March the roll showed the defences were short of only 1,604 men and on 28 March the shortage was reduced to just 340, and even further over the next three days, mostly thanks to volunteers and the press gangs. It was a race against time, but the Admiralty won. On 2 April the Copenhagen defences were manned to the standards set by the Admiralty, in fact with a small surplus.

Enough – but good enough?
It was one thing having found enough men to meet the Admiralty's requirements. It was another entirely as to whether enough was the same as good enough. And although every vessel in the defence line was manned correctly quantitively, were they manned equally qualitatively?

Two vessels stood out from the rest. The crew of the frigate *Elven* consisted entirely of experienced seamen because her role as signals frigate required that she was able to manoeuvre quickly and safely. And the crew of the artillery barge *Hajen* consisted entirely of craftsmen and soldiers because that was all there was left by the time she, as the last vessel, was to be manned. On board the other sixteen vessels it was the proportions of the three different categories of men – regulars and seamen, volunteers and pressed men, and soldiers – that demonstrated the difference. And the soldiers were far from a decisive component of the forces; on most ships they represented less than a quarter of the crew. The real difference lay in the ratio of regulars and seamen to volunteers and pressed men.

In this respect the *Dannebrog* was in a class of her own. She had not a single volunteer or pressed man in her crew, and the soldiers on board represented one third of the manpower. But the other two-thirds were all professionals, either regulars or seamen. She was also one of the first ships to be on her station and able to exercise her gun crews hardest. She also fully met the requirements of the flagship of the Defence Line in terms of manning, with the expectation that she would survive the longest.

The division of the two main categories of men was determined by Olfert Fischer and it reflected his analysis of how the enemy would press his attack. In the eight ships to the north of the *Dannebrog* forty-two per cent of the crew were volunteers or pressed men; but in the eight ships to the south of her that figure was fifty-eight per cent.

IN THE COPENHAGEN ROADS

When Olfert Fischer hoisted his flag as Commander-in-Chief of the Copenhagen Roads defences on 11 March he *knew* the British would come. What he did not know was *when*. On 23 March he knew that they would be in the Roads in a matter of hours if they had a favourable wind, that is, from the north. This made no difference to the task at hand. His job was still to get the defence vessels into position and moored, and as ready for action as possible. What it did mean was that everything had to be done with an even greater sense of urgency.

In this situation efficient communications was an important element of his power of control. Each vessel under his command, and Trekroner Fort, had its own signal number: and from the *Dannebrog*'s stump of a mainmast, a fluttering stream of signals was flown. Many of the vessels had difficulty in understanding the signals and in sending a reply to that effect. This was part of naval life least familiar to the contract lieutenants. Olfert Fischer, therefore, ordered an officer from each ship to report on board the *Dannebrog* every afternoon, weather permitting, when his adjutant gave a briefing on the orders for the next twenty-four hours, as well as notifying them of the password of the day. On special occasions he ordered the presence of the commanding officers in his great cabin aboard the flagship. And from time to time Fischer himself, or one of his staff officers, called on each of the defence vessels to boost morale and to present the necessary orders.

Olfert Fischer's defence

The most pressing problem Olfert Fischer faced in these hours was to get his vessels in position. Signal after signal was sent to vessel after vessel to expedite the warping and mooring, and those ships that were already in position were ordered to assist the latecomers with boats, warping anchors, cables and men. The larger ships in the southern section of the line were particularly slow in getting into position, but those in the middle section were also tardy. And on 23 March signals assumed a note of greater urgency. To the *Charlotte Amalie*: "Work day and night, with greatest despatch, to moor to four anchors; take on your powder and allocate men to your guns"; to the *Indfødsretten*: "Moor to four anchors without delay," and similar messages to the *Wagrien*, *Jylland* and *Kronborg*.

During the process of placing the Defence Line in the King's

Deep a change of plan became necessary. Originally the *Wagrien* was to have been the most southerly of the vessels in the line of defence. But when the *Prøvestenen* sprang a leak Fischer had to redispose his forces. On the morning of 23 March the *Wagrien* was ordered to stop mooring ship. In the afternoon Commander Risbrich received instructions for the *Wagrien* to take *Prøvestenen*'s position. Fischer was concerned that the *Prøvestenen* would sink and decided that the safest course would be to move her to a position where she would have only two or three feet of water under her keel. If she sank there, she would settle happily on her extra two keels and still be capable of fighting. Instead, Risbrich moored the *Wagrien* dead astern of the *Prøvestenen*, as the southernmost vessel, making the southern end of the King's Deep line now two hundred metres further north than originally planned.

This meant that the whole line was shorter and that the distance between ships was less. That in itself was of advantage to Fischer. What he feared most, and had warned against, was that the British would break through the Line and fire on the Danish vessels from astern or ahead, where they were most vulnerable. This was also why he dropped the original plan for an inner and outer line and placed his ships on what was effectively a single line. He had already placed one of the converted cavalry barges, the *Rendsborg*, in the outer line in the gap between the blockships *Wagrien* and *Jylland*.

After the arrival of the British squadron off Kullen Fischer decided to move all his ships into the outer line. He correspondingly instructed the manoeuvrable cavalry barges *Aggershus* and *Nyborg* to moor to only two anchors, so that they were ready to "take position between any opening in the line". He therefore positioned the lightly armed signals frigate, the *Elven* (with only ten guns), so that her guns could cover the large gap between the *Dannebrog* and the *Kronborg*. Then he moved the three small artillery barges, the *Søhesten*, *Sværdfisken* and *Hajen*, into the line proper. And on the morning of 30 March, when he could hear the British battling their way past Kronborg Castle, he ordered Fleet Battery No 1, then in Trekroner Fort's harbour, to "position herself in front of the *Aggershus* or where she best could find a place" in the King's Deep line.

Gunboat flotilla
The gunboats also had the task of preventing a breakthrough of the line. They were to use their bow chasers against the bows of any

British ships-of-the-line that attempted to put themselves between the Danish vessels.

The eleven gunboats had both oars and sails; they had two masts, a crew of sixty-nine and were armed with two 18-pounder bow chasers. On 21 March Fischer briefed the commanders of the two divisions as to their preliminary orders for the imminent action. They were to take up position behind the southern sector of the King's Deep Line and south of the *Dannebrog* so as to leave a clear range for Steen Bille's squadron.

But two days later the chain of command of the gunboat flotilla was changed, and it was a change that could have been crucial. Command was divided, in a way that was far from clear, between Olfert Fischer and Steen Bille. The reason behind the change was that the flotilla's most experienced men came from Steen Bille's squadron. With this change, it was decided that the flotilla should be tasked both to follow orders from Steen Bille and signals from Olfert Fischer. The immediate consequence was that it was Bille who, in his usual energetic fashion, took over the training of the flotilla. They started with what today would be called Officer-of-the-Watch manoeuvres in response to signals from their divisional leader – weigh anchor, form line of battle, alter course in turn, alter course together, reduce distance and make ready to anchor. Bille was an experienced leader of men who understood the psychology of men cheering in unison as a ship's company. On 27 March the watchkeeping officer noted in the *Dannebrog*'s log: "3 o'clock, both divisions of gunboats exercised under oars and as they passed us, hailed us with three cheers, which we returned as they passed us again."

Lieutenant Captain Steen Bille was a skilful and independent officer. In 1801 he had an independent command and it was the vessels of his squadron that were to serve as the eyes of the defence line. The naval brigs, *Sarpen* and *Nidelven*, that were patrolling in the Sound to observe the movements of the British Fleet were part of his command. On 23 March Bille gave orders to his squadron to clear for action: "10 o'clock – lower decks cleared and reminded of the oath of fidelity they had taken and to maintain their courage against the enemy that was now threatening the country, at which the crew, as one man, burst out cheering, to be repeated with three-fold huzzas and cries of fighting to the last man. The men were divided into gun crews and began gun drill and small arms practice." The same evening Bille had a spring attached to the

Danmark's anchor cable to allow him to direct a broadside against the enemy, no matter which quarter the attack came from, because he knew that there would be an attack.

On the same day he had received orders directly from the Crown Prince to open fire if the British should attempt to outmanoeuvre Olfert Fischer's fixed defences. "As it was possible that the British, without opening fire, may attempt to double the ships of the defence line, it is your duty in such circumstances to take the initiative of using the necessary force the King has authorized you with." Nelson's tactics from Aboukir of splitting a line of ships by doubling were already well-known by the Danish Navy.

Gun drills

The battle the defence line was to fight would be a pure artillery duel. Commander Risbrich was perfectly correct when he said that rate and accuracy of fire would be decisive as "we can expect to be engaging an enemy who is professional and experienced". On March 23 Olfert Fischer expressed the same concerns as the *Wagrien*'s captain when he cooly reported to the Admiralty that "most of the ships of the defence line are manned by only two officers and the crews barely trained. Indeed, on the last vessels to be moored almost completely untrained. I wish only for fair weather to allow me to get them moored, manned and drilled."

Training of the crews was something Fischer had stressed from the beginning. On 15 March, at a time when very few of the vessels were even in position, he gave orders that "the crews are to be exercised in gun drills at every opportunity, morning and afternoon". From 17 March signals to that effect were sent from the *Dannebrog*, with some hours' exercising action stations in the morning and two or three hours' gun drill in the afternoon.

In view of the fact that many of the crews had never even seen a gun before, it was essential to get them trained, to some degree at least, before things hotted up. The six-man crew of each gun should be capable of going through the drill automatically when the time came for the drums to beat to action, get to their stations and each carry out his specific role in the ritual of firing a naval gun: "open port, load, run out" and so on. They would have to be able to go through the procedure of popping a powder cartridge into the muzzle of the gun, tamping it down to the bottom of the barrel, loading a ball, tamping again and running out. When the heavy artillery piece – and a 36-pounder and carriage weighed three or four tons – had been fired, the recoil sent it hurtling back until it was arrested by the breaching ropes, as thick as a man's arm, bolted to the ship's side. It then had to be sponged out to douse any glowing powder remains and the whole procedure repeated.

It was gruelling work, and new to many. It was not only on the gun deck of the *Prøvestenen* that cheap laughs were to be had when a keen but green volunteer rating loaded the ball before the cartridge. In a situation like this the professional rating was worth his weight in gold. Fischer was therefore a happy man when he could report to his officers on 25 March that senior gunners from the Naval Artillery Company would be boarding the *Prøvestenen*, *Wagrien*, *Jylland* and *Charlotte Amalie* as supernumaries "to train the gun crews but return ashore before any action begins". They went aboard all right, but they were not as easy to get rid of as Fischer had ordered. The commanding officer of the *Prøvestenen* wrote of 45-year-old gunner Caspar Johansen: "On April 2, as the British were about to engage me and every man was at his appointed station, I ordered him ashore as he was not part of the ship's company (a boat was propitiously alongside). He requested that he be allowed to remain on board and join a gun's crew, which was his great desire. He thus remained on board and was allocated to the upper gun deck where, during the ensuing action, he showed himself to be as efficient as he was courageous." At Johansen's home in Rævegade, his eldest son of fourteen was a gunner's boy in the Naval Artillery Company. What was he to say to him if he were sent ashore when the enemy was at the door? Caspar Johansen did return home to the naval houses in the quarter known as Nyboder after the battle, unscathed and intact. In fact, he even made the newspapers and was decorated on 2 April 1802 for his valour during the Battle.

The training of the gun crews was the most pressing task, but it was far from the only one. Many of the vessels had not received gun carriages for all the pieces when they were warped out. Ashore, work was proceeding at full speed to complete the work and as late as the afternoon of 29 March, an anchor vessel was warped out of Holmen dockyard with seventeen sledge carriages – twelve for the *Jylland* and four for the *Charlotte Amalie*, with the *Kronborg* having to settle for one. These carriages were much more cumbersome than the usual wheeled trolleys. Despite the shortage of men, Fischer managed to get the Admiralty to accept an increase in the size of a gun's crew, from six to nine, for those fitted with sledge carriages. Furthermore, with such inexperienced ratings, it was essential to make the elevation and training of the guns as simple as possible. To that end Fischer urgently requested that sights be fitted and instructors provided to demonstrate their use, and issued orders for all such mechanisms to be fitted with clear instructions.

Powder was to be collected from the magazine in the Citadel. Fischer wanted to be supplied with at least thirty cartridges per gun, twenty rockets, grenades and hand grenades. He also stressed that the two ships-of-the-line *Sjælland* and *Holsten*, which carried masts and spars, should be fitted with swivel guns in the tops to be used against the men on the upper deck and rigging of the enemy ships.

State of readiness

Olfert Fischer made ready to face the enemy. On the morning of 24 March his commanding officers were told to report on board the *Dannebrog*. One of the items in his briefing was how they were to administer the oath of loyalty to their ship's companies. On board the *Elefanten* the people were charged to "fight for king and country, which was answered under oath with an 'aye' from all on board". On the afternoon of March 26 the Commander-in-Chief of the Danish forces, Crown Prince Frederik, went aboard the *Dannebrog*. He was greeted with a twenty-one gun salute as he arrived. On his return journey he was cheered by the ships as his barge passed. On the *Hjælperen* and *Mars*, the crews were lined up along the ships' sides and gave three cheers as the officer of the watch saluted; those in Bille's squadron gave their cheers from the shrouds.

The defence line was now ready. Its primary task was to be prepared for British fireships. This was clearly evident at Divisions on the afternoon of 25 March. The ship's company was told that "His Majesty has most graciously proclaimed that any man who diverts or destroys a fireship will receive in reward 100 rigsdaler if an officer or petty officer and 50 rigsdaler if a rating. He has also declared that any battery that succeeds in setting an enemy ship afire will be rewarded with 100 rigsdaler, for every mast shot away 50 rigsdaler and for every shot below the waterline 50 rigsdaler."

It was clear to the officers on the *Dannebrog*'s quarterdeck, hearing the Commander-in-Chief's orders at Divisions on 21 March, that the situation had changed. Apart from worrying latecomers into place and mooring, Fischer also issued the following order: "Officers and men of the vessels of the defence line are to remain on board unless ordered to leave in the service of His Majesty.

All ships are to keep a careful lookout to prevent surprise attacks."

The surprise attacks Fischer was so anxious about were not from the British Fleet, which the *Sarpen* and *Nidelven* were watching like hawks up at Elsinore. What worried him was that "a small vessel could be despatched close inshore down the coast to attempt to set our ships afire".

Fire-watching was thus a serious duty in the defence line. Each vessel had one of its own boats in the water, rowing round the ship throughout the night and they took turns in sending a patrol boat around the northern and southern flanks of the King's Deep line between 2300 and 0200. Both types of patrol boat were equipped with grappling irons to tow any enemy fireships, or their own ship's on fire, out of harm's way. Gradually the state of alert was escalated. On 27 March three large armed boats pulled out of Holmen; they were to carry out fire patrols every night between 2000 and 0400. They were manned by a hand-picked crew under the command of a naval officer and carried grappling irons attached to iron chains. With the evening patrol of 29 March, when it was clear that the British were preparing to pass Kronborg, the state of readiness was increased even more: "every ship is to have armed men at the ready and boats cleared for launching at night if help should be required by the ship or line patrols". The Defence Line was terrifyingly vulnerable to attack by fire. If one single ship were to go up in flames, it could spread to those close nearby, so everything possible was done to avoid such a catastrophe.

Increased readiness
The arrival of the British squadron off Kullen on 22 March triggered even greater alertness. The next day orders flew from the *Dannebrog* in a steady stream: "All officers and men are hereby ordered to show extra care in lookout and watchkeeping duties by day and night"; "Any ship's boys on board the vessels in the line who are too small to fetch and carry powder are to be sent ashore"; "Ships ordered yesterday to take on powder must ensure this is done as soon as possible as neither the gunner nor any of the men should be ashore in the event of the enemy engaging" and "Petty Officers are to be aware that a signal consisting of two black and white chequered flags means all boats ashore are to return to their ships immediately; attention will be drawn to this signal by the firing of a single shot".

The British could arrive with no warning. This time they did not come but the state of readiness was maintained. At 0730 on 24 March a signal was sent from the *Dannebrog* to all commanding officers to report on board the flagship. When they had all gathered in the great cabin their ears rang to the following instructions: "In the event of hostilities, make every effort to delay the enemy. In the event of a ship being doubled, the cavalry barges *Aggershus* and *Nyborg* are to do everything in their power to provide fire support for those ships whose batteries on the side of the vessel facing the city are not yet ready. Those ships who do not carry dressings and medicine chests on board are to pick them up at their earliest opportunity. The frigate *Elven* is to position herself between the *Dannebrog* and the *Kronborg*, a quarter of a cable to the west of them in order not to foul the range of the *Trekroner*'s and *Danmark*'s guns."

In political terms Denmark and Britain were not yet at war and the first hostilities had not yet taken place. But the Danish orders for war had been given the day before. Steen Bille had received direct orders from the Crown Prince to open fire if British ships put themselves on the blind side, between the defence line and the city. The same day, 23 March, Fischer had asked the Admiralty "whether I should regard England and Denmark as being in a state of war – if not, I await further instructions." The Admiralty replied in its most convoluted civil service style, far from the plain speaking the Crown Prince had used in his orders to Steen Bille. It authorized Olfert Fischer as Commander-in-Chief of the Defence Line to act as he saw fit: "When and if the English men-of-war arrive, the Commander-in-Chief is hereby ordered to demand of the commander of these vessels the nature of his intentions, which declaration will determine the Commander-in-Chief's subsequent actions." The Danish government had no desire to be seen in the eyes of the rest of the world as having been responsible for firing the first shot. But from 23 March Fischer was given blanket authority to open fire as he saw fit.

Enemy in sight
Around noon on 24 March the wind had been from the north. Later in the afternoon it veered to the south, and there it stayed. The wind was Denmark's ally and the readiness of the defences therefore needed no further preparation. All efforts could now be turned to the forthcoming action.

On 25 March Fischer sent the order for "all ships to have three guns loaded with double shot on each side". Two days later this was followed by another order: "All ships are to have enough shot on deck so that there will be no delays during the action." The orders of 28 March concentrated more on warping into place and mooring the last of the latecomers. The next day the orders assumed a more urgent note, stating that the British could weigh anchor at any time and set sail for Copenhagen. During the briefing that afternoon Fischer reported that "When a flashing light is lit at night, that is the signal for clearing for action." And as a last and very human reminder, "Commanding officers will be kind enough to ensure that no ladies board their ships and that other officers refrain from bringing them aboard as long as we await the arrival of the enemy."

Fischer now expected the enemy at any moment. Early in the morning of 29 March the brig *Nidelven* returned from her station south of Elsinore with the news that the British squadron had anchored close to Kronborg, an indication that they soon intended to make the passage past the fortress. The same afternoon the *Nidelven* made her way northwards again to observe the British ships. At the same time the *Sarpen* was tasked to lay off the Hollander Deep "and stop all ships from the south making passage northwards, whatever flag they may be flying". If her commanding officer saw the *Nidelven* sailing towards Copenhagen from the north with a British Union Flag flying from her foretop he was to remain where he was, but if she also fired signal shots he was to proceed immediately to the Kronløbet Channel.

At last, during the night of 29 March the wind backed to the north and the signals fluttering from the *Dannebrog* shortly after dawn left no one in any doubt that Fischer expected the imminent arrival of the British battle squadron. At 0500 the *Elefanten* was ordered to "keep a close watch"; at the same time an officer from the *Danmark* was ordered to report on board the flagship. Fifteen minutes later the vessels in the defence line were given the order to clear for action. At four minutes to six Fischer sent the signal that all contact with the shore should be broken. After the gunfire from Kronborg had been audible for half an hour Fischer issued orders that "ships are to open fire as soon as the enemy is within range".

The British were on their way. The *Nidelven* came flying from the north under full sail with a British flag at her foretop and firing the agreed signal shots. Together with the *Sarpen*, she made her way into the Kronløbet Channel, where the two brigs anchored astern of the blockships *Elefanten* and *Mars*. At 0800 Olfert Fischer signalled Sub-Lieutenant Peter Willemoes aboard his Fleet Battery No 1 to leave harbour at Trekroner Fort and take up position in the large gap in the defence line between the *Dannebrog* and the *Sjælland*. With the choppy sea washing over the low deck and her crew wading in water up to their ankles, Willemoes warped out of the protection of the harbour and took up his assigned station at 0900. Precisely one hour later the first British ship-of-the-line dropped anchor in the Copenhagen Roads.

Much honour, little hope

The long period of waiting was over, but the artillery barge *Hajen* was still not in her position in the three-kilometre line in the King's Deep. She was the only absentee. Fischer had abandoned the original plan for an inner and outer line. Instead, in accordance with the tactics agreed between him and the Defence Commission, he strove to "reduce the distance between the ships in the line". He made no bones about his reasons. As he explained in a later report: "I was firm in my conviction to move the Fleet Battery, the artillery barges *Søhesten*, *Sværdfisken* and *Hajen* and any vessel that bore a gun of any kind into the gaps in the line to make any breakthrough as difficult as possible."

The defence of the King's Deep Channel ranged north to south in a single line, not close in to the Refshale Shoal but out in the Deep itself, so far out that the northernmost ships stood the risk of being doubled by the enemy. Fischer was aware of this danger and had allocated extra hands to allow them to man the guns on both port and starboard. His reason for deploying the line so far from shore was the necessity to keep control of the wide King's Deep Channel. He had chosen to place the northernmost ships in a position where they could protect the incomplete Trekroner Fort, whose soldiers were without any but the most primitive form of protection and severely exposed. An officer with Steen Bille's experience had his doubts as to how long the Fort would be able to keep up any effective resistance.

As Commander-in Chief of the Defence Line, Olfert Fischer had made maximum use of the resources at his disposal. But he had made it plain both to his military and political masters that the forthcoming battle could not be won and that Danish control of the King's Deep could not be maintained. Two members of the government reached precisely the same conclusion after they had

107

been on board a number of the defence vessels on 30 March. Minister of Finance Ernst Schimmelmann and President of the Slesvig-Holstein Chancellery Cay Reventlow had been greatly impressed by the courage and resolution of the men in the line of defence, but on the boat journey back to Copenhagen they confessed that the position of the Danes in the Copenhagen Roads was disturbingly parallel to that of the Spartans at Thermopylae: Much honour, little hope.

DENMARK'S ALLIES

With Denmark in the League of Armed Neutrality, she could expect, in theory, the assistance of the other members, and Denmark's League allies were Britain's natural enemies.

The question is whether Denmark, on 30 March with the British fleet at anchor in the Copenhagen Roads, actually had any League comrades or any other allies? And did she really expect any help from them?

The French First Consul would appear to have been the person who could provide the fastest and most effective help to Denmark. With massive numbers of troops along the Channel coast and by ordering the combined squadrons of France, Spain and Holland to leave Brest, Rochefort and Texel, Bonaparte could have contained the British Channel Fleet and North Sea Fleet to its own waters and thereby force Britain to drop its plans to attack the member states of the League of Armed Neutrality. The Tsar had already made such an appeal to Bonaparte in January. The Danish Foreign Minister had also explained to the French envoy in Copenhagen how his government could be of assistance to the Nordic countries. But not until the Fleet was in Danish territorial waters did he make a direct appeal for assistance.

Bonaparte reacted with enthusiasm. As a former artillery officer he was full of helpful advice and encouragement about the use of heated cannon balls; he offered to send two or three hundred of his most experienced gunners to Copenhagen by coach and he promised unequivocally to put his squadrons at Brest, Rochefort and Texel to sea and that, together with four hundred gunboats deployed along the Channel coast ready to invade Britain, they would be able to contain a force of at least forty British ships-of-the-line. But when the Danish envoy applied pressure to get the

Dutch squadron to sea, Foreign Minister Talleyrand replied with his usual venom that it was just as difficult for Bonaparte to get any action out of his allies as it was for Denmark to get any out her Swedish friends.

The political reality was that relations between France and Russia were still far from settled and that Bonaparte had other and more important goals for his navies and armies. On the other hand, it was politically expedient for Bonaparte to demonstrate the closeness of his relations with the Tsar and the League of Armed Neutrality. On the evening of April 1 the Danish envoy in Paris received Bernstorff's direct appeal for help and immediately sought an audience with Talleyrand. The next day, whilst the smoke of gunfire hung thick over the King's Deep, he received the Foreign Minister's reply, with a promise of a French diversionary move against the British. And the same evening the First Consul's personal equerry, General Lauriston, left Paris by special coach with a personal message from Bonaparte to the Crown Prince.

In fact, there was absolutely no hope of any help from France. France was not obliged to provide it and Denmark had shown tangible coolness towards Bonaparte's régime until the British attack forced the Danish government to change its stance.

Russia and Prussia

The Danish government knew that Prussia had only joined the League of Armed Neutrality because it had no alternative and, that in late March, it had only broken off relations with Britain because of the unrelenting pressure from St Petersburg and Paris. It had no fleet; furthermore, the areas of northern Germany in which the Prussian army could operate in support of the League were also areas in which Prussia and Denmark had widely differing political, military and financial interests. Behind a façade of harmony and loyalty, the governments in Copenhagen and Berlin were watching each other very closely. The Danes knew that Prussia was only fulfilling its obligation to the League because of pressure from the Tsar and Bonaparte, whose political concorde the Danish government predicted to be a short-lived affair. Denmark had no ally in Prussia, nor had she made any attempt to woo one.

Russia was the recognized political and military leader of the League of Armed Neutrality and its strongest partner, but no help could be expected from that direction. Basically, the Tsar regarded the Danish and Swedish fleets as an extended arm of the defence of the Russian coastline and ports.

And even if the Tsar had wanted to come to Denmark's assistance, he was physically unable to do so. The ice made it impossible for the squadrons in Reval and Kronstadt to put to sea so early in the year. The people of Copenhagen, however, believed the Russians would come. And the worthy Russian envoy in the capital, Vasilii Grigorevich Lizakevich, did his utmost to keep the belief alive. But in the Government, the Admiralty and the Navy, it was a foregone conclusion that help from the south was a hope in vain. At least help in the form of the Russian fleet.

Danish-Swedish mistrust

But there was still the Swedish fleet. Would Denmark's arch enemy come to her assistance? For very good reasons, many said that was a pipe-dream. The unfailing goal of Swedish foreign policy was to acquire Norway. The King of Sweden had made this abundantly clear to the Tsar during his visit to St. Petersburg in December. And the Danish government knew it. It also knew that the Swedish offer of playing a part in the defence of the Sound had an ulterior motive – to regain its toll-free status in the Sound at the same time as getting a share of that toll.

On the other hand Denmark and Sweden had a vested interest in the League presenting an outward appearance of unity and decisiveness. This was the prime reason for Sweden allowing the Norwegian troop convoys through their country. It was also a major point in the Danish-Swedish defence discussions. And it was the reason for a meeting in Helsingborg between Crown Prince Frederik and his cousin, King Gustav IV Adolf of Sweden.

In mid-February the Swedish Naval Minister, Vice Admiral Cronstedt, arrived in Copenhagen as the personal emissary of the King. With him he brought the Swedish Order of the Sword for the Crown Prince's favourite, Lieutenant Captain Steen Bille, and a letter from the King to the Crown Prince himself in which Cronstedt was authorized to present the King's plan for a common policy of the Sound's defence.

Cronstedt had accompanied the Swedish King on his visit to St. Petersburg and had taken part in the military planning together with the Tsar. The plan the Tsar and the King had agreed upon, against the protestations of Rosenkrantz, the Danish envoy in St. Petersburg, was for a Danish-Swedish naval force to protect the passage of ships across the Drogden Shallows between the islands of Amager and Saltholm, just south of Copenhagen. From the Danish point of view, the plan was unacceptable because it left Copenhagen exposed, hence Rosenkrantz's objections. But under the pressure of the impending threat, the Danish government reluctantly accepted it. After his return to Stockholm, the King had issued orders that seven ships-of-the-line and three frigates should be fitted out in Karlskrona as the Swedish contribution to the League's squadron, ready to put to sea by the end of March. On his way to Copenhagen Cronstedt had taken a small diversion to Karlskrona to discuss the project with the Swedish naval Commander-in-Chief. In Copenhagen he further went through the details of denying the British access to the Sound with Crown Prince Frederik, his naval adjutant Commander Hans Lindholm and Count Bernstorff. In the course of this meeting he promised that Sweden would also send twenty-four gunboats from Stockholm to join the Sound squadron. In return, the Danes revealed their defence plans for Copenhagen. The Swedish admiral, who had battle experience from the American War of Independence and the war between Sweden and Russia in 1788–90, assessed the Danish defence measures as adequate and, together with Hans Lindholm, he discussed preventive measures against British fireships and the use of heated shot.

Another task in Cronstedt's mission was to arrange a meeting between his King and the Danish Crown Prince, a meeting the King wanted to take place on Swedish soil. The Danes were more than interested in signalling the bond between the two countries and it was agreed the meeting should take place in Helsingborg.

On the morning of 6 March Crown Prince Frederik arrived in the town just opposite Kronborg Castle, accompanied by Steen Bille and the naval and army adjutants, Hans Lindholm, and Captain Kirchhoff of the Danish Army. After inspecting a guard of honour the Crown Prince and the King of Sweden spent two hours in discussion.

The main item on the agenda was the common defence of the Sound. The Crown Prince accepted that it should be based at the Drogden Shallows and a system of common communications signals was devised. The question of the establishment of Swedish artillery batteries in Helsingborg was briefly touched upon and just as quickly evaded. It was much too hot a political potato. King Gustav chose to accept the Crown Prince's claims that the guns at

Kronborg were quite capable of defending the entrance to the Sound on their own, a claim both knew to be untrue. The Swedish batteries were not set up.

The meeting of the two royal houses in Helsingborg ended in being exactly what the Danes had intended, a political demonstration. The only result of the meeting was confirmation of the Danish-Swedish defence plan for the Drogden Shallows that had already been drawn up and agreed upon. The defence of Copenhagen was not mentioned. That remained what it always had been, a purely Danish matter.

Admiral in a tight spot
The arrival of the British fleet in the Kattegat two weeks later changed the picture radically.

At that time the Swedish King was in Gothenburg organizing his coastal defences. From the coastline he saw the ships arrive. He reacted by sending a courier to the Tsar with a request to expedite the sailing of the Kronstadt squadron and its joining up with the Swedish squadron, and by sending Cronstedt on a new mission to Copenhagen. Shortly afterwards King Gustav left for Landskrona, from where he was in direct contact with his Minister of the Navy in the Danish capital.

On the surface of it Cronstedt's task was little short of mission impossible. The letter he conveyed from the King was politically non-committal. And in the Danish capital there was already a feeling of resentment among the general public that the Swedish fleet had not ventured into the Sound. Cronstedt was in a tight spot and politically embarrassed; and personally unhappy about the critical feelings towards Sweden.

Shortly after his arrival the Crown Prince offered to despatch eight floating batteries with Danish crews – the navy's sand barges armed with 18-pounders – up to Helsingborg to defend the entrance to the Sound. But, for political reasons Cronstedt had to give an evasive answer. He pointed out, and with all justification, that as there were no shore batteries in Helsingborg to support the floating batteries, and as their guns were not powerful enough to do any real damage to the British ships, he would have to limit his acceptance of the offer to forwarding the proposal to the Swedish king. In fact his answer was a point blank refusal, and thus was it perceived by the Crown Prince. And even as level-headed an officer as Lieutenant Michael Bille reacted vehemently: "Unbelievable! As

1. Lieutenant Michael Bille of the *Prøvestenen*.

2. The *Freya* affair, 25 July 1800.

3. Sir Hyde Parker.

4. Commodore Olfert Fischer.

5. Danish ships in convoy 1781 (*T. E. Lønning*).

6. Commander Peter Krabbe.

7. A dynasty of Danish foreign politics. For sixty years, with but a few years' interruption, the Foreign Minister of Denmark was named Bernstorff. From left: Johan Hartvig Ernst (from 1751 to 1770); his nephew Andreas Peter (from 1773 to 1797); and his son Christian (from 1797 to 1810).

8. Lord Spencer.

9. Tsar Paul I.

10. Lord Grenville.

11. Henry Dundas.

12. Sub-Lieutenant Peter Willemoes on his fleet battery.
(Courtesy of Willemoesgaarden/Assens, Denmark).

13. Lord St Vincent.

14. Lieutenant Captain
    Steen Bille.

15. Vice Admiral Lord Nelson in 1801.

16. The battle at noon (*C. A. Lorentzen*).

17. Crown Prince
    Frederik.

18. Sub-Lieutenant Peter Willemoes.

19. Captain Thomas Foley.

20. The White Flag.
(*C. A. Lorentzen: courtesy Det Nationalhistoriske Museum paa Frederiksborg/Hillerød, Denmark*

1.

Lord Nelson has directions to spare
Denmark when no longer resisting but if
the firing is continued on the part of Denmark
Lord Nelson will be obliged to set on fire all
the floating batteries he has taken, without
having the power of saving the Brave Danes
who have defended them. Dated on board His
Britannick Majesty Ship Elephant
Copenhagen Roads April 2nd 1801

Nelson & Bronte Vice
admiral under the command of
admiral Sir Hyde Parker

To the Brothers of Englishmen
the Danes

21. Lord Nelson's first letter.

yet I will not confess that the Swedes are traitors; more than likely it is lack of initiative on the admiral's part. And it's just as unbelievable that we have not already taken steps to strengthen the Swedish defences. It was obvious that Kronborg could not engage any ship on the Swedish side. I think that some misplaced jealousy and caution on our side has provoked this appalling negligence. Had the Swedes after our pressing request refused to establish these batteries, then we should have put floating batteries on the shoals ourselves."

Cronstedt knew of the ill-feeling in the Danish authorities and he was aware that he had made things worse by his refusal. When the Crown Prince therefore proposed that the Swedes send fireships from the Swedish coast towards the British fleet, Cronstedt recommended it enthusiastically to the King. He certainly believed such a plan was highly doubtful from a military point of view, but it would have a considerably mollifying effect on the Danish authorities.

Even so, he had to accept that the distrust and bitterness towards Sweden was growing day by day. And when King Gustav, only two days later, generously offered to let the Karlskrona squadron join the Copenhagen defence line, it was something that had to be wrapped in the utmost secrecy.

Swedish ships in the King's Deep?

The 23-year-old Swedish king had witnessed from Helsingborg how the British Fleet shot its way past Kronborg and anchored threateningly off Copenhagen, and it was in this situation that he suddenly reached his decision to come to Denmark's assistance. His offer to allow the Karlskrona squadron to join the defence of the Danish capital was genuine enough and an example of how both mind and heart have their roles to play in reaching crucial political decisions. It was an emotional reaction in a tense situation and the offer was hardly in accordance with the long-term objectives of Swedish foreign policy. At the same time the King was realistic enough in his politics to know that his chivalrous offer of assistance to his and the Tsar's ally in their hour of need would have favourable repercussions in St. Petersburg.

Originally the Karlskrona squadron (comprising the ships-of-the-line *Gustav III*, *Vladislaff*, *Wasa*, *Dristigheten*, *Tapperheten*, *Försigtigheten* and *Manligheten* and the frigates *Bellona*, *Camilla* and *Fröja*) was to have been ready to sail for the Sound in early April. But on 20 March King Gustav had sent new orders from

Gothenburg: the squadron was to depart for the Sound at the earliest opportunity. There it was to take up station near the Drogden Shallows and the Flinterenden Channel between Saltholm on the Danish side and Malmø on the Swedish. And it was to take with it vessels that could be sunk to block those channels. On 29 March Admiral Wachtmeister reported that the squadron would be ready to sail on 1 April.

King Gustav received his report late in the evening of 30 March and the very same evening a messenger rode from Landskrona at full gallop with new orders for the Karlskrona squadron. It was to sail on 2 April. Its destination was still the Sound, but it was now to join the defence line in the Copenhagen Roads.

The King's military reasoning was that he wanted to make the League of Armed Neutrality's naval power in the Sound so strong that the British fleet would not dare to cross the Drogden Shallows and enter the Baltic with so much firepower at its rear. Therefore he also gave instructions to the Swedish envoy in Copenhagen to ask the Danes to delay the British with sham negotiations. So, on 31 March it was a delighted and relieved Cronstedt who received orders from his King to inform the Danish Crown Prince that the Swedish fleet was on its way and to agree on the most advantageous positioning of the Swedish ships.

The Swedish offer of help was completely unexpected by the Danes. A Swedish contribution to the defence of the Baltic approaches in the form of batteries at Helsingborg would have been politically unacceptable to Denmark as it would have provided Sweden with an argument for demanding its share of the Sound toll. But it was something else entirely for a Swedish squadron to take part in the defence of the Sound and of Copenhagen. This was a development under the aegis of the League of Armed Neutrality and the Danish government had no reason to harbour any political concerns about accepting help from a member of the League.

From mid-March ten Elsinore pilots had been stationed in Dragør, on the southern end of Amager, ready to take the Russian and Swedish squadrons across the Drogden Shallows. These pilots were now put on immediate readiness. One was despatched immediately overland to Karlskrona and a number of small ships were made ready in Dragør to sail at a moment's notice to warn the Karlskrona squadron if the British made a move to enter the Baltic. On 31 March the positioning of the Swedish ships was finally agreed on: the ships-of-the-line were to position themselves at the southern end of the King's Deep, stretching like a tail swept across the channel. The 40-gun frigates were to moor behind the King's Deep line. The line had 690 guns mounted; the Karlskrona squadron would add a further 574 guns. What the Swedish king promised was effectively almost a doubling of the firepower of the Copenhagen defence line.

But the joy in Copenhagen was short-lived; the help from Sweden did not turn up. When the squadron was ready to leave on 2 April the wind was unfavourable. The southerly wind that made it possible for Nelson to attack the King's Deep made it impossible for the Swedish squadron to work its way through the skerries of Karlskrona. The King's bitterness and his dismissal of both the squadron commander, Rear Admiral Palmqvist, and Admiral Wachtmeister for negligence and insubordination reflected his emotional involvement in trying to help Denmark. But it was entirely without justification. The Karlskrona squadron had done everything humanly possible.

Even if it had been able to wear the skerries and take advantage of the southerly wind and run for the Sound on 2 April, it would have arrived too late. Nelson had seen to that. Whilst his fleet was still in the Kattegat he had realized the necessity of placing the fleet in such a way as to prevent the members of the League from joining forces. That had been one of the reasons why he had wanted to make the passage through the Great Belt, and it had been one of the reasons why he had wanted to attack the King's Deep from the south. On 1 April he weighed anchor with more than half the Baltic Fleet's ships and manoeuvred south through the Hollander Deep. That evening he and his division dropped anchor between the King's Deep and the Drogden Shallows. Copenhagen was definitively cut off from its allies.

That same evening Cronstedt begged an audience with the Crown Prince to ask how the Swedish squadron could now be of assistance. At the time the Crown Prince had come to the conclusion that, even if the Swedish ships had been able to get through and enter the Copenhagen Roads, they would suffer greater losses than the British and the advantage gained would be too small compared to the risk. In such a situation the Crown Prince thought it only fitting to release the King of Sweden from his obligation.

And thus it was that Nelson did not have to take on the Swedish fleet, even though Cronstedt, late on the afternoon of 2 April, whilst sporadic gunfire was still being heard from the blockships in the

King's Deep, was still watching eagerly for the Swedish squadron to emerge from the south and prayed that it would arrive in the nick of time and hurl itself into the action.

For twenty-four hours there had been an opportunity to reinforce the Copenhagen defence line – reinforcement on such a scale that could have caused Parker to reassess his situation and abandon his plan. But the reinforcements did not arrive and the chance had been there for but a single day, at a time when it was far too late in the day to regroup the Danish defences. Those ordered by the Danish government on 27 December had at no time been based on promises or expectations of help from the country's allies and League members. From the very beginning the defence of Copenhagen had been regarded and planned as a purely Danish operation.

Chapter 7

THE BATTLE OF COPENHAGEN
– PROLOGUE

THE LAST THREE DAYS

The long wait was over. On the morning of 30 March the opponents were at last drawn up in sight of each other: the Danish line of ships in the King's Deep and the forest of masts of the British Baltic Fleet some seven miles distant in the Copenhagen Roads.

War became a reality that morning when the Commandant of Kronborg Castle opened fire on the *Monarch*. But neither the Danish government nor Olfert Fischer knew precisely what the enemy's objectives were. Did they intend to make an all-out attack on Copenhagen? Or did they merely want to pass the city and move into the Baltic for a confrontation with the Russians and Swedes? Three days were to pass before the answers to these questions became terrifyingly obvious.

Parker's orders were crystal clear – the target was Copenhagen. And five days previously, after a disastrous display of doubt and uncertainty, he resolved to follow them to the letter. He already knew, more or less, the strength and disposition of the Copenhagen defences and the plan of battle was already finalized. The opening gambit was for Nelson to attack the King's Deep line from the south with half the fleet, whilst two fireships were sent against the block-ships in the Kronløbet Channel. The end game was the storming of the Trekroner Fort. Quite what the middle game would be was not so certain.

On the morning of 30 March there was little for Fischer to do other than worry the last of his vessels into position, exercise his guns crews, be on guard against surprise attack, observe the movements of the British and try to deduce what their intentions were.

The first move was made by Parker. He had to reconnoitre the Danish defences and he had to reach a final decision on how the attack was to be launched, and his was the final word and the ultimate responsibility in the planning of the attack his second was to lead.

Parker and Nelson wasted no time. The moment the anchors were let go and holding ground they began their observations of the line and made preparations to sound the waters of the Hollander Deep, where the Danes had removed all seamarks. Barely had the *Elephant*'s anchor disappeared under the waves before Nelson ordered the *Bellona*, *Ardent* and *Elephant* to prepare twelve barrels as dan buoys, anchored with barshot, to mark the Middle Ground Shoal. As soon as he had issued these orders Nelson boarded the lugger, *Lark*. With him went Parker, Graves, Colonel Stewart and Captains Domett, Otway, Foley, Fremantle and Riou. Escorted by the frigate *Amazon* and the brig *Cruizer*, the *Lark* made her way down towards the northern end of the Danish defence line, where she shortened sail to slow down and allow Parker and his officers to study the situation closely through their telescopes. The nearest of the Danish ships, the *Elefanten*, *Hjælperen* and *Indfødsretten*, and Trekroner Fort, opened fire but the range was too great and shortly before 1300 Fischer gave the order to cease fire.

After two hours' reconnaissance the *Lark* headed back for the *London* and Parker and his retinue went aboard to discuss their observations. They had now seen the defences with their own eyes, observed the vessels and estimated their armament. They were all agreed on at least one point – the Danes had made use of the waiting time to beef up their defences. But they could not agree on just how strong the line actually was. Many were concerned about the numerous shallow-draft ships and about Trekroner Fort. Parker admitted pessimistically that the King's Deep line was "considerably more formidable than we had been led to believe". Nelson, however, was of another opinion, as he expressed in a letter to Lady Hamilton: "It looks formidable to those who are children at war, but to my judgement, with ten sail of the line, I can annihilate them; at all events, I hope to be allowed to try."

The final decision to attack was not made on 30 March. Parker wanted to carry out another reconnaissance of the defences the next morning and he wanted the artillery officers from the bomb vessels along with him.

Clear for action

But, as mentioned before, there was not a great deal left for Olfert Fischer usefully to do on 30 March. That morning he plugged the large gap between the *Dannebrog* and *Sjælland* with Fleet Battery No 1. In the afternoon he sent one of the gunboat divisions to a position behind the southern sector of the King's Deep line. That evening they were joined by three more from the other division. During the afternoon he did not call the officers from his ships for a briefing aboard the flagship but sent two of his staff around his command with orders as to who was to carry out patrols and fire watch during the night. Further orders were issued to the effect that "all ships are to have boats ready and armed to remove fireships, against which the most attentive watch is to be maintained, and to assist in patrolling duties." Following the arrival of the British there was a new item in his daily orders: "Ships are to prepare for action. Commanding officers are to ensure their people get what sleep they can during daylight hours when duties permit."

On the night of the 30 March half the men of the defence line, therefore, were sleeping on deck next to their guns whilst the other half kept watch. It was bitterly cold, and more than one captain that night recalled Crown Prince Frederik's order "not to be economical with spirits or money" and issued an extra ration of aquavit to their shivering crews.

Council of war aboard the Elephant

On the morning of 31 March Parker went aboard the *Amazon* with the same group of officers as the previous day to carry out his second reconnaissance of the Danish line. With them were two artillery captains and five artillery lieutenants from the bomb vessels. Throughout the forenoon the *Amazon* tacked back and forth in the waters north of the Middle Ground Shoal and a good way down the Hollander Deep. Once again shots were fired from the Danish ships but to no avail. The British frigate kept tantalisingly out of range, but not out of sight.

With the reconnaissance completed, Parker ordered a written report from the seven artillery officers on the possibilities of bombarding the Danish navy's establishment at Nyholm. Their assessment was clear and unambiguous – bombardment *would* be feasible if the defence line in the King's Deep were removed, but only if.

So Parker had as much intelligence as he could obtain. A council of war was therefore held aboard the *Elephant* that afternoon. Present were Parker, Nelson, Graves, Domett, Foley, Fremantle, Murray and Riou. What the Commander-in-Chief was keen to hear was their views as to whether to attack the defence line or not, and from Nelson, Graves and Domett he wanted those views in writing. It soon became apparent that opinion was divided. Rear Admiral Graves was adamantly opposed to an attack, whilst Parker's Captain of the Fleet, William Domett, was equally adamant in his enthusiasm to engage.

During the debate the issues of Denmark's allies and their battle fleets were raised. At this point Nelson strode up and down the deck of the *Elephant*'s day cabin, visibly exasperated at all the doubt and dithering that was going on. When the Swedish fleet was mentioned, he tersely replied, "The more the better", and when the discussion turned to the Russian fleet, "So much the better; I wish they were twice as many, the easier the victory, depend on it." Nelson was hungry for a scrap and held no high opinion of the tactics of the Nordic fleets. He knew well the French and Russian fleets from his confrontations in the Mediterranean and his experience had taught him: "Close with a Frenchman, but outmanoeuvre a Russian".

The conclusion of the council of war was that Parker stuck to his decision to attack – and to attack from the south. Nelson repeated his offer to lead the attack with the forces he had already been given and Parker accepted. He left the detailed planning to Nelson and "with sound discretion, and in a handsome manner" gave him two more ships than he had asked for. Captains Murray and Fremantle of the *Edgar* and *Ganges* were not slow in coming forward and gaining their Commander-in-Chief's approval that it should be *their* ships that should be detached to Nelson's division.

During the reconnaissance and council of war the rest of the fleet had not been idle. First thing that morning the shallow-draft armed vessels and men from Parker's division were sent across to Nelson; in the afternoon some of Parker's ships were detached to Nelson's division and in the evening and throughout the night the sounding and buoy-laying in the Hollander Deep was carried out according to Nelson's instructions, under the charge of Captain Brisbane of the *Cruizer*.

The old blue trousers

There was just as little for Fischer to address on 31 March as the day before. He now knew that the gap between the *Dannebrog* and the *Kronborg* would be closed before the arrival of the British; the *Hajen* was on her way. At 0730 that morning Sub-Lieutenant Müller had reported on board the *Dannebrog* as captain of the artillery barge. But, as it turned out, it was to take longer to get her into position than estimated; during the warping across the Refshale Shoal she went aground and was not afloat again until the next morning.

The enemy was in sight and aboard every vessel gun drills were being carried out incessantly. Nevertheless, there was a strange feeling of calm along the defence line. On board the blockship *Elefanten* 25-year-old reserve surgeon Søren Wendelboe, who had married only eight days before, found the time to write to his beloved Maren Kirstine about life on board a man of war: "I am very comfortable on board among so many fine men. I mess with the officers and the senior surgeon who was here before me. If only you were by my side, I should indeed be quite happy; because, despite the fact that we have the English in sight, there is a mood of calm as they are doing nothing yet. I am aware that people in the city are more concerned than we are – here there are happy faces and good humour and it is difficult to believe there is an enemy fleet at our door. The only inconvenience I suffer is that I cannot know when next I will be able to go ashore, as no one may leave their ship, nor may I ask for you to visit me as no ladies are allowed on board in this threatening situation."

Søren Wendelboe wrote in blissful ignorance of the fate Nelson had planned for his ship – to send the Baltic Fleet's two fire-ships against the *Elefanten* and *Mars*. The young reserve surgeon's thoughts were on more domestic matters: "Would you be so kind as to send me a pound of tobacco, half a pound of roast and ground coffee beans, a bottle of cream and some sugar, a pair of clean woollen stockings, a clean shirt, my old hat and long boots and my small pipe. Please also send the old blue trousers that you will find in the pine chest of drawers – they are good enough to wear here on board."

On board the *Dannebrog*, Olfert Fischer was somewhat less blasé about the situation on 31 March. He organized no general officers' briefing that afternoon either. But he did order his commanding officers on board. Once more he emphasized the importance of patrolling the line and each ship in it, of keeping fire watch and of arming and equipping the boats with grappling irons to tow away any fireships. The crews of the gunboats were messed in various of the largest ships in the line. Commanding officers were instructed to ensure that the spirit levels on the guns were functioning correctly and he ordered the highest state of readiness for the coming night. It meant another night of being chilled to the marrow, both for the watchkeepers and those who slept on the deck by their guns.

Prepare to weigh

But the next morning, 1 April, the uncertainty of the British intentions was beginning to dissipate, everyone on board could see what was going on with their own eyes.

Since 30 March the British fleet had been riding to anchor in two divisions. The previous day certain ships from Parker's division had joined Nelson's division. But with sunrise on 1 April Parker's entire division weighed anchor and headed south, where it anchored once again with Nelson's ships. The entire fleet now lay north of the Middle Ground Shoal.

Nelson used the forenoon to complete the sounding and marking of the Hollander Deep, a process that was crucial to his being able to carry out the attack. Before 0700 he was aboard the *Amazon* and from Captain Riou's frigate he took charge of the final stage of the sounding and marking, assisted by the smallest vessels in the fleet, the *Harpy*, *Fox*, *Lark* and *Eling*, which earlier that morning had taken masters on board from the major vessels. Edward Riou had the reputation of being a superb seaman. In 1790 he saved his ship, the frigate *Guardian*, bound for Australia with convicts, after she encountered an iceberg off the southern tip of Africa. And on 1 April he delighted Nelson with his lightning reactions; the *Amazon* went aground on Saltholm Flats but Riou immediately ordered all sail set and literally sailed her off the bank.

Around noon the job was done. The Hollander Deep was sounded and clearly marked with dan buoys. Two of the minor vessels anchored to mark Saltholm Flats, the brig *Harpy* marked the Middle Ground Shoal and Captain Brisbane put the *Cruizer* at the northern tip of the same shoal to mark the entrance to the Hollander Deep. The passage was clear and the wind was from the north.

At 1330 Nelson called on his Commander-in-Chief to receive his final orders. At the same meeting Parker issued orders to three of the ships-of-the line in his division, the *Defence*, *Ramillies* and *Veteran*. They were instructed to weigh at the same time as Nelson started his attack on the line of defence from the south, tasked to "menace the northern part of the enemy's line, as well as to be ready to render assistance to disabled ships coming out of action". These orders were part of the overall strategy for the impending action. Neither the Commander-in-Chief nor his second wasted much time pondering over the fundamental weakness of the plan: Nelson would be attacking with the wind and tide under him, whereas Parker would be working against both. Their diversionary action, therefore, would only take effect relatively late in the game.

At that time Nelson was highly preoccupied. It was vital for him to make the passage of the Hollander Deep while the wind was still from the north. On the way back from the *London* to the *Elephant*, he personally hailed each ship in his division as he passed them and shouted orders to prepare to weigh anchor.

On board the *Monarch* Midshipman Millard spotted a boat being rowed towards his ship from the north: "On directing my spying-glass towards her, I observed several officers in her, but at the end of the boat was a cocked hat put on square, with a peculiar slouch, so as to be at right angles to the boat's keel. I immediately ran to the officer of the watch and assured him Lord Nelson was coming on board, for I had seen his hat. My information did not receive much credit, till in process of time the old checked surtout was discovered; and soon after a squeaking little voice hailed the *Monarch*, and desired us, in true Norfolk drawl, to prepare to weigh."

As soon as Nelson was through the sally port of the *Elephant*, he hoisted the signal for his division to weigh, a signal that was answered by every ship with loud hurrahs. It was now 1500. Most of the ships set sail, a light northerly breeze taking them through the Hollander Deep, with Captain Riou and the *Amazon* in the van.

Behind them they left Parker's reduced division, comprising the two three-deckers *London* and *St. George* (very similar in size to HMS *Victory*) and the remaining six ships-of-the-line.

At 1700 they dropped anchor at the southern end of the Middle Ground Shoal. An hour later, the division's gun brigs weighed and followed suit, anchoring close to the larger ships at about 2100.

Nelson was now in the starting blocks and the trap was sprung.

Final precautions

Olfert Fischer followed the movements of the British fleet closely from the *Dannebrog*. During Nelson's last sounding operations the *Prøvestenen* and *Rendsborg* had fired several shots, but the range being more than 3,000 metres, Fischer sent a signal to cease fire.

He had several reasons not to react to the British buoying of the channel: neither he nor his government had any firm assessment of the British plans (their objective *could* have been the Baltic, in which case there was no point in poking at a hornet's nest), but also, and this is a crucial point, there was absolutely nothing Olfert Fischer could do to prevent it. The seaworthy vessels in his fleet, the frigates *Elven* and *Hjælperen*, and the converted cavalry barges *Aggershus*, *Nyborg* and *Rendsborg*, were all moored and could not be spared from the King's Deep line. And, with the British fleet just off the northern end of Middle Ground Shoal, it would be a risky business sending the gunboats after them, let alone Steen Bille's squadron in the Kronløbet Channel. In the last twenty-four hours before the battle Danish control of the Copenhagen Roads extended no further than the effective range of the guns in the King's Deep.

But where Fischer could do something useful, he did. Nelson's surveying of the waters could have been carried out with the intention of placing his bomb vessels on the Middle Ground Shoal itself, from where their incendiary shells could reach Nyholm and the indispensable battle squadron being fitted out in the dockyard. At sunrise on 1 April, therefore, he sent instruction to the largest ships, the ships-of-the-line *Sjælland* and *Holsten* and the blockship *Jylland*, "to have longboats ready, with warping anchors and two cables". They were also given verbal orders "to have these boats ready by night and day until further notice, and that their fire patrol longboats should be armed. This will allow the artillery barges and the Fleet Battery to haul themselves closer to the shoal to cause as much delay as possible." The King's Deep defence line was firmly and more or less permanently moored, but it would be possible to warp the small armed gun vessels over towards the shoal, under the covering fire of the heavy guns in the line, and engage the British bomb vessels in such shallow water.

On the other hand the movements of the Fleet on 1 April gave no cause for alarm aboard the vessels of the defence line. On board the *Elefanten*, Søren Wendelboe wrote reassuringly to his wife, "This evening broadsheets were handed out to both officers and men with songs written by the very best poets and sung by all on deck. So you see, my dearest good wife, that we are enjoying ourselves. Do not fret for me and enjoy these days as best you can in the company of our friends, as you must do without mine. Nor should you be concerned that this missive is addressed to myself. I have done so as is it not fitting for an officer to write to his wife at this time."

Yet, despite the apparent calm and good humour, the fact remains that on the evening of 1 April there was an enemy fleet of forty ships just south of the entrance to the King's Deep, only 3,000 metres from the blockship *Prøvestenen* and Stricker's Battery. A battle could break out at any moment.

On board the artillery barge *Hajen*, which had been refloated off the Refshale Shoal that afternoon and slowly warped herself out into the King's Deep, the crew were very attentive to what the British were up to. Sub-Lieutenant Müller manned his guns, loaded the twenty 18-pounders with roundshot and handed out side arms. With his ship in position and her armament ready to open fire, Müller was rowed across to the *Dannebrog* to make a report to that effect. The farewell he was given when he left was indicative of the mood among Danish naval officers about the next day. At the gangway 22-year-old Sub-Lieutenant Wulff, who had joined the *Dannebrog* two days before, sent his comrade-in-arms off with the words, "Good night. At this time tomorrow I shall either be a captain or an angel."

On the morning of 2 April Rasmus Wulff was killed at his post on the upper deck.

Stricker's Battery

When Parker's ships weighed that morning and joined up with Nelson's division Olfert Fischer's reaction was to issue orders to the line to present their broadsides to the enemy. As Nelson's division moved down the Hollander Deep he gave the signal to prepare for action. Whilst Nelson made his passage, Fischer called his officers together for the final briefing before the battle. He informed them what signal they were to send if they ran out of powder during the action; he drew their attention to the necessity of maintaining the highest state of readiness: "All boats are to be armed and carry grappling irons. The sharpest lookout is to be kept."

As the Danes had no inkling of the British plan, Fischer was preparing for every eventuality – attack by fireship, by boat and by shelling from the Middle Ground Shoal. Ashore, the assessment by such a professional officer as Vice Admiral Cronstedt was that the British had no immediate intention of engaging the defence line but were attempting to unsettle it with their gun brigs and bomb vessels. Crown Prince Frederik had arrived at the same evaluation. At his own initiative, the Commandant of Holmen dockyard had given the order to call all men to arms when Nelson had moved in to the Hollander Deep. The Crown Prince was irritated by this display of independence and countermanded what he considered to be an unnecessary order made in a state of panic.

With evening creeping on, the ships in Nelson's division lay closely together, riding to anchor south of the Middle Ground Shoal, in range of the mortars at Stricker's Battery. Army Lieutenant Stricker therefore sought the approval of the commanding officer of the Artillery Corps to open fire on the enemy. Colonel Mecklenburg, however, was not prepared to issue any such order off his own bat. After discussion with naval officers at Holmen, he had his doubts that the British would attack the King's Deep line. It was much more likely, in his opinion, that they would continue south and enter the Baltic. And if they should decide to attack from their present position, he did not want to reveal the presence of the battery before the battle, as it was defenceless against amphibious attack.

The Colonel did, however, seek an audience with the Crown Prince. And at 2000, after nightfall, the Crown Prince gave the order for Stricker's Battery to open fire against Nelson's division.

Three shells were fired from the battery's mortars. From his spotting post Mecklenburg deduced that the mortars did not have the range and ordered them to cease fire.

But from sea it looked very different. On board the *Hajen* Sub-Lieutenant Müller saw three shells land right in the middle of the British ships. And on board the *Elephant*, there was great consternation when the mortars opened fire, and equal astonishment when they ceased. Nelson's ships were in a particularly vulnerable position. He was not able to see a target and, at night and in uncharted waters, it would be foolhardy to try and move his division. They had to stay where they were, static targets for the Danish mortars. But, ashore, Colonel Mecklenburg was also in command of Stricker's Battery. And his decision it was to cease fire.

To a southerly wind and victory

In his geographical position, a keen lookout and vigilant guard boats were just as important to Nelson as they were to Fischer and at 2000 on 1 April the guard boats pulled away from their ships. The water most keenly patrolled was the 3,000 metres between the British ships and the Danish defence line. Those guard boats that got closest to the Danes discovered they were not asleep on the job; they were cleared for action and they were keeping a sharp lookout.

In the King's Deep vessels men were sleeping at their guns, with the ships cleared for action. On Nelson's ships hammocks were slung and the off-watch men were getting a good night's rest before the sun rose on 2 April.

Many of them, however, were not turned in. The previous evening Nelson had sent the signal to clear for action. And the bulkheads on the gun decks had to be removed, every unnecessary item stowed away, the guns prepared and sidearms issued. On two of the ships, the fireships *Otter* and *Zephyr*, the preparations were rather different. Powder and shot were offloaded to other vessels and the crew – the captain, a midshipman and eight ratings – completed their preparations so that their ships could be transformed into blazing torches within the space of a few minutes.

Nelson's most pressing problem that evening was one of navigation. From his reconnaissance patrols north of the Middle Ground Shoal and in the Hollander Deep he knew how many ships there were in the defence line and what guns they carried. What he did not know was precisely where in the Deep they were moored. Were they in the middle of the channel or close in to the Refshale Shoal? Or had the Danish Commander-in-Chief of the Defence Line taken advantage of the shallow draft of his ships and positioned them on the shoal itself? Nelson had no way of knowing. One thing he did know, however, was that when his ships entered the King's Deep he could not count on the channel being more than 900 metres wide. It was a precondition for a successful attack that he was able to communicate to his commanding officers the course they should sail to avoid going aground.

The first thing Nelson did, therefore, when *Elephant*'s anchor was let go that afternoon was to discuss the problem with the masters and skippers with experience from Baltic trade, who were on board acting as pilots. At nightfall he attempted to take soundings of the entrance to the Deep. But despatching sounding vessels was a risky business: the creaking of the oars in their rowlocks could give them away. His last question to the boats sent on the mission was "Are your oars muffled?" When he was assured this had been done, he said, "Very well, should the Danish guard boat discover you, you must pull like devils and get out of his way as fast as you can"

Nelson was in desperate need of all the intelligence he could obtain about the waters he was to sail into. At the same time he also realized the Danes were keeping a keen lookout and he did not have in mind to send his men on such a hazardous mission, so close among the Danish blockships, which meant he would have to do without information that could play a vital role when he moved his ships into the entrance of the channel where the battle was to take place.

The fleet lying at anchor south of the King's Deep that night was a large one. It comprised the ships-of-the-line *Elephant, Defiance, Edgar, Ganges, Monarch, Russell, Bellona, Polyphemus, Ardent, Agamemnon, Glatton* and *Isis*; the frigates *Amazon, Desirée, Blanche, Alcmene, Arrow, Dart* and *Jamaica*; the brigs *Cruizer* and *Harpy*, the gun brigs *Sparkler, Biter, Teaser, Force, Bouncer* and *Tigress*; the fire-ships *Otter* and *Zephyr*; and the bomb vessels *Discovery, Explosion, Hecla, Sulphur, Terror, Volcano*, and *Zebra* – and their tenders.

With his ships snugly at anchor, Nelson invited some of the officers closest to him for supper, among them Captains Foley, Fremantle and Riou, and Colonel Stewart. Nelson was in fine form and with his band of brothers made a toast for a southerly wind and victory. But with everybody having last-minute jobs to attend to, supper did not last long. The commanding officers returned to their ships to make sure all was ready for action. Only Riou stayed behind. And together with Foley and Riou, Nelson put the finishing touches to his plan of battle.

NELSON'S PLAN

When Nelson withdrew to his day cabin with Foley and Riou it was between nine and ten o'clock. He was physically exhausted from the labours of the past few days, but mentally, as always, he was as sharp as a pin; it was only his body that needed rest. And what Foley and Riou were incapable of getting Nelson to do, his servant of many years, Tom Allen, managed with some ease. In situations like these he was the one with the authority. He had Nelson's cot moved into the great cabin and persuaded him to lie in it.

Nelson's plan was elegant in its simplicity. His objective was to fight for control of the King's Deep and the means he had at his disposal were adequate for the job. He outgunned his opponent, his men were highly professional and well trained, and he was in the position of putting a manoeuvrable force against a fixed one.

He chose to direct the first wave of attack against the middle section of the defence line. If successful, he knew from experience that this would destroy the enemy's command and communications.

The attack was to be led by the 74-gunner *Edgar*, which was to anchor opposite the 54-gun blockship, *Jylland*. Then the *Ardent* (64) was to pass in the *Edgar*'s lee, anchor and engage the *Sværdfisken* (18) and *Kronborg* (22). Finally the *Glatton*, a converted East Indiaman with the heaviest armament in the wave (twenty-eight 68-pounder carronades on the lower gundeck and twenty-eight 48-pound carronades on the upper), was to pass to the east of the *Ardent* and anchor opposite the *Dannebrog* (60) and her supporting barge the *Hajen* (18).

The second wave would be directed against what Nelson had always believed was the Achilles heel of the Danish defence line, its southern end.

The smallest of the British ships-of-the-line, the 50-gunner *Isis*, was to enter the King's Deep as number four and let go her anchor opposite the 52-gun *Wagrien*; *Agamemnon* (64) was to follow in her wake and put herself opposite the *Prøvestenen* (58). Outgunned in this section of the line, Nelson solved the problem with the help of the smaller ships of the fleet. The frigate *Desirée* (36) was to run as close inshore as she could to the south of the Danish line. From this position Captain Inman should be able to rake not only the *Prøvestenen* and *Wagrien* but also the converted cavalry barges *Rendsborg* and *Nyborg*, both with 20 guns. Captain Rose of the *Jamaica* (28) was given charge of a flotilla of six 14-gun brigs, the *Biter*, *Bouncer*, *Force*, *Sparkler*, *Teaser* and *Tigress*, also with orders to take up positions from where the four most southerly Danish vessels could be raked. So against the 150 guns of the southern section of the defence line, Nelson had placed 262, on top of which was the added destructive effect of the raking on the moored Danish ships, with any shot hitting their bows or transoms hurtling down the length of their gundecks, leaving carnage behind them. Nelson had every right to believe, therefore, that the four most southerly ships in the line would be put out of action at a very early stage in the battle. With that done, the ten ships involved could be redeployed against the northern sector.

The *Agamemnon* and *Isis* were to cut their anchor cables and sail immediately north, where they were to take up station ahead of the most northerly of the British battleships, the *Polyphemus*. Captain Rose was to take the *Jamaica* and her flotilla of six gun brigs and head north to provide fire support to the attack there.

The third wave was planned to be put against the northern sector of the King's Deep line and the two blockships at the entrance to the Kronløbet Channel.

In the wakes of the *Isis* and *Agamemnon*, the 74-gun *Bellona* was to enter the King's Deep. Captain Thompson was to anchor ahead of the *Glatton*, where he was to support Captain Bligh (of *Bounty* fame) in his engagement with the *Dannebrog* and *Hajen*, at the same time firing upon the three small vessels near the Danish flagship: Fleet Battery No 1 (20), the cavalry barge *Aggershus* (20) and the signals frigate *Elven* (10). Hereafter Nelson himself was to follow with the 74-gun *Elephant*. As his opponent, he had selected the most heavily armed vessel in the line, the *Sjælland*, which he saw for himself during the reconnaissance was a 74. Ahead of the *Elephant* he had placed his old friend and comrade-in-arms at Tenerife, Captain Fremantle, who, with the *Ganges'* 74 guns, was to engage the blockship *Charlotte Amalie* (26) and the artillery barge *Søhesten* (18). At this stage Nelson decided to put ship against ship – the *Monarch* (74) against the *Holsten* (60), the *Defiance* (74), flying Rear Admiral Graves' flag, against the *Indfødsretten*, the *Russell* (74) against the *Elefanten* (70) and *Polyphemus* (64) against the *Mars* (64).

There was only one ship in the Danish defence line that Nelson had decided not to engage – the defence frigate *Hjælperen* (16). During his reconnaissance Nelson was uncertain of what kind of vessel she was, but classified her as a 24-gunner fitted with bombs. He was unwilling, therefore, to waste one of his ships-of-the line-against such a small vessel. In addition to these capital ships Nelson also had a flotilla of frigates that were to act as a manoeuvrable reserve: *Amazon* (38), *Blanche* (36), *Alcmene* (32), *Arrow* (30) and *Dart* (30). Under the command of Captain Riou aboard the *Amazon*, in Nelson's chess game these were his bishops, those highly manoeuvrable pieces. Riou also had the two fireships *Otter* and *Zephyr* and was to act under Nelson's direct signals.

Finally, Nelson positioned the seven bomb vessels. Five of them, the *Discovery, Explosion, Terror, Volcano* and *Zebra*, he put in the lee of the *Elephant*, from where they were to bombard Nyholm. The other two, *Hecla* and *Sulphur*, were to head north and take up positions from where they could bombard not only Trekroner Fort but also Lynetten, which the British believed, wrongly as it turned out, to be a 20-gun fort.

Nelson's armada

Nelson's plan called for the ships-of-the-line, frigates, gun brigs and bomb vessels to bludgeon the Danish vessels and Trekroner Fort into submission. Actually taking them was left to an armada of armed boats with ratings and soldiers at their oars. First the Danish ships were to be taken, after which the Fleet would engage the Fort. Finally, the Fort was to be taken by storm attack. The British took an optimistic view of their chances of beating and taking Trekroner Fort. There was enough water to allow the British ships-of-the-line to engage it at close range. It extended only ten feet above sea level and its men were virtually unprotected. The primitive construction with its hordes of men would be a prime target for the British battleships' guns and carronades.

The flotilla of boats Nelson could put together was large. Each ship-of-the-line in his division was to have a flat-bottomed boat in her lee, armed and fully manned. Parker would send similar boats from his division, armed with carronades and with thirty soldiers in each, under the command of the *London*'s First Lieutenant. He was charged to place his vessels in the lee of the *Elephant* and follow Nelson's orders. Parker was also to send four longboats with anchors and cables, likewise with orders to stand ready in the lee of the *Elephant*. In addition there were all the boats from the other ships in his division. Together they formed a veritable armada, mobilized and ready to play their part in the forthcoming battle.

Superiority

With this plan Nelson outgunned the Danes by more than fifty per cent. In reality his superiority was far greater: firstly because he had the advantage of manoeuvrability against moored ships, both in ship-to ship-engagements and in the fact that he was able to move ships from one section of the line to another; secondly because his battle-hardened and professional crews would be facing an opponent who was neither; and thirdly because he would have the support of Parker's ships-of-the-line at the northern end of the line.

The plan, as already stated, was simple. It promised a quick victory, with minimum loss of men and materiel.

But there were two variables that posed a threat – the wind and the water depths. To attack forcefully, he had to have a southerly wind and when he could expect that was anyone's guess. But he knew it would come, if not tomorrow then the day after, or the day after that. Water depths were another matter entirely; this was not merely a question of time. Before the attack he must know the course to steer to stay well inside the King's Deep Channel.

Shortly after midnight the plan was complete and the writers went to work at producing fourteen copies of the battle orders, one for each ship-of-the line, one for the commander of the frigate flotilla and one for the commander of the gun brig flotilla.

Meanwhile, Nelson lay in his cot in the after cabin and urged the writers to completion. Sleep was impossible for him; the combination of excitement and exhaustion was too overpowering. At regular intervals he received reports about the wind and they sounded more and more promising. At midnight it had been flat calm with a breeze from the east. But the wind was slowly veering to the south and gaining in strength. As daylight began to loom behind the grey overcast on the morning of 2 April he had the wind he needed, a half gale from the south-east.

Nelson was up and about early. The writers were still hard at it. But at 0600 the last i was dotted and the last t crossed; the fourteen copies were ready for delivery. By this time Nelson had already eaten breakfast. From the *Elephant*'s halyards the signal stood stiffly in the wind for the commanding officers to report on board. The battle was about to begin.

NELSON'S IMPROVISATION

Nelson's plan failed, however, and because of one of the variables it could not cater for, the water depths. During the passage into the King's Deep Channel he had to improvise an emergency plan at just a few minutes' notice.

The hours of the morning and forenoon watches were hectic for the signals officer aboard the *Elephant*. As soon as dawn had broken the first signal was aloft with orders to individual ships. Shortly before eight Nelson called his commanding officers on board to receive a copy of the battle plan and hear a briefing of his intentions. Shortly after that the general signal was hoisted for all ships to clear for action and prepare to anchor by the stern with springs on the cable.

Most of the commanding officers had anticipated this order

hours before. They had already flaked out a heavy-duty anchor cable aft along the lower deck, led it out through a gun port right aft, then back along the ship's side to the fo'c'sle where it was made fast to an anchor. A spring had also been bent on to the cable, so that the ship could be swung into the best angle relative to the enemy. Most of the work in clearing for action was already completed.

On board the *Monarch* the bosun's pipes had sounded at 0600, spreading the word to lash up and stow hammocks. William Millard had been kept busy throughout the previous evening and, with no respite, taken the middle watch from midnight to four. But he did manage to get a couple of hours' sleep before the drums beat the ship's company to action stations. He rushed up on deck, inspected the guns under his charge and dashed to the quarterdeck to report them as ready to the *Monarch*'s First Lieutenant. The ship was ready for battle; not until then could the ship's company be piped to breakfast. On his way back to his post after breakfast he passed what was probably the most gruesome sight imaginable aboard a man of war shortly before an engagement; the surgeons were making their preparations to treat gunshot and splinter wounds and to perform amputations. One of the tables in the cockpit was bedecked with knives, saws and scissors of all shapes and sizes. Another very solid table was placed in the middle of the space. "As I had never seen this produced before, I could not help asking the use of it, and received for answer 'that it was to cut off legs and wings [arms] upon'. One of the surgeon's men, called loblolly boys, was spreading yards and yards of bandages about six inches wide, which he told me was to clap on to my back." Humour was an excellent safety valve for the tension everyone was under. One of Millard's fellow midshipmen said to the doctor, "Damn you, Doctor, if you don't handle me tenderly, I will never forgive you," and was given the unnerving reply, "By George, sir, you had better keep out of my clutches, or depend on it I will pay you off all old scores."

Uncharted waters

The British fleet was now in all respects ready to weigh anchor. Every eye was turned towards the *Elephant*. Time passed agonizingly slowly, but still there was no signal from Lord Nelson.

The navigation problem had reared its ugly head. Or rather navigation problems, because there were two. The first was whether all the ships had come far enough south of the Middle Ground Shoal when they let go their anchors the night before. The second was what course they should steer when they entered the King's Deep Channel.

Sounding the waters at the southern tip of the shoal would take time, but it could be done. A flotilla of boats set off from the ships. An hour later the soundings had been taken and the gun brig *Cruizer* anchored to mark the southernmost tip of the shoal.

Sounding the entrance to the King's Deep, however, within range of the Danish guns was impossible.

At that time Nelson was close to a nervous breakdown. In front of him to the north lay a grey and unbroken expanse of water. Somewhere out there, he knew, were the Middle Ground and Refshale Shoals. But where? The position of the Danish line was of no help to him whatsoever. It could be out in the King's Deep itself, or it could, as many on board surmised, be right up against the Refshale Shoal. And none of the pilots the fleet had taken from Britain for this express purpose dared suggest a safe course for the entrance to the King's Deep. Nelson was furious to see "the honour of our country intrusted to pilots who have no other thought than to keep the ship clear of danger and their own silly heads clear of shot". He appealed to the pilots to pull themselves together and arrive at a decision. At length Alexander Briarly, who had been master of the ship-of the-line *Audacious* during the precarious navigation at the Battle of the Nile, declared that he was willing to take responsibility. He indicated the bearings that were to be maintained to keep the larger ships on a course up through the deepest part of the channel. Nelson immediately sent him aboard the *Edgar* to assist Captain Murray, who was to be the first to enter the Deep.

By this time it was ten o'clock. Only then could Nelson make the signal to weigh anchor. The *Edgar*, with Briarly on board, had already weighed and set course for the King's Deep. At 1015 Nelson signalled the ships-of-the-line *Ardent*, *Glatton* and *Isis* to weigh, follow the *Edgar* into the Deep and anchor opposite the enemy vessels as laid out in his battle orders.

Victims to the Middle Ground Shoal

At last the attack was under way. But things did not go as Nelson had planned. His most dangerous enemy on 2 April turned out to be the Middle Ground Shoal. Its first victim was the ship-of-the-line *Agamemnon*.

134

According to the plan the *Agamemnon* should have been the fifth ship to enter the King's Deep and was to have anchored opposite the *Prøvestenen*. The soundings around the southern tip of the shoal now showed that the *Agamemnon* was east of the shoal. When the signal was made to weigh, the *Agamemnon* had therefore set all sail. But the current and wind were too great for the bulky ship to work her way south. In fact she began to drift and Captain Fancourt had to let go his anchor to avoid going aground. All efforts were now concentrated on warping the ship southwards. Again the current was too strong and the anchors did not hold. From the vantage point of the Hollander Deep Fancourt and his crew had to settle for being spectators to the battle and take comfort from Nelson's understanding promise that they would have the opportunity later on to get their share of action against the Russians.

But the Middle Ground Shoal was to claim more victims. The vessels that were the last to sail through the Hollander Deep on 1 April were all in positions east of the shoal. This meant that they would either not be able to get to their appointed stations before the battle was over or that they would arrive in its death throes. The frigate *Jamaica* and her flotilla of six gun brigs worked like terriers to round the southern tip of the Middle Ground Shoal, but she did not make it, and the six gun brigs did not arrive as a combined force but in dribs and drabs, one by one, and not until the afternoon. The seven bomb vessels suffered the same fate. *Discovery*, *Explosion* and *Terror* did not reach their appointed positions behind the *Elephant* until between 1200 and 1300; *Volcano* and *Zebra* between 1400 and 1500; and *Hecla* and *Sulphur*, which were to have bombarded Trekroner Fort, did not arrive at all.

Measured in numbers of guns, the loss to Nelson was a modest one. But the loss of the *Jamaica* and the six gun brigs meant that the pressure he could exert on the southern end of the defence line was considerably weakened and that none of his ships-of-the-line could be released from the southern sector during the battle to reinforce the northern end.

Engage the enemy more closely

Nelson reacted immediately to the navigation problems. His lightning improvisation produced a new plan allowing him to maintain gun superiority and retain the attack waves against the middle and southern sectors of the Danish line. According to his plan the *Agamemnon* should have anchored as the most southerly of the

135

British ships-of-the-line. As soon as she had signalled that she was unable to round the Middle Ground Shoal, Nelson decided to allocate her appointed position to the battleship that had originally been tasked to be the most northerly. The *Polyphemus* was ordered to enter the King's Deep immediately astern of the *Isis* and anchor opposite the *Prøvestenen*.

By now many of the British ships were under way and heading for the entrance to the King's Deep. Nelson followed their progress anxiously. Just before he signalled the *Polyphemus* with her new position he had sent a signal to number six, the ship-of-the line *Bellona*, that she was standing too far to the east and in danger of going aground. But it was too late. In her passage east of the *Isis*, the *Bellona* went aground and stayed aground. Nor was she to be the last victim of the navigational problem that had worried Nelson so much. As one of the last British battleships, the *Russell* entered the King's Deep, following closely in the wake of Rear Admiral Graves' flagship, the *Defiance*. As soon as Graves was within range he opened fire, as did the *Russell* a few minutes later. Everything was blanketed in gun smoke and the *Russell* lost visual contact with the *Defiance*. After a few minutes Captain Cuming could make out a mast top ahead, but its was the *Bellona*'s. Almost immediately a violent shuddering went through the ship's hull. The *Russell* was now aground as well, immediately astern of the *Bellona*.

Nelson had lost two more of his capital ships. Again he reacted promptly. His first thoughts were to avoid any more groundings. That the *Bellona* and *Russell* had gone aground was really his own fault; that morning aboard the *Elephant* he had instructed their commanding officers to pass the ship ahead to the east to avoid coming too close to the Refshale Shoal. The moment he saw the two ships-of-the-line too far to the east he hoisted the signal that was to remain fluttering from the *Elephant*'s maintop throughout the battle – signal No 16: "Engage the enemy more closely". He himself kept to port and passed between his own ships and the Danish line. The ships astern of him followed suit and the Middle Ground Shoal claimed no more victims.

The loss of the *Agamemnon*, *Bellona* and *Russell* meant that he had to abandon his original plan: to attack the full length of the defence line and with fifty per cent more firepower.

As he altered course he decided to reshuffle the positions of his reduced force of battleships. He ordered Captain Foley to put the *Elephant* in the *Bellona*'s place and anchor her just a quarter of a cable (fifty metres) ahead of the *Glatton*. Nelson left the *Elephant*'s quarterdeck and strode to her gangway. From here he hailed the *Ganges* as she passed and ordered Captain Fremantle to anchor in a new position, ahead of the *Elephant* with the *Sjælland* as his opponent. Shortly before 1100 he had signalled the ships-of-the-line still under sail to form close line of battle. The two last ships, the *Monarch* and the *Defiance*, followed the orders, which meant they had new opponents. When they let go their anchors they were now just fifty metres from each other. The *Monarch* was just ahead of the *Ganges*, within range of Fleet Battery No 1, the *Sjælland* and the *Charlotte Amalie*, and the *Defiance* just ahead of the *Monarch*, with the *Charlotte Amalie* as her primary target but also within range of the *Søhesten*.

By this time the frigate *Desirée* was already in her appointed station in the shallow waters south of the *Prøvestenen*, from where Captain Inman could open fire on the four southernmost Danish vessels and rake their bows. At roughly the same time the frigates were following in the wake of the battleships and at the entrance to the King's Deep. Before they sailed, Nelson had instructed Captain Riou to head north and support the most northerly British battleships in their attack on the blockships in the Kronløbet Channel. Riou therefore raced his frigates behind the British line, which was already in action. When he observed that the remaining ships-of-the-line were unable to engage the Danish line north of the *Søhesten* he took the bold decision to put his five frigates in the positions originally allocated to ships-of-the-line. He anchored his own frigate, the *Amazon*, ahead of the battleship *Defiance* and ordered the frigates astern of him to anchor so as to extend the line in an arc towards the Kronløbet Channel, within range of the guns of Trekroner Fort.

Nelson's presence of mind

In his difficult position, Nelson had a choice: he could either allow his remaining nine ships-of-the-line to engage the entire defence line that was originally to have been attacked by twelve; or decide not to attack the northern sector of the line. Or, put more simply, either to fight a battle in which he would be outgunned or one in which he would still have fifty per cent superiority in firepower.

When Nelson had to improvise his new plan most of his battleships were in position and already in action. At this time he had only four ships-of-the-line – the *Elephant*, *Ganges*, *Monarch* and

Defiance – to play with. He knew that if he set them against the entire northern sector of the line and the blockships in the Kronløbet Channel he would be putting his 296 guns against 442 from the Danish vessels and another 66 from Trekroner Fort.

He had only a few minutes to make up his mind if he were to stop the four ships making their way northwards. He used those minutes to make a momentous decision: to concentrate his attack on the middle and southern sectors of the Danish line and postpone the attack on the northern sector and the blockships in the Kronløbet Channel. His original plan was based on a British line of some two and a half miles, the improvised line was barely one and a half.

Nelson succeeded in implementing his emergency plan and in focusing on fifteen of the twenty vessels in the Danish line. But he did not succeed in fighting at such close quarters as he had planned and ordered. He had issued orders to the effect that his ships-of-the-line were to anchor at a distance of 1½ cables (about 300 metres) from their opponents. The British masters and pilots, meanwhile, were convinced that the Danish line was close to the edge of the Refshale Shoal and were concerned about going aground if they closed their Danish opponents. And when the lead, which was cast continuously, showed a depth of 9.5 metres, they insisted on letting go the anchor. Had they only moved over to the west side of the King's Deep the lead would have shown deeper water, and, even if they had laid themselves close up to the Danish ships, they would still have had plenty of water under their keels. As it was, the battle was now being fought at twice the range Nelson had ordered, with the result that it was to last twice as long as he had told Sir Hyde Parker it would.

The battle on 2 April was thus fought to Nelson's improvised plan. But the principles of the original plan, that is greater firepower and manoeuvrability, were maintained. His expectations, when he issued his battle orders, for a quick victory were still alive when his ships anchored in their new positions and the King's Deep echoed with the rumblings of the first shots.

Chapter 8

THE BATTLE OF COPENHAGEN – ACT I

THE FIRST SHOTS

On 2 April, Maundy Thursday, the sun appeared over the horizon at 0545, but twilight began more than an hour before that. Down the line in the King's Deep the hands were called and stiff limbs were stretched and rubbed back to life after another cold night on the hard decks next to their guns.

The first signal of the day was hoisted aboard the *Dannebrog* at 0500 – clear for action. Fischer did not know what Nelson's plans for the day were, but, with the wind veering to the south-east during the night, it became plain that Nelson could attack, if he still wanted to, that is.

0500 also sent 'Call the Hands' ringing around the decks of the artillery barge *Hajen*, which only twelve hours before had finally arrived in the line close under the *Dannebrog*'s transom. But breakfast would have to wait. Sub-Lieutenant Müller realized only too well that if his people were to have any chance of surviving there was something more important than bread and aquavit they should be given: gun drills. So as the morning light slowly brightened the *Hajen*'s novice crew of craftsmen and soldiers were given their first, and only, training in manning a naval gun. Not until then were they given any breakfast, because today they were to meet Lord Nelson.

The low-lying artillery barge did not offer Müller the best observation post. But further to the south, from the deck of the blockship *Wagrien*, Commander Risbrich had a grandstand view of the dense clump of British ships south of the Middle Ground Shoal, and he was an experienced observer. He knew better than anyone what the plethora of signals and the many boats plying back and forth between the ships meant. As a young lieutenant he had served in the Royal Navy during the American War of Independence and been in battle many times. The ship he studied most closely was the large, yellow two-decker, with the black strake running the length of her hull between the upper and lower gundecks, the ship with the flag of Vice Admiral flying from her foremast. Commander Risbrich spent a long time watching the *Elephant.* Then he turned to his officers, Sub-Lieutenants Claus Henne and Gotfried Hagerup, and Contract Lieutenants Peter Groth and Christian and Lauritz Stæger, and said in his customary staid fashion, "I can see that they will soon weigh anchor and attack us. So let us go below, gentlemen, and enjoy our breakfast. Because we shall have much to do this day."

Telescopes were pointing at Nelson's ships from the *Dannebrog*'s quarterdeck as well. Olfert Fischer read all the activity in the same way as Risbrich. Nelson was going to attack and he was going to do it now. At 0900, therefore, he repeated the signal to clear for action and for the ships in the line to haul in on their anchor springs to present their broadsides to an attack from the south. The captain of the *Holsten* also took the time to lay out warping anchors and no sooner had she swung herself onto her firing bearings than the crew could see for themselves that the British were indeed on their way. They had been expected for months and work had been going on for just as long to give them as warm a welcome as possible. For three days now they had been in sight without anybody being able to more than guess at whether they would attack or sail on into the Baltic. All that waiting was now over. At 1015 they could see the British ships-of-the-line south of the Middle Ground Shoal weighing anchor and making sail for the passage in the King's Deep. To the north they could also see Parker's ships getting under way and that his powerful battleships were heading down towards Trekroner Fort and Copenhagen. As they watched, Olfert Fischer gave the signal for the vessels in the defence line to open fire as soon as the enemy was within range.

The British war machine
At that time every eye in the defence line, at the shore batteries, among the thousands of spectators who had gathered ashore and in the British ships was trained on one ship; the bulky, yellow two-decker, the *Edgar.* By Nelson's plan Captain Murray had been given the honour of leading the attack. With her square sails trimmed to perfection, the big 74-gunner sailed slowly up the

140

King's Deep on a course that took her between the defence line and the Middle Ground Shoal, some five or six hundred metres from the most southerly Danish vessel.

On board the *Prøvestenen*, Lieutenant Michael Bille had command of the lower gun deck, where the blockship's biggest guns, the heavy 36-pounders, were placed. They had been loaded and run out hours ago. Bille peered out of the first gunport up in the port bow. At 1030 the *Edgar* loomed into range and Bille fired the first salvo at the British ship. The guns on the upper deck roared in echo. Captain Murray returned fire. The battle had begun.

For years afterwards the picture of the attack on the Danish defence line was burned into William Millard's memory. His post at action was aft on the *Monarch*, which was to be one of the last ships to enter the fray. His gaze followed the *Edgar* as she sailed into the Deep: "A more beautiful and solemn spectacle I never witnessed. The *Edgar* led the van, and on her approach the battery on the Island of Amak [Stricker's battery on Amager] and three or four of the southern-most vessels opened their fire upon her. A man-of-war under sail is at all times a beautiful object, but at such a time the scene is heightened beyond the powers of description. We saw her pressing on through the enemy's fire, and manoeuvring in the midst of it to gain her station; our minds were deeply impressed with awe, and not a word was spoken throughout the ship but by the pilot and helmsmen; and their communications, being chanted very much in the same manner as the responses in our cathedral service and repeated at intervals, added very much to the solemnity."

One by one Nelson's ships followed the *Edgar* into the King's Deep, where they opened fire as soon as they were within range. From the Danish vessels at that time, it was impossible to see that the *Agamemnon* had had to let go her anchor east of the Middle Ground Shoal, that the *Bellona* and the *Russell* had gone aground and that Nelson was going to have to improvise. What they could see, however, from the upper deck of the blockships, from the gloom of the gundecks in glimpses through the gun ports, and from the small artillery barges and converted cavalry barges dwarfed by the imposing hulls of the British ships, was a war machine functioning with the precision of a chronometer. Apparently unconcerned with the Danish gunfire, the British ships-of-the-line moved majestically up the Deep in line-ahead formation, guns barking at the defence line, until, on arriving at precisely their appointed positions, they let go an anchor aft and concentrated their fire on the opponent Nelson had selected for them.

In the *Edgar*'s wake, followed the *Ardent*, whose 24-pound carronades on her upper deck were greatly feared at close range. And rightly so. But there were also guns aboard the Danish vessels. As the *Ganges* entered the scene, a cannonball ripped an arm off the pilot and killed the master outright, leaving Captain Fremantle to navigate and manoeuvre his ship alone to the position right ahead of the *Elephant* that Nelson had hailed to him minutes before.

At 1100 the *Monarch*, the last battleship but one, entered the channel. As she did so Captain Mosse saw that the *Russell* was aground. He waited to fire his first broadside, therefore, until he was just off the Danish vessel that was engaging the grounded ship, and from the *Russell* three loud cheers were heard in thanks and as a sign that the *Russell* had not lost her spirit. Nor did the *Monarch* reach her chosen position without taking losses. During the entrance into the channel, with the Danes firing independently as the enemy came within range, Captain Mosse had been standing on his quarterdeck with Nelson's instructions in his left hand and a speaking trumpet in the other. As the *Monarch* reached her position he shouted, "Cut away the anchor!" That was the last time Midshipman Millard saw his Captain alive. As soon as the anchor was gone he dashed to his post at the aftermost guns. A few minutes later the body of Captain Mosse was carried past him and laid in the stern walk, covered with an ensign. The captain of the *Monarch* had been killed in precisely the spot Millard had been standing minutes before. The *Monarch* had been given a very exposed position. Not only was she under fire from the ships opposite, she was so far to the north that she was also within range of the guns at Trekroner Fort. They were to slay and maim many of the gun crews in the forrard part of the ship. When the *Defiance* took up her position ahead of the *Monarch*, and even closer to the Fort, she soon became aware of the hostility of her new neighbour. With her stern anchor holding and with spring attached, a quarter of a cable ahead of the *Monarch* she took a salvo that damaged her mainmast, mizzen and bowsprit.

The first shots had been fired at 1030. One by one the British ships had engaged their Danish opponents, with the exception of the three furthest to the north – the *Holsten*, *Indfødsretten* and *Hjælperen*. At 1100 every British ship-of-the-line was in action.

Raking

As the most southerly Danish vessel, the *Prøvestenen* had exchanged fire with almost every British ship-of-the-line during their passage into the King's Deep. After they had passed, she was left to face her own opponent, the *Polyphemus*. But Commander Lassen had not been in action for long before it became clear that he had more than one aggressor to contend with. Over on the Middle Ground Shoal there was the *Russell*. As soon as she went aground her crew got to work training the guns so they could engage the *Prøvestenen*. And just south of her was the *Desirée*. Captain Inman had followed Nelson's instructions and manoeuvred his 36-gun frigate into the shallow water south of the Danish line, from where he could fire on the *Prøvestenen*'s port bow without her being able to return fire. So Commander Lassen concentrated on the *Polyphemus* and *Russell*, and put his trust in Stricker's Battery on Amager to help him out with the frigate.

The *Wagrien*'s main opponent was the *Isis*, lying so close by that she appeared to be almost on top of the *Wagrien*'s north-eastern mooring anchor. But the *Wagrien* was under attack by more than one ship. Commander Risbrich was soon to become aware that he was within range of the grounded *Bellona* and that, just like Commander Lassen, he was defenceless against raking fire on his bows from the *Desirée*. He was very conscious of the superiority in enemy firepower and therefore instructed his gun commanders not to aim for the enemy's masts and rigging but the hulls, and hope to put some of her guns out of action. Risbrich was full of admiration for the efforts of his gun crews.

North of the two blockships lay the cavalry barges *Rendsborg* and *Nyborg* and the blockship *Jylland*, all of which had exchanged fire with several British ships as they passed before engaging in single combat with their main opponents. And north of them was the small artillery barge *Sværdfisken*, which, with only 18 guns, seemed puny against the large British 74. But her captain, thirty-year-old Sub Lieutenant Søren Sommerfeldt, had nothing but praise for his people and their courage in this uneven fight.

After the battle the *Sværdfisken* reported: "Began the action when the enemy was within range. In the first salvo had loaded three guns with double shot. Fired continuous horizontal shots, alternating between round shot, bar shot and grapeshot. Also had the opportunity to fire five incendiary and other shells. Soon after the engagement began, regretfully lost No 53 of the Naval Artillery

Corps, Christen Sørensen, killed in action. The calm and discipline he had instilled continued, however, despite gunner's mate No 13 of the 4th Division of the First Artillery Company Mons Nielsen's relative inexperience. Contract Lieutenant Randleff followed my orders to the letter, laying down as much fire from the forrard guns as he was able. But after a short time he was wounded in the arm and had to leave the deck. Despite the fact that I had lost two Petty Officers, everything was going well. I cannot praise highly enough the courage and zeal with which the Norwegian men defied a superior opponent. Without needing to be ordered, they filled the places at the guns vacated by the enemy's countless salvoes of grapeshot. This greatly encouraged the volunteers, many of whom displayed outstanding bravery. Although I had done my best to ensure the nettings were covered with old cordage and hammocks, an enemy ship directed a salvo against me that took away almost half my gunwale, splinters from which killed and wounded many of my men. A ball passed through the bread room, killing a man and wounding the senior writer and a man passing powder."

The vessels north of the *Sværdfisken* also discovered at a very early stage that they were up against a professional and superior force. One of the first shots the blockship *Kronborg* received killed a 26-year-old Contract Lieutenant, merchant mate Poul Hansen Bohne from Copenhagen. The artillery barge *Hajen*, just to the north of her, however, took very few losses in the opening phase of the battle; even though she faced the *Glatton*'s carronades, only four men were wounded. There were two reasons for this good fortune: the first was her very low bulwarks, covered with sail bags filled with hammocks and cordage that protected the crew from the dreaded splinters that killed and wounded so many during a battle; the second was that the British ship-of-the-line concentrated her attentions initially on the *Dannebrog*, flying Commodore Olfert Fischer's pennant. For the same reason the others in the gaggle of small ships in the vicinity of the *Dannebrog* – the *Elven*, *Aggershus* and Fleet Battery No 1 – came through the opening phase relatively unscathed. Lieutenant Fasting of the *Aggershus* was unfortunate enough to lose two of his ten port guns when they were damaged whilst firing her first broadside.

North of the middle of the Danish line the British engaged three other vessels in the opening move – the *Sjælland*, the *Charlotte Amalie* and the *Søhesten*. Early that morning Commander Kofoed followed Fischer's signal to swing his stern over to the east, an advantage if the attack came from the south, but not so when the British ships put themselves into a position from where they could engage the old China ship from the north and present her with a poor line of sight. With her flush deck and low freeboard, the *Charlotte Amalie* was extremely vulnerable to grapeshot fired from the *Monarch*'s quarterdeck and fo'c'sle: "Ten men were constantly engaged in throwing the dead overboard and taking the wounded to the lazarette."

The line is broken

After the first broadsides the combatants were enveloped in a thick blanket of smoke that drifted across the Danish line. This made it difficult for the Danish gun crews to sight their targets. But at that early stage of the battle, with the British concentrating on man-oeuvring, anchoring and training their guns against the strange collection of ships, the smokescreen offered them protection. It is also probably the reason why Nelson's ships-of-the-line, despite their greater firepower, were successful in breaking through the King's Deep line only at the very south in the opening gambit.

Here Captain Murray had anchored the *Edgar* in a position where his main opponent was the blockship *Jylland*, but from where he could also fire on the *Rendsborg*, anchored in the line between the *Jylland* and the *Wagrien*. This was a very exposed position for such a small ship and one that Olfert Fischer had only given her after a great deal of deliberation. And as early as 1115, after only forty-five minutes of action, the *Rendsborg* had to abandon her place in the line.

Lieutenant Commander Egede had no other choice: "With the enemy's second salvo, I took a ball below the water line that also took away my bower anchor. The ship swung stern on to the enemy and I immediately took several shots in my transom that caused considerable damage. I cut my bower anchor cable in order to swing myself broadsides again and cut the anchor spring; with the help of a foresail and the mizzen topsail, I managed to put her aground not far away, so that I could still bring my guns to bear and in perfect order."

It would have meant certain death to stay in such a position, with her stern exposed to the British battleships, begging to be an-nihilated with raking fire. The *Rendsborg*'s captain took the only course of action open to him when he cut his mooring and sought refuge on the Refshale Shoal. He put his ship in a position where she could continue fighting until he had to strike his colours. But she left a large gap in the Danish line.

A breakthrough of the line, followed by raking fire from the British, was what Fischer had feared most of all. But with the greatest of good fortune for Fischer, Nelson was not able to capitalize on the breakthrough. At that time the British gun brigs, which were the only vessels capable of manoeuvring in these shoal waters and placing themselves in the gap between the *Jylland* and the *Wagrien*, were still east of the Middle Ground Shoal, struggling against wind and tide to round it and enter the King's Deep.

The ships-of-the-line would have found it impossible to carry out complicated manoeuvres in uncharted waters and under fire from the enemy. But they did what they could: although they could not actually move into the gap created, they could get a better shot at the enemy by hauling in on their anchor spring. That is certainly what Captain Murray did. When the *Rendsborg* had pulled out of the line he hauled the *Edgar's* bows west, allowing him to fire on the *Wagrien* over her port quarter, without Risbrich, who already had his hands full with the *Isis* and *Bellona*, being able to return the *Edgar's* fire.

Gunboats in action

Olfert Fischer had taken every precaution possible to prevent a British breakthrough of his line. He had reduced the distance between ships to an absolute minimum by moving most of his vessels into the line itself, and he had formed a manoeuvrable force of eleven gunboats under the command of Steen Bille's second-in-command, Commander Christian Walterstorff. His task was to fire on any British ship that tried to put herself between two ships in the line.

On 1 April ten of them had moved to a position behind the southern end of the King's Deep line. And early the next morning the last gunboat, the *Flensborg*, under the command of Lieutenant van Deurs, had warped out from Trekroner Fort and joined the flotilla.

When the first shots were fired the gunboats had moved towards the gaps in the line and fired on the British battleships with their bow chasers. But the thick pall of smoke that was drifting over the Refshale Shoal made it difficult for them to get a decent sight of their targets and in some cases the ferocity of the British guns made them pull back from the line.

The gunboats were commanded by regular naval officers and crewed by experienced ratings from Steen Bille's squadron to man the oars, sails and two bow chasers. On board the *Christiansund*, Sub-Lieutenant Grove had a gun commander, not normally part of the Admiralty complement for such a vessel. When the *Christiansund* had left the dockyard, Grove's junior surgeon, Bent Bentzen, begged his commanding officer to place him in command of one of the guns until the time came for him to tend to the wounded. Grove "found this such a source of encouragement for the rest of the crew that once he had demonstrated to my satisfaction that he could handle a gun, I put him in charge of an 18-pounder. Later, when the Admiral of the British fleet closed me at such short range that I could open fire on him across the *Wagrien*'s stern, Bentzen's rate of fire and coolness was such that I could not but admire this man who was not trained for combat."

The warrior surgeon was decorated for his action on 2 April, but the gunboat flotilla was poorly led and its activity was of no significance.

The only signal Fischer sent to the flotilla – that it should plug any gaps in the line – was hoisted at 1100. At that time the signal was superfluous, partly because the commanding officers had already done so on their own initiative and partly because the thick smoke prevented Fischer from being able to see the gunboats and them from seeing his signal. And it was not until this point, so late in the game, that Commander Walterstorff went aboard the *Stege* to take command of the flotilla.

A little later, at about noon, the flotilla moved north, firing between the Danish ships as they went. It remained behind the northern sector of the line until about 1430 and when the action here ended Commander Walterstorff gave the order for the flotilla to move inshore and anchor in the lee of Trekroner Fort. The commanding officers of the gunboats reported after the battle that few shots had been fired and few casualties taken. The gunboats had never been intended to be put against ships-of-the-line and they should never have been used.

The shore batteries were equally irrelevant to the outcome of the battle. From Stricker's Battery, the outermost ramparts and Quintus Battery, the distance to the British ships was 1,600–1,700 metres; not only that, but the Danish ships had fouled their range. The few shells that were fired were as ineffective as the attempts of the Quintus Battery to play ducks and drakes with their round shot through the gap that appeared when the *Rendsborg* cut her moorings and drifted on to the Refshale Shoal.

Artillery duel

At 1100 fifteen of the eighteen Danish vessels in the defence line were in action. But for the three most northerly ships, the *Holsten*, the *Infødsretten* and the *Hjælperen*, the fray was yet to begin. And at 1200, one and a half hours after they had heard the *Prøvestenen* fire the first shot, they could still do nothing more than peer through the smoke and listen to the battle raging, without being fired at and without the enemy coming within range.

They were out of sight, but not out of mind. Out of sight because, in the southern sector, Nelson could put 496 British guns against 244 Danish guns and 352 against 202 in the middle of the line. This was exactly the superiority that Fischer had warned the Defence Commission about in February when he told them the King's Deep line would be unable to withstand an attack. But they were not out of mind because they were to play a role later.

The last signal Olfert Fischer sent to the ships in the line, before the gunsmoke made communications impossible, was hoisted at 1015. It was to engage the enemy as soon as he was within range. Nelson's last signal was sent to the maintop, where it remained for the duration of the battle, as Captain Foley let go his anchor opposite Fischer's *Dannebrog*. It was signal No 16 – "Engage the enemy more closely".

By now it was 1100. The manoeuvring was over. The decisive artillery duel had begun.

THE COLLAPSE OF THE MIDDLE SECTOR

At 1100 the Battle of Copenhagen was boiling. The gunsmoke lay in a thick layer under the overcast sky and the combatants could not see beyond their own ships and the closest opponent. Aboard the Danish vessels the crews toiled at their guns, but the British firepower was clearly superior. They had a higher rate of fire and they were more accurate. Almost as soon as the action had started Nelson was convinced that it was only a matter of time before the Danish resistance was overcome.

In the middle of the line he had placed the battleships *Glatton*, *Elephant*, *Ganges* and *Monarch*. His own opponents were the blockship *Dannebrog* and her seconds – the artillery barge *Hajen* and Fleet Battery No 1, the *Sjælland* and the two small vessels behind the line, the converted cavalry barge *Aggershus* and the signals frigate *Elven*.

For the *Monarch* the action began as soon as she let go her anchor. Anchoring a large ship-of-the-line was a delicate manoeuvre under normal conditions. First the way had to be taken off the ship by luffing up into the wind, then the anchor let go and the cable paid out until the ship was stationary; then the duty watch was piped to the capstan to haul in the cable until the ship was in position. But the battle of 2 April was not fought under normal conditions. There was neither room nor time to luff up and get the way off the ships; this was done by letting go the anchor from the stern whilst the ship was still making way. The result of such a brutal procedure was a great lurch throughout the ship that left her trembling from stem to stern. Captain Mosse had therefore put four men on the huge wheel to keep the ship stable after the anchor had gone. They were still fighting for control when a round shot whipped through the aftermost gunport, smashed the wheel to smithereens and killed or wounded three of the four helmsmen.

Shortly before this incident Captain Mosse was himself killed. When he fell, his second-in-command took over automatically. And from his post on the quarterdeck, Midshipman Millard watched as Lieutenant Yelland took command of the *Monarch*. "This brave veteran had taken care to have the decks swept, and everything clean and nice before we went into action. He had dressed himself in full uniform with his cocked hat set on square, his shirt-frill stiff starched, and his cravat tied tight under his chin as usual. After the fall of our Captain, he [Lt. Yelland] sent me down to desire the lieutenants from the different quarters to come on deck, when he informed them of the Captain's death and appointed himself, of course, commanding officer; the remaining officers having, as it were, sworn fealty to him, returned to their different stations. How he escaped unhurt seems wonderful: several times I lost sight of him in a cloud of splinters: as they subsided I saw first his cocked hat emerging, then by degrees the rest of his person, his face smiling, so that altogether one might imagine him dressed for his wedding-day."

On board the *Elephant* Nelson paced his quarterdeck unceasingly. By his side, when he was not commanding a carronade aft or relaying Captain Foley's orders around the ship, was the commanding officer of the British soldiers. As Lieutenant Colonel Stewart phlegmatically put it, "I never passed so interesting a day in the course of my life or one which so much called for my admiration of *any* officer". The small, skinny admiral, with the empty sleeve pinned up to his breast, was pursuing an excited but very composed conversation with the tall, broad-shouldered officer in his scarlet infantry uniform. And when a shot hit the mainmast and sent a shower of lethal splinters flying, Nelson turned to Stewart with a wry smile and said, "It is warm work, and this day may be the last to any of us at any moment. But mark you, I would not be anywhere else for thousands."

The psychology of courage
The vessels in the Danish line in the King's Deep were all very different, and their crews were very different, varying from ship to ship. The same was true of the officers' abilities to mould a crew out of such a group of men. The fortunate among them had had two weeks' training to prepare, but one crew had only joined ship a few hours before the battle

One thing, however, was common to them all – the conditions under which they worked and fought. Those of them fighting on the upper decks could actually see the enemy and their own ships, and the smoke was not so blinding or choking. The price for such a grandstand view, though, was high; most casualties were among those on the upper deck, where they were easy targets for musket fire and grapeshot of their opponents.

Be that as it may, conditions on the lower gun decks were horrific. The only light was that coming through the gunports and, as the battle progressed, through the holes punched into the ship's side by British shot. The acrid powder smoke burned throats and lungs, and the explosion when a gun was fired consumed all the oxygen around it, leaving the crew gasping for breath. In the gloom and smoke they toiled at loading their gun, running it out and training it at the appointed target, using handspikes to inch it round. And when the gun captain applied the glowing fuse to the touch hole primed with loose powder, everyone jumped for their lives as the gun fired and hurtled backwards until the recoil was arrested by the breechings running between the gun carriage and the ship's side.

Gunnery was physically demanding work, as the Danish crews

found out during the gun drills before the battle. But then it had only been a few hours' training at a time; now it was backbreaking labour with no end in sight, with their very lives at risk and in a din so infernal that it was almost impossible to distinguish one sound from another – the shouted orders, the cries of warning, the screams of those wounded by fragments of metal and splinters of timber, the moaning and praying of the dying. This nightmare symphony was drowned intermittently by the roaring of their own guns, the jarring thud as an enemy shot ploughed into the stout timber of the ship's side and when the dreaded raking fire sent round shot and bar shot screaming and whining along the length of the gun deck.

On the lower gun decks battle was a living hell. But the men kept at it – the national serviceman ratings, the soldiers, the volunteers and the pressed men; fighting to the bitter end, on and on until the order was given to cease fire. Or most of them, at least.

That each and every man could stand it, that they did not try and flee, out of their minds with terror, below deck or break down into gibbering wrecks is incomprehensible.

Escape through the hatchways, however, had been considered: soldiers with loaded muskets were posted at each one with orders to shoot to kill if anyone made an attempt to go below unless it was in pursuance of their duties. But they were superfluous; all the men stayed at their posts.

It was called courage – whatever that means – and still is. Fear and the instinct for survival undoubtedly kept many at their posts doing what they must, whether ordered to or on their own initiative. Many, in all the categories of ratings, displayed unbelievable coolness and resolution; some were commended and decorated for their valour. But a gun's crew was more than just a collection of individuals. It was a team, with the pressure that can come from so being. Most feared the enemy, but there was another, more compelling fear – that of letting down their comrades, of showing fear itself.

What the crews of the British ships accomplished that morning was no less remarkable, but they were hardened and trained professionals, under the command of officers with combat experience, and they were used to winning. The crews of the defence vessels in the King's Deep had neither training nor routine to keep them going. What they experienced on 2 April, those who survived to remember it that is, was something new, and quite terrible.

The Dannebrog*'s destiny*

From the very beginning the *Dannebrog* was one of the prime targets for Nelson's attack. In the opening phase both the *Elephant* and the *Glatton* concentrated their fire on the Danish Commodore's flagship. At 400 metres Captain Bligh could make effective use of his carronades and also bombard the blockship with incendiary shells. So the *Dannebrog* had only been in action for half an hour before the situation on board became very serious. The numbers of dead and wounded were already too high; her hull had taken a beating and the British shot had almost swept the gundecks clear of men. Fire had broken out, too, and despite every effort it proved impossible to get it under control. Olfert Fischer himself was one of the wounded on the upper deck. Very early on he had been struck a glancing blow on the temple and neck by a splinter from the *Dannebrog*'s cat-heads. During the battle he did not pay it that much attention. But by evening it proved to be concussion that was giving him "unbearable headaches" and making it difficult for him to concentrate.

After only half an hour's action Fischer did not believe the *Dannebrog* could take much more. He reached the decision, therefore, as Admiral Niels Juel had done 125 years before him at the Battle of Køge Bay against the Swedes, to shift his flag to another ship and carry on the battle from there. But which ship? To the south he could *hear* the bark of artillery barges. Because of the smoke of battle, he could not see any Danish vessels in the southern sector of the line. His impression was that they would not be able to keep going for very long either. But the ships at the northern end of the line were not even involved in the battle yet. So Fischer moved to the ship-of-the-line *Holsten*.

Since 11 March Fischer's broad pennant had flown above the blockship. Now a seaman went aloft and replaced it with a command pennant, after which he plummeted to the deck, Fischer's pennant flag clutched to his chest, shot by a British musket ball.

At 1130 the Commodore, his aide and secretary boarded a boat and were rowed northwards to the *Holsten*, where his broad pennant went aloft immediately.

The *Dannebrog* continued fighting under Commander Braun's command pennant while his crew continued their fight to get the fire aboard under control. She took some of the heaviest losses of the day. Sub-Lieutenant Wulff was killed at his captain's side. Shortly after that Braun's right hand was blown off – his payment,

152

as he bitterly expressed it, for the rich ship owners and neutrality speculators being able to serve two kinds of champagne at their dinner parties. He was forced to leave the deck and hand over his command to his second, Commander Lemming. Contract Lieutenant Lützen was wounded in the leg and had broken his arm. Contract Lieutenant Kornbeck was wounded in the right arm and face, and Contract Lieutenant Mollerup received serious burns to both hands. Between a third and a quarter of the *Dannebrog*'s crew were dead or wounded.

In the end she was fighting with only three guns. At this point the captain struck his colours; the fire was still not under control and spreading all the time. Commander Braun wanted to cut his moorings and drift over to the British line to make sure he took one of the enemy with him, but the wind would not allow it. Instead he concentrated his efforts on rescuing the able-bodied and wounded he had left. Her had no clear idea of just how many had been killed, but when he left his blazing ship, "the lower gundeck was so full of dead that you could hardly avoid treading on them".

Most of the *Dannebrog*'s wounded were rescued by Danish or British boats, but not all. The flag was hauled down at 1430. The burning ship stayed in her position until the flames caught the last of the four mooring anchor cables. Then she started drifting slowly north with the current. At 1630 she was 300–400 metres north of Trekroner Fort. At that time the fire reached the magazine and, with a deafening explosion, the *Dannebrog* blew up in a pillar of flame, smoke and flying wreckage.

The first withdrawal

One reason for the British ships-of-the-line concentrating their fire on the *Dannebrog* was that the four small vessels around her were little more than an irritation to the huge battleships and that three of the four withdrew at an early stage.

The first to pull out of the battle in the middle of the line was the signals frigate *Elven*, the most weakly armed in the line. When she was warped out, she bore six guns and on 29 March took four howitzers on board. But her prime role was not to fight, but to act as relay for Fischer's signals.

When the British battleships anchored opposite the Danish line the *Elven* opened fire between the *Dannebrog* and the *Hajen*. To begin with the crew had used the new flintlocks on their guns, but, as they were unfamiliar with their use and did not care for them,

Lieutenant Commander Holsten gave them permission to use fuses, which they were used to. Quite what effect the *Elven*'s guns were having was very difficult for her commanding officer to ascertain as the smoke was so thick "that from time to time we could barely make out the enemy ships".

The effect of the carronades aboard the *Elephant* and the *Glatton*, however, was another matter. He was in no doubt about their effect. The *Elven* may have been a small target, tucked behind the King's Deep line, but after just under an hour's action nine of her eighty-eight crew had fallen, seven were in critical condition and two more slightly wounded. And as one of the few Danish vessels that could manoeuvre, she had suffered most of those losses because of her masts and rigging.

From his position fifty metres or so behind the *Dannebrog*, at about 1230 Holsten noticed that her battle ensign was gone, as did Colonel Stewart aboard the *Elephant*. Stewart interpreted it as a disagreement between the captain and his crew as to whether the ship was to go on fighting. In fact the ensign had been shot away and a new one was later hoisted. But Holsten did not wait for that. He was convinced that the *Dannebrog* had struck her colours and decided to pull out of the fray to save his ship and crew. He cut the two anchor cables, attached buoys to mark the anchors and got his frigate under way. At this point one of the Norwegian petty officers, Thorgeir Svendsen, "amidst the perpetual howling of shot, displayed extraordinary courage by going repeatedly aloft when the sails were released, by gathering cable ends together that had been shot away and single-handedly getting the anchor a-cock-bill". It was 1230 when Holsten cut his moorings, headed north in the lee of the Danish line and anchored behind Trekroner Fort, from where he began warping his frigate down the Kronløbet Channel.

Aggershus *and* Nyborg

The next ship to pull out of the action in the middle of the line was the converted cavalry barge *Aggershus*. She too lay tucked behind the line some distance from the gap between the *Dannebrog* and Fleet Battery No 1 and just to the north of the *Elven*. She had opened fire at 1100, as soon as the *Elephant* and *Ganges* were within range. An hour later her commanding officer, Sub-Lieutenant Fasting, reported that he "had only three guns left that could speak. With these, I fought on for another hour. As the spring on the starboard anchor aft was shot through, the ship swung bows on to the enemy, whose intense fire, particularly in the last hour, had so decimated my crew that I was unable usefully to present my broadside again, I decided, in an attempt to save the lives of those men who were still alive and those who were wounded, and to prevent my ship from falling into enemy hands, to cut the moorings. I left the spring from my port quarter to allow me as much as possible to swing away from the enemy's fire and our own line."

But that was not enough to get the *Aggershus* out of trouble. "Raised the foresail, which was immediately shot away. Released the fore topsail to no avail as the sheets were gone and which proved to be more of a hindrance than a help as the braces were also gone and it was only with the greatest difficulty that we could use our rudder as the wheel was also shot away. As the wind and current were from the south and as I had no way of steering the ship and believed I would not drift free of the most northerly ships in the line, I allowed most of the able-bodied and as many of the wounded as possible to be rowed ashore in the ship's boats, which were under orders to return to the ship as soon as possible as I intended to sink her where she was and leave with the rest of my crew."

It was just before the stroke of one when Lieutenant Fasting cut his moorings and pulled the *Aggershus* out of action. The cavalry barge was badly damaged and more than a third of the 214 men aboard were killed or badly wounded. The mizzenmast was shot away, the foremast damaged and, with her rudder missing and rigging shot to pieces, the *Aggershus* was no longer under command. Fasting had to face up to the fact that his ship could sink at any moment, taking with her many of the crew.

But just as he was about to give up hope help arrived through the wraiths of smoke in the form of her sister ship the *Nyborg*.

She was coming from the south, where she had lain snugly behind the line between the *Rendsborg* and the blockship *Jylland*. When the *Rendsborg* had had to withdraw from the battle after only 45 minutes' action, the *Nyborg* had been left in a very exposed position and the number of killed and wounded aboard was almost as high as that of the *Aggershus*.

Just after 1230, therefore, Lieutenant Commander Rothe had reached the decision to pull out of the battle. Both hull and rigging had suffered heavy damage but he had succeeded in getting a sail on the foremast. With the wind and current under her, the *Nyborg* was able to make her way north behind the Danish line. And now she showed up, just as Lieutenant Fasting had given up all hope of saving his *Aggershus*. "Then the artillery barge *Nyborg* came drifting up to us. She secured a line between us, set more sail and towed us west of Trekroner Fort, where we received assistance of vessels taking the wounded ashore and taking ships in towards Kalkbrænderiet to the north, where, having discovered that the water we were taking on board from the hits we had taken below the waterline was increasing and seeing that we were drifting further and further north, I decided to scuttle her in about 2½ fathoms in the bay north of the Lime Kiln."

So the *Aggershus* never made it into Copenhagen. The *Nyborg* was taken under tow down the Kronløbet Channel. Just before she reached the boom, however, she sank off the Customs Quay. According to a newspaper report, "The bowsprit was shot almost completely away, there was but a short stump remaining of the fore-mast, the cabin was stove in, rigging and sails hanging in tatters, her bulwark shattered by one shot after another. Only one of her twenty guns was useable. The deck was covered with dead bodies and torn off limbs."

Sub-Lieutenant Willemoes

The third of the small vessels to pull out of the middle of the line was Fleet Battery No 1. Her position in the King's Deep line proper, between the *Dannebrog* and the *Sjælland*, left her even more exposed than the *Elven* and the *Aggershus*. The large raft, 13 × 47 metres, lay low in the water opposite the British ships-of-the-line. That was its tactical strength. But its weakness was well known to the Danish Admiralty as well: "Its sides between the timber stanchions may soon be shot away with carronade fire. The seas that will then wash aboard unhindered may weaken the crew's strength and the lack of protection their spirit."

The Fleet Battery came into action just before 1100. Her opponents were no less than the *Elephant* and the *Ganges*. And although the two battleships had been concentrating their fire on the *Dannebrog*, seventeen-year-old Sub-Lieutenant Peter Willemoes and his crew had received more than their fair share of British round-shot, bar shot and grapeshot over their unprotected deck. The guard rails were reduced to matchsticks and the crew was wading in ice-cold water up to their ankles as the fresh wind whipped the waves across the deck. One gun blew up, another had its trunnions blown off and five of the twenty on board were destroyed. The noise level on the open raft was infernal and one of the pressed men, Hendrik

Lemberg from Elsinore, "lost his mind during the battle and died immediately afterwards".

After just over an hour and a half's fighting the Fleet Battery had lost forty-six men, dead or wounded, that is 35 per cent, the highest losses on the Danish side. At that point Olfert Fischer's pennant was no longer flying from the burning *Dannebrog*. And shortly before, the two vessels inshore of the fleet battery, the *Elven* and the *Aggershus*, had cut their moorings and pulled out of the battle.

In this situation, just before 1300, Sub-Lieutenant Willemoes also decided to withdraw. In accordance with regulations, he marked his four mooring anchors with buoys. Having cut his moorings, he was unable to work his way clear of the next Danish ship to the north. Slowly the cumbersome raft drifted closer to the *Sjælland* and rammed her side with a great bang and creaking of timbers. Many of her men clambered aboard the *Sjælland* to what they thought was safety. The Fleet Battery was alongside for only a short while before she started drifting northwards again. The ships in Kronløbet Channel sent their boats to assist in warping the heavy raft into the harbour.

It was a very dazed and bewildered seventeen-year-old commanding officer who went ashore and presented his report and at the first opportunity sat down and wrote a comforting letter home to his parents and younger brothers and sisters at home in Odense on the island of Funen. "I am, thank God, still with all my limbs, which I least expected to keep possession of. As I had about my small battery Admiral Nelson and two British ships-of-the-line, who fired incessantly with grapeshot, round shot and bar shot, I did my duty and have been praised by the Crown Prince and the admirals, as well as all my colleagues, for standing firm. They told me they never believed I would escape with my life."

Midshipman Millard of the Monarch

The ship-of-the-line *Sjælland* had more guns and men than any other Danish vessel in the King's Deep. In his original plan, Nelson had picked this large 74 for himself, but the emergency plan changed all that. Instead, she was faced by two British 74s, the *Ganges* and *Monarch*.

But the *Sjælland* was a worthy opponent and, with 56 dead and 164 wounded, the *Monarch* took more casualties than any other ship in the British fleet on 2 April.

When Captain Mosse was killed it made a deep impression on

Midshipman Millard. But, despite his tender age, he realized that "employment was the surest mode to escape those unpleasant sensations which must arise in everyone's breast that has time for reflection in such a situation. I therefore pulled off my coat, helped to run out the gun, handed the powder, and literally worked as hard as a dray horse.

"Every gun is supplied at first with a portion of shot, wadding &c., close by it; but when these were expended, we applied to a reserve placed by the main mast. It immediately occurred to me that I could not be more usefully employed than in conveying this supply, which would enable the stronger ones to remain at the guns, for the men wanted no stimulus to keep them to their duty, nor any directions how to perform it.

"The only cautions I remember to have been given were hinted to me by the gunner before the action, viz to worm the guns frequently, that no fire might remain from an old cartridge, to fire two round-shot in each gun, and to use nothing else while round shot could be had."

In the *Monarch*, all the seamen were manning the guns. Soldiers from the 49th Grenadiers under the command of Lieutenant Colonel Hutchinson had been sent on board to take part in the concluding storm of Trekroner Fort. They were dressed in full uniform and lined up on the quarterdeck and the gangway between the quarterdeck and the fo'c'sle, from where they took potshots at the upper deck crew of the *Sjælland*. They themselves were fired at with such tenacity that they were ordered down. The other soldiers, in their working jackets, were distributed among the guns.

The officers of the regiment were without any gainful employment other than that which they found for themselves. One of them was Lieutenant James Dennis. He came up on deck just as a shot took away the *Monarch*'s wheel and spread death and destruction around it. His sabre, still in its scabbard, was fractured in three places and a piece of flying timber lacerated the ends of the fingers of his left hand. He could not feel his fingers but lifted what was left of his sabre and shouted, "Look here, Colonel!" When Hutchinson drew his attention to his hand, he bound his handkerchief around it and set up a series of cheers that was soon echoing round the ship. Such cheering, Millard knew, was "of more importance than might generally be imagined; for the men have no other communication throughout the ship; but when a shout is set up, it runs from deck to deck, and they know that their comrades are, some of them, alive and in good spirits."

As the battle raged on, Lieutenant Dennis dashed around the ship and when he found any of his men wounded carried them in his arms to the cockpit.

The colonel of the regiment was also desperate for something to do. When the battle commenced, Millard records, he did not leave the deck "but walked backward and forward with coolness and composure; till at length, seeing the improbability of being ordered away [to attack Trekroner Fort] he begged I would employ him if I thought he could do any good. I was at this time seated on the deck, cutting the wads asunder for the guns; and the Colonel, not withstanding the danger attending his uniform breeches, sat himself down and went to work very busily. Indeed, afterwards, I was often obliged to leave the charge of my guns to the Colonel, for I was now the only midshipman left on the quarterdeck, and was therefore employed by Mr Yelland, the commanding officer, as his aide-de-camp, and dispatched occasionally into all parts of the ship. On my return, the Colonel made his report of what had passed in my absence."

The seventeen-year-old Midshipman and the Commanding Officer of King George's 49th Grenadiers quickly found out that rank and etiquette were meaningless on board a ship-of-the-line in battle. They did their duty wherever and however they could. And they were lucky enough to escape unscathed, or practically unscathed, by the Danish shot that cost so many of the *Monarch*'s crew their lives and limbs. One of Millard's fellow midshipmen was so badly wounded by splinters all over his body that he had to be taken below. Millard accompanied another who suffered the same fate, but only as far as the companionway down to the cockpit where the horrific amputations were being carried out as fast as the doctor could cut and saw, whilst his assistants lay across the wounded man to hold him down. At the top of the companionway he turned back.

William Millard did not completely avoid the flying splinters that constantly flew through the air like angry wasps and killed and wounded many more men than the Danish shots. "When I passed backwards and forwards between my quarters and the mainmast, I went on the opposite side to that which was engaged, and by that means probably escaped a severe wound; for as I was returning with two shot in one hand and a cheese [or packet] of wads in the other,

I received a pretty smart blow on my right cheek. I dropped my shot, just as a monkey does a hot potato, and clapped my hand to the place, which I found rather bloody, and immediately ran aft to get my handkerchief out of the coat pocket."

Colonel Hutchinson examined Millard's jaw, fearing it to be broken, but when he felt there was no serious damage allowed the midshipman to return for his shot.

The *Monarch* took a great deal of punishment, a battering William Millard was to witness at close hand. After an hour's action he was ordered to run the length of the ship, right up to the forrard magazine to collect the special quills used to fire the guns. "When I arrived on the maindeck, along which I had to pass, there was not a single man standing the whole way from the mainmast forward, a district containing eight guns on each side, some of which were run out ready for firing; others lay dismounted; and others remained as they were after recoiling." But there was not a living soul in this grizzly burial chamber and Millard had to pull himself up by his boot straps before he could bring himself to stride over the body of a soldier.

Most of *Monarch*'s casualties were in the forrard part of the ship and most of them had fallen to Trekroner Fort's guns. Shortly after Millard returned to his guns on the quarterdeck he saw another midshipman come up top, his head and throat wrapped in a gruesome mess of blood and brains. He came with three ratings to report for duty. They were all that was left of the gun crews on the fo'c'sle, where one of Millard's midshipman friends had had both his feet blown off, lying alongside twenty dead or wounded seamen. The four survivors reported to Lieutenant Yelland and were immediately put to work at the guns on the quarterdeck.

Death sentence for desertion

The *Monarch*'s losses were high, but so were the *Sjælland*'s.

When the battle came to the *Sjælland* at 1000 her commanding officer, Commander Harboe, stood on the quarterdeck. As in all the other large ships in the defence line, his second-in-command, Lieutenant Commander Schultz, had charge of the upper deck and Lieutenant Hoppe of the lower gun deck. On the upper deck Sub-Lieutenant Dietrichson was stationed at the after guns and Contract Lieutenant Justesen at the forrard; also on the upper deck was Contract Lieutenant Wedelée; on the lower gundeck Contract Lieutenant Bærentzen. The commanding officer of the soldiers on board, 94 men from the Norwegian Regiment, was Staff Captain Westerholt, who had placed himself on the quarter-deck with a number of his red-coated musketeers to direct their fire. The ship's company was divided between the guns and other essential posts whilst at action, and on the starboard side of the ship, in her lee, a quartermaster and a detachment of seamen were manning the ship's pinnace, the captain's barge, a longboat and a yawl.

At a very early stage the guns on the *Sjælland*'s quarterdeck had been dismounted by British shot and Westerholt and his mus-keteers were ordered down. He was moved to the lower gundeck to organize the supply of powder and ensure that the wounded were taken to the lazarette. The smoke on this deck was now thick and heavy, and, not long before, a British incendiary shell had struck, belching choking smoke that made it almost impossible to see anything.

As the battle progressed, the *Sjælland*'s losses grew. The men on the upper deck were gradually blown away from their guns. Wedelée was killed and Justesen took a ball in his left foot. Her masts and yards were shot away, her port side was almost a colander after the British bombardment and the ship's carpenter and his assistants were working non-stop to plug and shore up the 20–30 holes below the water line and make sure the pumps were kept manned and working. But it was not this damage that was Harboe's greatest worry; it was the fact that the *Sjælland* was finding it increasingly difficult to fight back against the battering she was taking. The casualties among those who had been trained to man the guns were high and most of the gun carriages were shot apart and the guns reduced to useless pieces of scrap. But just before 1300 she was still putting up a fight, firing from the aftermost guns on both decks. Not long afterwards all fire from the upper deck ceased as there were not enough hands to tend the guns.

At this point a fear began to spread around the ship that she was sinking. On the upper deck, where the ensign had been shot away but the command pennant was still flying from the mainmast, Lieutenant Commander Schultz could see that the *Dannebrog* was in flames and that the Fleet Battery was drifting towards the *Sjælland*'s starboard side, where it would probably crush the ship's boats, the crew's only escape route if the ship were to sink.

Throughout the battle he had carried out his duty as second-in-command and kept up the spirits of the gun crews on the upper deck. But at this point he fell apart. He ran down to the lower gundeck, leaped overboard through one of the gun ports into the longboat and thence to the pinnace. And, with the captain's barge and fifty or so able-bodied and wounded men, steered the boats for Trekroner Fort. By the time he went ashore in the Fort he had regained control of himself and returned to his ship. But he had deserted – and the crew knew it. A moment's panic later led to the death penalty for cowardice for the *Sjælland*'s second-in-command and a humiliating pardon in front of the firing squad.

Commander Harboe was not aware of the desertion of his First Lieutenant until the battle was over. But he had observed that his ship-of-the-line was almost without hands to man the guns or put up any further resistance. He had therefore gone below and at 1300 given the order to cut the two heavy anchor cables forrard, which until then had held the ship in her position in the King's Deep line.

Just after that the Fleet Battery crashed into the *Sjælland* and some of the men from the low raft scrambled aboard the ship. In this situation nobody had a clear idea of what was happening on the lower gundeck and the crew was without any form of leadership. And yet another of the ship's officers lost control of himself. Staff Captain Westerholt had not spared himself during the battle. He had been as close to the action as anyone. A few minutes earlier, a shot had whistled past him so close that it took away the tails of his coat. But in all the confusion in the lower deck he was also struck by panic. Together with some of his soldiers, he jumped down into the ship's yawl and headed for the Customs Quay, where the same fate awaited him as Lieutenant Commander Schultz.

When Harboe gave the orders to cut the anchor cables he had hoped that the wind, at that time from the south-south-east, would put the ship aground south of Trekroner Fort. But he could see that instead they were heading straight for the battery itself. He therefore let go his emergency anchor "to stop the ship immediately and not foul the battery's range. Paid out as much anchor cable as possible to free the *Hjælperen*'s range also and to allow me to use what few guns I had left on the lower deck. But as the enemy continued to fire on us with great energy and we knew we were no longer in a position to defend ourselves, I decided to strike my colours. But when the battle suddenly subsided shortly afterwards, I left the pennant up and started throwing powder and shot overboard."

Sub-Lieutenant Müller and Admiral Nelson
At about 1300 the battle in the middle of the line changed character. The frigate *Elven* was gone; the converted cavalry barge *Aggershus* was gone and Fleet Battery No 1 was gone. The *Dannebrog* was still fighting, but the fire was spreading and the intervals between shots were becoming longer and longer.

But, astern of her, the artillery barge *Hajen* was still firing. The British had never encountered a vessel of this sort before. They were of such low freeboard that it was difficult to depress the guns enough and the heavy smoke made them difficult to sight. To begin with the British line-of-battleships had concentrated their fire on the *Dannebrog*, with the result that, in the first hour of battle, the *Hajen* took only four casualties. But when the four vessels in the middle of the line pulled out, and as shots from the *Dannebrog* began to dwindle, the artillery barge was the centre of all the attention it could desire.

The *Hajen* came under terrible fire, also from the *Glatton*'s carronades. The breechings and blocks on the carriages were destroyed and more and more guns were dismounted. The crew were also close to exhaustion after two or three days' unending hard labour. This engendered "utterances that the time had come to stop fighting, which complaints were silenced by the encouragement of the captain and the issue of aquavit, and the battle from the *Hajen* continued with renewed energy and full determination." Sub-Lieutenant Müller urged his craftsmen and soldiers to fight on, but they were tired and inexperienced in serving the guns. So Contract Lieutenant Lind took over as gun captain on the most forrard of the guns, while the captain himself and gunner Jacob Müller from the Naval Artillery Company kept the others firing. But they were running out of powder and Müller flew a signal for more to be rowed out from the shore.

From the *Elephant*'s quarterdeck Nelson and Stewart followed the *Hajen*'s actions. Stewart was impressed by the small Danish artillery vessels, which in his opinion were just as hard to defeat as the blockships. He was particularly impressed with the *Hajen*, which was continuing to fight with such resolution and sticking it out longer than the others of her class. She struck her colours only when the ships-of-the-line opposing her directed the full concerted might of their guns against her and opened fire with shot and grapeshot.

In this predicament the *Hajen* had no other choice than to surrender. At 1445, after four hours' fighting, Müller ordered her flag to be hauled down. But the British kept up their fire and Müller ordered all his men to take cover below deck as he and gunner Møller spiked their guns and attempted to build a raft that could convey their men to the safety of the shore. Shortly afterwards the *Hajen* was boarded by two armed longboats and Müller and his crew were taken aboard the *Elephant.*

As a token of respect, the British allowed this young officer to keep his sword. On the quarterdeck, Colonel the Hon. William Stewart complimented him on his valour, and he was presented to Nelson.

In the *Elephant*'s great cabin, Müller stood face to face with his opponent: "small, lean and very erect, dressed in a green kalmuck overcoat and a small cocked hat". The *Elephant*'s captain was also present: "a tall, handsome and somewhat older gentleman in full uniform bedecked with decorations". Captain Foley assured Müller that "the English had never had such a warm day as this, neither against the Dutch, the French or the Spanish". Nelson, pacing up and down in his cabin, said, "It pains me what has happened today, and as proof I have already sent an envoy to negotiate a cease-fire. Should it transpire that this is not acceptable, I will have to take Trekroner Fort and burn the Arsenal."

Müller was in awe at meeting the hero of the Nile, but not so excited as to stop him from replying, "There are certain things about the Trekroner battery, which, if you were aware of them, would make you understand that it will not be as easy to take as you may possibly think. As far as the Arsenal is concerned, my country-men are not so stupid as to leave anything behind when they see it under attack."

Nelson had other things to attend to than discussing his plans with a Danish Sub-Lieutenant. He concluded the interview, there-fore, with the wish that Müller's time as prisoner might be short and that every attempt would be made to make him comfortable. He then saluted him and Müller went up on deck.

Beaten but not taken
The battle in the middle of the line in the King's Deep was over. Nelson had beaten the vessels there by 1300. The *Dannebrog* kept on firing sporadically until 1430 and the *Hajen* a quarter of an hour longer. But in military terms the Danish resistance in the middle of the line had been broken after two hours.

However, the long-term resistance of the Danes was to have an influence on what happened later, because Nelson's intentions were not to annihilate the Danish vessels but to conquer them and make room for the British bomb vessels. A whole armada of British boats with seamen and soldiers aboard was afloat throughout the battle, behind the British ships-of-the-line, ready to board and take the Danish vessels, but when Lieutenant Home of the *Monarch* pulled away with the ship's flat-bottomed boat and longboat to board the defeated Danish vessels that had struck their colours the Danes opened fire on them. Another boat on the same mission was sunk by a shot from Danish guns. Lieutenant Home had to turn his prize-taking spree into a rescue mission, pick up the survivors and return to the *Monarch*.

Nelson had won a military victory in the middle of the line. The vessels that were left were beaten, but as long as they lay in their positions, and as long some of them were capable of firing on the British boats that attempted to board them, he had still not accomplished the objectives he had set for himself. He had won with his guns and carronades, but they did not enable him to capitalize on his victory. He would have to adopt other measures.

Chapter 9

THE BATTLE OF COPENHAGEN – ACT II

THE NORTHERN FLANK

The battle on the northern flank lasted longer than that in the middle of the line. There were several reasons for this. One was that when Nelson had to improvise an emergency plan it was from the north that he took the ships he was suddenly in need of; another was that the battle was fought at a slightly greater distance than in the middle and the south; another was that the guns at Trekroner Fort contributed to the weakening of the most northerly of the British line-of-battleships; finally, the vessels in the Danish northern flank did not all go into action at the same time. Although the blockship *Charlotte Amalie* and the artillery barge *Søhesten* joined in at the same time as the vessels in the middle of the King's Deep, those north of them, the ship-of-the-line *Holsten*, the block-ship *Indfødsretten* and the frigate *Hjælperen*, only opened fire an hour later.

That morning the *Charlotte Amalie* and the *Søhesten* had followed Fischer's orders and swung their ships to present a broadside to the south. They had watched as the *Edgar* entered the Deep, seen the *Prøvestenen* fire the first shot and the *Edgar* return fire. But after that the smoke was so thick in the southern sector, gradually spreading north to the middle, that they could see nothing of how the battle was developing. The captain of the *Charlotte Amalie* could truly affirm that "If the Commander-in-Chief has sent any signals during the battle, I have been unable to see them because of the smoke". The Danish and British lines were almost fighting in an enclosed space, defined by the limits of the smoke. As Nelson described the conditions so succinctly, "Here was no manoeuvring: it was downright fighting".

The Charlotte Amalie

At about 1100 Commander Koefoed of the *Charlotte Amalie* observed a British line-of-battleship "close my side, anchor from the stern with a lead of almost a cable. I was suffering from his grapeshot as my deck was flush and I was vulnerable to the guns on his quarterdeck and fo'c'sle."

With her twenty-six guns, the *Charlotte Amalie* was the second smallest blockship in the line and on the low-lying vessel's open deck the men were completely without protection from the guns on the British battleships' upper decks, but it was only when the middle sector collapsed that the *Monarch* and the *Ganges* could concentrate their combined forces against the *Charlotte Amalie*. For Koefoed, therefore, the first two hours of battle were less bloody than the last.

"When the line-of-battleship *Sjælland* to the south of us drifted with the current, her opponent hauled himself around and engaged me with raking fire; my people were mown down at such a rate that I had difficulty in removing them. All the ships to the south of me were lost and I felt my crew was in great danger. They were able to carry out their gunnery duties only very slowly and some of my gun carriages were shot to pieces. I realized that I was unable to inflict any more damage on the enemy, as I was facing a greatly superior opponent and would be sacrificing my brave and courageous men to no useful purpose. I believed it was my duty as a human being to strike my pennant and flag, having first thrown my signals book overboard, with the full intention of surrendering my ship and my crew to the enemy."

It was the *Ganges* that eventually struck the death blow, forcing the *Charlotte Amalie* to surrender. But the battle had been long and hard. From the *Elephant*'s quarterdeck Colonel Stewart had watched with admiration how the small blockship had sustained the action so much longer than the *Dannebrog*.

Only now could Koefoed spare the time to attend to his wounded. He was not economical in his praise of his surgeon: "In the lazarette, where I went down for a short time after I had struck my colours to see my much distressed and wounded men, I saw to my amazement the care he had taken in dressing every man and the conscientious attention he was giving each of them".

When Koefoed hauled down his colours it was 1445, but the British kept firing. They had had too many experiences of Danish ships whose colours were gone but who still kept on firing at boats that were sent to board them. But Koefoed was most disgruntled: "When they shamefully, against all the rules of war, kept firing at me and wounding my men still on deck, I felt it my duty to get as many of my officers and men as I could into the boats and ashore to Trekroner Fort, to be of more service, if possible, against the enemy. Having arrived there, I sent the longboat back to the ship to pick up more men, whom Contract Lieutenant Willems was leading with great character under the hailstorm of shot, despite the fact that he had twice been wounded and was close to exhaustion. He made one more visit to the ship to remove the wounded but was forced to turn back when he discovered that the ship had been boarded by the English."

They managed to save 167 of the *Charlotte Amalie*'s crew of 241. But 39 were dead and wounded and 28 were taken prisoner, and the Admiralty was never able to trace 7 of the 66 volunteers and pressed men.

Where is the rascal?

The *Charlotte Amalie* fought a tenacious and determined battle, and the *Monarch* paid a high price for defeating the small block-ship. When Midshipman Millard was sent up top to hoist a signal towards the end of the battle there was not a man alive on the quarterdeck. The signals midshipman was wounded and his yeoman had had a leg shot off and had crawled down to the cockpit where he bled to death while he waited for his turn to be held down by the loblolly boys on the operating table. A shot had crushed a leather bucket full of pistols and scattered them around the deck; a musket was lying with its barrel bent backwards in a semi-circle, hit just at the moment a soldier had put it to his shoulder to fire it.

At that time, around 1400, an unusual scene unrolled on the *Monarch*'s deck. Millard had seen "Mr Yelland storming and raving, stamping and swearing, as if he had been in a high state of delirium". Several of his officers were trying to calm him down. "Mr Bateman, who was quartered in the after part of the lower deck, had discovered a man with an axe just about to cut the cable by which the ship rode. The man declared that he had been called from above to do so, but Mr Bateman chose to have better authority upon so serious a point, and for this purpose came on deck with the Master, to enquire of Mr Yelland. The very mention of it nearly upset the old gentleman, for some time he could only say, 'Where is the rascal? Who is the rascal? &c., and had he fallen in with the poor man he would most certainly have run him through the body without much further inquiry. When they had quieted him a little, they had some trouble to convince him that the mischief was not actually done. 'Are you sure, Mr Bateman, you stopped the villain in time? Mr Grey, go down yourself and see all fast.' 'Sir, I come from thence.' 'Go again, sir'."

What had happened was this: the small bower anchor had been shot from the cat-heads and its spring prevented the ship from being swung to the east so that the forrard guns could be brought to bear on Trekroner Fort. Someone had then shouted, "Cut it away". This was repeated from man to man along the deck. In all the noise and confusion one of the men forrard had mistaken the spring hawser for the anchor cable that held the *Monarch* in her position in the Deep.

When all hope is lost

Just after the *Charlotte Amalie* entered the battle the artillery barge *Søhesten* immediately to the north became the next combatant. At 1100 Lieutenant Middelboe gave the order to fire and the *Søhesten* delivered her first broadside. "Kept up continuous fire to the best of my abilities, despite the fact that many men were killed in the first few minutes; particularly at the four guns aft, where the muzzles of two were shot away, unfortunately killing six to eight men each time."

The small barge, whose broadside of nine guns was almost immediately reduced to seven, had a hard time of it after the collapse of the middle of the line. Just after 1300 "our aftermost hawser was shot away. Immediately cut the forrard cable to prevent the vessel from turning bows on to the enemy; laid a warp on the shoal to get free of the *Holsten* who threw us a line; kept up fire for only a short time as this line was also shot away, at which we swung bows on to the enemy again; took another line from the *Holsten* and recommenced firing and continued until we could man no more than two guns as the others were damaged or without men to serve them. At that time I observed two enemy ships-of-the-line swinging to train their broadsides at us and rake our bows."

By this time it was 1430. The *Søhesten* crews had been fighting for three and a half hours against the British line-of-battleships, during which the men had been turned alternately from serving the

169

guns to manoeuvring the vessel. Lieutenant Middelboe was a professional naval officer and knew of the demands placed on a commanding officer in action by paragraph 752 in King Frederik V's Articles of War: "He is at all times to defend his ship with courage and fight bravely to the end, without striking his colours or surrendering as long as the slightest possibility exists for preserving his ship; but when all hope is lost for the ship and her crew, the ship may be put aground, scuttled or set on fire, having first ensured that no orders, logbooks or papers fall into enemy hands, and it is better that he surrender than cause so many of our brave subjects to suffer injury or death."

There was no longer any hope for "the safety of the ship and her crew". With the prospect of being raked by two British line-of-battleships, any further resistance would instigate meaningless massacre. The flag was hauled down and Middelboe got to work spiking the guns. He had succeeded in sealing the touch hole of a single gun when British boats arrived alongside the *Søhesten* and the captain and his crew were taken prisoner.

Arenfelt of the Holsten

Just to the north of the *Søhesten* lay one of the most powerful ships in the Danish line, the line-of-battleship *Holsten*. That morning Commander Arenfelt had hauled in on his warping hawser, paid out in his anchor spring and swung the ship so as to allow her to fire at the British ships as they moved up the King's Deep. But he was to have a long wait. "At 35 minutes past 10 o'clock, the *Prøvestenen* opened fire, soon returned by the English van. Since then each of our vessels in the south has engaged one by one. With the dense smoke the battle created, we lost sight of the enemy. Our guns were ordered to train as far forrard as possible without endangering the *Søhesten*."

Time passed and still the *Holsten*'s gun crews were unable to practice their craft against the British. But the waiting time was not uneventful. Just over an hour after the first shot had been heard from the south a boat appeared out of the smoke and came alongside the *Holsten*'s starboard side. Suddenly the Commodore, his aide and secretary were on board. Arenfelt's command pennant was hauled down from the mainmast and replaced by Olfert Fischer's broad pennant. At 1130 tactical command was transferred from the *Dannebrog* to her sister ship, the *Holsten*.

The nerve-racking waiting continued. Arenfelt and his men were still keeping a keen watch, peering through the clouds of smoke to the south. They could not actually see the British ships but they did get occasional glimpses of a ball in the air or the flash of a British muzzle, "even though they were some way off. Our guns were therefore elevated above the horizontal and trained towards the unseen enemy."

When Nelson had to improvise his plan he ordered the *Defiance* to anchor in a position where she would have the *Charlotte Amalie* as her main opponent but still be capable of firing on the artillery barge *Søhesten*. This she had done, riding to a stern anchor fitted with a spring hawser, and here she was to remain. Weighing anchor as normal and moving to a new position was impossible. She could always cut her anchor cable, but if she did, the wind and current would take her out of the King's Deep.

She was not completely stymied, though. By hauling in on the spring she could swing the hull and bring her guns to bear on the Danish vessels north of the *Søhesten*. And she had one more decisive manoeuvre open to her: she could pay out on the anchor cable aft and allow the current to take her further north. With a cable that was 185 m long, a line-of-battleship like the *Defiance* could move herself at least 100 m north of her original position without weighing anchor.

This is precisely what Rear Admiral Graves did. On board the *Charlotte Amalie*, the second-in-command, Lieutenant Bardenfleth, followed the manoeuvre at close quarters without really understanding it: "At about twelve o'clock the *Defiance* surrendered her station to the *Ganges* and moved abeam of the *Holsten*, where she anchored again and remained there until the end of the battle". Thus is his written account of it, but the *Defiance* had not re-anchored, merely paid out her cable to its maximum. On board the *Holsten* they saw a large British 74 with the flag of a Rear Admiral loom out of the smoke. Olfert Fischer had only been aboard his new flagship for fifteen minutes when he had to accept the fact that "the enemy closed the *Holsten* broadside on".

For Arenfelt and his crew this was the time when the waiting ended. "At that moment a shot entered the lower gundeck between the third and fourth gun port from the bows. At 48 minutes past eleven our lower gundeck opened fire, followed immediately by the upper deck and quarterdeck. The enemy shot was raining down like a hailstorm and almost all the men at the three first guns were killed. At the fourth gun at this time Lieutenant Haas informed me there was only one man remaining. I gave the order for those who were left to join the other gun crews. On the lower gundeck the enemy's first salvo passed through a gun port and took away its halyard; the port fell shut and we were unable to open it again, putting that gun out of action; the hinge on another port was shot away; and the rear trucks of another gun destroyed but continued firing throughout the battle. Four breechings were shot away and replaced with spares from the naval stores, allowing the guns to remain in action. The best bower cable and the sheet anchor were hit just aft of the bits; this shot killed many of the men on the lower gundeck; they were replaced by men from the other guns where they could be spared."

With her 74 guns, the *Defiance* clearly outgunned the Danish 60-gun ship-of-the-line and the speed and accuracy of the British gunners sealed the fate of the battered flagship. After an hour and three-quarters Olfert Fischer regarded the *Holsten* as done for and decided to transfer his command – again. There were almost no men left to man the guns. His personal log, left on the deck by his secretary, was shot overboard. The Commodore was convinced that the *Holsten* would "soon have to strike".

But where could Fischer move to? He had to leave the *Holsten* if he were to avoid being taken prisoner while his forces were still fighting. He had to admit the chances were few. "I was considering moving north to the others, but soon afterwards I saw that the *Indfødsretten* had struck her colours. As this option of saving the northern sector was closed to me, I left the *Holsten* at half past one and transferred my command to Trekroner Fort as the final choice, which would have to be taken with sword in hand."

The Commodore's broad pennant was hauled down once again. Fischer and his entourage left the ship and the command pennant was again hoisted to the maintop.

Arenfelt and his crew continued the battle, but the *Holsten* had only a short time left. "The enemy's fire was ferocious. All firing in the southern sector had ceased. The *Sjælland* drifted alongside, as did the *Søhesten*, and the Fleet Battery, which was apparently unmanned. Observed that the *Dannebrog* was adrift and on fire. The *Indfødsretten* had struck her ensign. Commodore Fischer ordered me to strike his broad pennant; hoisted my own pennant; he left immediately for the Fort. With the entire defence line now in shreds, and having taken the fire of five ships-of-the-line and three frigates as they passed, and with another four on their way from the south, we took a salvo aft from a ship to the north, so, although I was prepared to sacrifice all, we were in a position where we were unable to continue with any advantage to the country." He gave the order to strike.

The situation on the northern flank was hopeless when Arenfelt hauled down Fischer's pennant and hoisted his own again at 1415. Only now did he have the time to inspect his ship: "Quickly estimated how many shots we had fired: lower gundeck 20 or 21, upper deck 19 or 20, quarterdeck and foc's'le 16 or 17 shots per gun; all guns were spiked. The guns on the lower deck that were run out were hauled in and the ports closed to protect the survivors from grapeshot and to put a list on the ship so that the shots taken below the waterline would not cause her to sink."

It was a dying ship that the captain inspected. "Had taken a shot through the gunner's store-room . . . another through the gangway between the bread room and the cartridge-filling room, another through the provisions store, the gangways, the sail locker and the bread room. Throughout all this, the men kept up their fire. Saw we had taken 13 shots below the waterline and more than 150 through the gundecks; a fearsome number in the shrouds, stays and yard arm blocks; all masts and yards were damaged or shot away. The mizzen and foremasts were useless; after the shot took away the bits, the anchor fell and was hanging over the lower gundeck; ordered its cable and the spring cut without being buoyed; man shot dead in the maintop. The three boats lay to starboard under shelter of the hull but a shot from the Kronløbet Channel went through the longboat and yawl. Ordered a carpenter to apply lead patches and sent Lieutenant Linstow ashore with as many men as we dared put in the boat. The dead and wounded cannot be numbered, but, of the officers, Contract Lieutenant Sonne was badly injured in the eyes and Contract Lieutenant Haas in the thigh."

Shortly after the *Holsten* struck, she was boarded by British boats and Commander Arenfelt and his officers and men were taken on board the *Elephant*, though Arenfelt was granted permission to return to his ship to tend the wounded. All of them, with the exception of one seriously injured man, however, had been taken ashore. Later that afternoon the prisoners from the *Holsten* were transferred to Parker's flagship, where the badly wounded man's legs were amputated. He did not survive the operation. During the night six of the other wounded from the *Holsten* also died. On the morning of 3 April Arenfelt and his officers conducted the Danish Navy's burial service on the deck of the *London* and the men were committed to the deep.

Riou's squadron

Furthest to the north the battle had assumed a different character. According to Nelson's original plan, the ships-of-the-line were also to have been deployed here and, before the passage into the King's Deep, Nelson had instructed Captain Riou, together with his frigates and fireships, to follow the larger ships and support their attack on the two blockships at the entrance to the Kronløbet Channel. But navigational problems created a completely new situation at the very north of the line and Riou elected to act on his own initiative, having assessed the situation confronting him.

The frigate flotilla reached the north end of the King's Deep at about 1130, behind the British line and within hailing distance of Nelson, while they fired between the gaps in the British line. The *Amazon*, the flotilla leader, anchored from the stern with a spring attached in front of the northernmost line-of-battle ship, the *Defiance*. The *Blanche* anchored ahead of the *Amazon* and the *Alcmene* ahead of the *Blanche*. The last two frigates, the *Arrow* and *Dart*, took up position in the arc the other three frigates formed as an extension of the British line north of Trekroner Fort. They concentrated their fire on the *Holsten* and the blockship *Indfødsretten*. They received heavy fire in return from the two Danish vessels, the frigate *Hjælperen* and the Fort itself.

Riou had the advantage of being able to choose his position and his decision was a bold one. The frigate flotilla suffered heavy losses, which would have been even greater if they had not shortly afterwards obeyed Parker's orders to withdraw from the battle. At the time the *Amazon* had been in action for almost half an hour, whilst the *Arrow* and *Dart* had barely let go their anchors and fired their first salvo. By then the *Amazon* had already lost fourteen men, with another twenty-three wounded. That was almost double those suffered by the *Elephant*. The last to fall was Riou himself. When the *Amazon* cut her anchor cable and turned off the wind to head north she was raked from astern by the Fort's guns. Riou had already received a head injury and had sat down on a gun to cheer up his crew when a shot cut him in half.

Early withdrawal

Exactly what kind of ship the *Hjælperen* was Nelson never discovered. Partly because she was a custom-built defence frigate, whose five-foot-thick sides at the midships waterline were the equivalent of armour plate and were intended to make her unsinkable; and partly because they were not given all that much time to study her at close quarters. She had pulled out of the battle on the northern flank before it really even got started.

Just before noon, when the British battleships reached their northernmost positions, the *Hjælperen* exchanged fire with both the *Defiance* and the *Monarch*. Just after noon she received the attentions of Riou's frigates as they arrived and anchored, and only an hour later she up-anchored and sailed across towards the Kronløbet Channel, where she anchored in the lee of Trekroner Fort.

Of her 269 men, six were wounded, three so seriously that they died of their wounds. But the *Hjælperen* herself had suffered almost no damage. When Lieutenant Lillienskjold "saw the state of the defences, he cut his moorings and sailed inshore to avoid needless sacrifice of his men without accomplishing anything to the honour of the flag". That, at least, is what he wrote in his report. It is also possible that the very sight of all the vessels in the middle sector that had withdrawn from the battle caused him to forget the admonitory words of the Articles of War to "fight bravely to the end".

Assistance to the Indfødsretten

On the northern flank, therefore, it was the 64-gun blockship *Indfødsretten* that lasted longest, remarkably long in fact. Certainly she entered the battle at a late stage, but she did remain in close action right up to 1500, and her fight was one full of drama.

She was moored to her four anchors with her bows pointing north-west, off Trekroner Fort, and so far north that the British ships really only engaged her with any enthusiasm once the other vessels to the north were vanquished.

The *Indfødsretten*'s first shot was a direct hit. One of the countless British boats, a longboat with twenty or so men on board, came within range and on the lower gundeck a musketeer in the Marine Corps, Anders Wessel, fired his cannon against the boat, which was hit and went down immediately.

The crew had been able to observe the *Prøvestenen*'s opening shot, as had every other Dane in the King's Deep. But, as stated before, from that time on everything was concealed behind the curtain of smoke. Not until two hours later did the men aboard the *Indfødsretten* begin to get an idea of how the battle was going and the impression they got was far from encouraging. "Between twelve and one o'clock, the cavalry barges *Nyborg* and *Aggershus* passed us and worked their way further inshore. Immediately afterwards, the *Elven* and *Sjælland* passed us, as did the Fleet Battery," wrote Contract Lieutenant Heich Meinertz of the *Indfødsretten*.

But at that time the bell began tolling for the *Indfødsretten*. "At one o'clock the first enemy ships came within range and engaged us with fierce fire. Half an hour later our commanding officer, Lieutenant Commander Thurah, fell, after which his second, Lieutenant Cortsen, continued the engagement with all the force he could muster. At two o'clock he fell too, at which juncture I assumed command and fought with every gun at my disposal until three o'clock."

Heich Meinertz wrote the truth about the *Indfødsretten*'s struggle, but not the whole truth. At 1330 her flag was no longer flying. Fischer had seen this from the *Holsten* and Lieutenant Lillienskjold from the *Hjælperen*, and both had understood it to mean she had struck.

Ashore on Nyholm Crown Prince Frederik, surrounded by numerous officers, had been following the battle, first from the Quintus Battery, and later, as the battle moved northwards, from Sixtus Battery. It was from here at 1330 that he issued orders for the crews of the northern vessels in the line to be supplemented with fresh men from ashore. He asked for volunteers among his officers and several responded immediately. A boat set off with Lieutenant Commander Schrødersee, and Lieutenants Nissen and Lützen with orders to head for the *Indfødsretten*.

He was never to assume command of her. The job of writing the assistance report fell to Lieutenant Nissen. "As soon as we arrived at the ship, Lieutenant Commander Schrødersee went aboard, followed closely by myself; Lieutenant Lützen remained in the longboat until the men had boarded. Lieutenant Commander Schrødersee asked immediately whether I had given the order for the men to board the ship, but, before I could reply, a shot went through him."

Schrødersee was killed just as his feet touched the deck of the *Indfødsretten*. Nissen assumed command: "I went thereupon to

176

the upper gundeck where there were but few men, but a Contract Lieutenant, whose name I never discovered, replied in response to my enquiry of who had hauled down the colours that it had been so ordered; I ordered him to hoist them again without delay, which action was performed as I went down to the lower gundeck, where Lieutenant Lützen came through the gangway. We were met with a situation of utter confusion – many men drunk, and only a few guns had been fired. We asked the officers, among them Lieutenant Rothe of the Marine Corps, who was the only one we knew, why the guns were not in action; he answered that they had been under intense fire for more than an hour without being able to return fire, but once they could present their broadside again they would open fire with every gun that could be used; we attempted to swing the ship but to no avail – the spring was stretched almost to breaking point and a thick splice was preventing us from paying it out of the gunport any further with the men in that condition."

In such a situation the reinforcements from Nyholm could do precious little. "It is the honest truth that the *Indfødsretten* was in great trouble. Two enemy ships lay ahead and astern of us, blasting the men from their guns without them being able to let off a single shot in their defence, and we deeply regret the deaths of the many brave men who accompanied us from Nyholm that occurred as soon as they set foot on board, without the comfort that can be derived from the satisfaction of fighting back."

Nissen saw plainly that he was completely unable to accomplish anything on the northern flank of the King's Deep. "At three o'clock, when it became apparent that further defence was useless, having called the officers together, there was unanimous agreement that we should do whatever was in our power to save the few men who were still unscathed and strike our colours. Having ordered the officers to ensure that all the guns were spiked and our ammunition jettisoned, we considered it the most correct action to take; our orders called for us to provide assistance to the ships under threat from the British ships at the north of the line. Boarded the longboat and set off thereafter for the *Elefanten*, which was still in action and remained so until the order to cease fire was given."

At 1500, when the *Indfødsretten* struck her colours for the second time, the northern flank of the Danish line of defence had ceased to exist.

The ships in Kronløbet Channel

At that point all that was left of the northern sector were the battery on Trekroner Fort and the blockships *Elefanten* and *Mars*, which were exchanging fire with Parker's ships-of-the-line *Defence*, *Ramillies* and *Veteran*. In the Kronløbet Channel, though, there was still Steen Bille's squadron, formally an independent force but in reality part of the defences, which is how Bille himself regarded them.

When Fischer had abandoned the *Holsten* at 1330 he had selected Trekroner Fort as his new 'flagship' because it was still intact. He realized only too well, however, that the Fort's turn would soon come and that it was imperative to reinforce its defence as much as possible. "I sent Lieutenant Uldall to HRH the Crown Prince to make a preliminary report on what had taken place and request reinforcements of 2–300 men for the Battery; there were still few men wounded and only one dead at this stage; but as the enemy approached, the men at the Battery would endure terrible suffering, so I considered it most prudent to keep a corps in reserve to man the guns."

Reinforcements from the shore were sent out to the Fort. By then it had been engaging the *Defiance* and *Monarch* for two and a half hours and inflicted heavy losses. The optimism Nelson and his commanding officers had felt before the battle about taking the Fort had dissipated and the doubtful issue of a storming of Trekroner Fort that had so preoccupied Olfert Fischer never took place on 2 April.

The two blockships in the Kronløbet Channel saw no real action. Whilst they tacked south, the *Defence*, *Ramillies* and *Veteran* opened fire on them from both sides; their shots went high. The *Elefanten* and *Mars* returned fire but the enemy was out of range. Nobody was killed aboard these vessels and the only two casualties, two wounded volunteers aboard the *Elefanten*, were caused by a shot from the British ships in the King's Deep.

So the King's Deep was out of range of Steen Bille's squadron, but by elevating the heaviest guns on the lower gundecks of the *Danmark* and the *Trekroner* (the ship that is, not the Fort), they could reach the northern sector of the line. But it was a risky business because between them and the British ships lay their own defence vessels. The *Trekroner* fired not a single shot – voluntarily; the only gun that did fire was detonated by a British shell that fell on her quarterdeck.

At about 1400 the *Danmark* fired a salvo or two, but the range was too great and Bille put a stop to it. Some of the British shells actually passed over the squadron. Forty-five minutes later a British shot passed through the *Danmark*'s side between the fifth and sixth aftermost gunports on the lower gundeck, where it killed a musketeer of the Danish Life Regiment and injured a rating.

Steen Bille's squadron was unable to play an active role in any part of the battle.

Northern flank defeated

When the *Indfødsretten* struck her colours at 1500 the King's Deep defence line was definitively beaten. It fact it had been since that ship fired her last shot. But no boats were sent to take her into British possession, partly because the guns of Trekroner Fort still controlled the water north of the King's Deep and partly because the commanding officers of the four most northerly British ships-of-the-line in the Deep knew, just after 1400, that Nelson had sent an emissary ashore under a flag of truce to bring an end to the battle. So there was no reason to risk boats and men on the potentially hazardous mission of boarding a defeated ship. In that situation the best thing to do was sit and wait.

The vessels on the Danish northern flank had lasted longer than those in the middle, not because they had fired faster and more accurately or that they had shown greater resistance than their sisters to the south, but because Nelson had not deployed his ships-of-the-line in the northern sector so as to concentrate his attack on the middle and southern sectors of the line, as Riou's frigates had withdrawn at such an early stage and because the Fort was a worthy opponent, as long as it was protected by the defence line vessels against gunfire and a combined operation to take it.

When the *Infødsretten* struck, the northern flank was done for. From her upper deck, the crew could see that the middle of their line was beaten and defeated, but they could still hear firing from the south, from the ships that had fired the first shots of the battle.

THE SOUTHERN FLANK

The first shot of the battle was fired in the southern sector of the line, and so was the last.

Danish resistance proved to be unexpectedly dogged, despite the early breakthrough of the line when the *Rendsborg* and *Nyborg* cut their moorings and despite the raking of the sterns and bows of the southernmost ships.

The withdrawal of the two ships split the King's Deep line into two definable sectors – the northern end, comprising the blockships *Jylland* and *Kronborg* and the converted cavalry barge *Sværdfisken*, and the southern, comprising the blockships *Wagrien* and *Prøvestenen*. The opponents in the north were the line-of-battle ships *Edgar* and *Ardent*; in the south the *Isis*, *Polyphemus*, *Bellona*, *Russell*, and the frigate *Desirée*, and, in the late afternoon, the gun brigs *Biter*, *Bouncer*, *Force* and *Sparkler*. The shore batteries were incapable of providing any effective support to the Danish ships in the southern sector for two reasons: one, the range was too great and, two, there was a considerable risk of hitting their own ships. Stricker's Battery, however, could annoy the *Desirée*, but not forcibly enough to persuade her to retire to another position; and against the swift Royal Navy gun brigs it was powerless.

The deck was running with blood

When the *Edgar* and *Ardent* moved into the King's Deep, the first players to make their entrance, they had been following Nelson's plan to the letter. They had anchored by the stern, with a spring, opposite their allocated opponents – the *Edgar* facing the *Jylland*, and the *Ardent* the *Sværdfisken* and *Kronborg*. None of the three Danish vessels had masts or rigging, so from the first minutes the British gunners could concentrate on pounding the hulls. The fight was long and bloody, with dead and wounded matching almost man for man on both sides.

The commanding officer of the *Jylland* was Commander Branth. His place during battle, along with his second-in-command, Lieutenant Commander Wleugel, was of course on the quarter-deck, while Lieutenant Risbrich had charge of the lower gundeck. The fire from the British guns and carronades spread death and destruction. "We replied with maximum fire, but in a short while most of our men at the aftermost guns were killed and the pieces damaged. The survivors were distributed around the other guns, where they continued to give of their best." Eventually there were only two guns left on the upper deck, with the lower deck suffering the same fate. Commander Branth had nothing but praise for his people. When the *Jylland*'s flag was shot away after two hours' fighting, the bosun replaced it and was killed by an enemy shot in the process. There were many in the ranks of the volunteers who distinguished themselves, among them Copenhagen butcher Christian Schultz, potter Claus Madsen Docke from Funen and Melchior Heymann from the city's Jewish community.

Getting on for 1430, though, after almost four hours' action, the battle was over for Branth and his crew: "As I could see that I was in a position where I was no longer able to do any serious damage or put up any meaningful resistance with the four guns I had left, I struck my colours to spare any more bloodshed and cut my moorings so as to drift aground on the Refshale Shoal. I had taken many shots below the waterline and was close to sinking."

The ship was lost, but there were still people that could be turned to useful work. "I sent Lieutenant Commander Wleugel with the longboat to the southern ships, where they might have been of assistance; I remained on board to make sure the wounded were taken ashore and to throw the many dead overboard and swab and hose down the deck that was running with blood. Whilst I was doing this a British officer boarded us and took the ship as a prize; he took me and Lieutenant Risbrich as prisoners aboard the *Ardent*, without allowing us time to change or take with us more than we stood in, which seemed to me to be an act of English barbarism."

Following his captain's orders, the second-in-command of the *Jylland* had taken twelve men in the longboat and was rowing them to the *Rendsborg*, but she was as much of a wreck as the one they had left. Wleugel's next wish was to head for the northern end of the King's Deep but there were so many British boats in the water that he chose to row across the Refshale Shoal and make for Trekroner Fort.

As the British were boarding the *Jylland* on her port side her longboat shoved off from the starboard side with Contract Lieutenants Frantzen, Holm and Rasmussen and the ship's coxswain. It was packed with wounded and able-bodied men and they managed to cover the 1,400 metres across the shoal and make it safely to the shore.

Now there is just the two of us left
The *Kronborg* and the *Sværdfisken* were less heavily armed than the *Jylland*, but they held out for just as long. On board the *Sværdfisken*, Sub-Lieutenant Sommerfeldt did as much as he could with the nine guns that were still trained on the enemy, but the British guns took

their toll of men and materiel and their superiority was crushing. "I kept up my fire until five guns were destroyed and the carriages of the rest were shot away in an effort to inflict most damage; men were falling around me; the enemy shots killed some of the wounded in the hold; splinters and grapeshot mowed down the men on deck; lost my best men, unable to tend more than one gun; had no alternative other than to strike." At 1430 Sommerfeldt hauled down his colours. "Used the short time available to me before I was captured to throw powder, four cases of artillery grenades and some of the roundshot overboard."

With twenty-two guns, the *Kronborg* was the smallest blockship in the King's Deep. When she took the enemy's first salvo Contract Lieutenant Poul Hansen Bohne was killed. After close to two hour's fighting the second-in-command, Lieutenant Søren Bille was so badly wounded in the right leg by flying splinters from the forrard capstan that he had to be taken down to the lazarette. The commanding officer, Lieutenant Hauch, then went to Contract Lieutenant Søren Helt, in charge of the guns aft, and told him, "now there is just the two of us left, shoulder to shoulder." As he spoke, a hail of grapeshot took an arm and part of his side away: "he sank into my arms and I took him midships."

When the commanding officer was killed, Helt was the only officer on deck and assumed command. And bosun Andreas Møhl, who had been the captain's aide, now acted as aide for the wounded second-in-command in the hold, bringing him reports and relaying his orders.

The *Kronborg* had a hard time of it. Gunner's mate Torgius Petersen was busy at his post; "the piles of dead bodies on the deck were growing so fast that we could barely get to our guns."

Lieutenant Bille continued fighting "with as much zeal as I could muster until all the guns were destroyed and, as one gun was put out of action, the men moved to another. Eventually we had only men enough to man the guns furthest aft and when their carriages were hit they moved to the last guns that could still be used. Soon, these too were hit and, as we had no further use for it, I ordered the powder to be thrown overboard."

The *Kronborg* was completely disabled. "Three shots passed through the magazine from one side to the other; the lazarette took nine round shots and two bar shots. The breeches hoist to lower the wounded hit three times – and on two of these occasions the men were killed by the fall as they were thrown into the hold. Dr

Wunderlich, who had joined ship a couple of days before the battle, was ill and when he went below to the lazarette he was killed at the main hatchway. Every man in the powder chain was dead; they were replaced by the men at the pumps as the shots we had taken below the waterline were causing no more flooding than three inches over the lower futtock."

Throughout most of the battle the crew of the *Kronborg* had fought with discipline, despite the odds against them. But in the end their fighting spirit failed them, as it was beginning to aboard the remaining Danish vessels in the King's Deep in the final stages of the battle – Fleet Battery No 1, the *Sjælland*, *Indfødsretten*, *Hajen* and *Prøvestenen*. The ranks finally broke on board the *Kronborg* when Lieutenant Bille ordered the pennant to be struck at 1430, by which time the ensign had already been shot away. Many of the men took to the boats lying off the starboard side. They were whipped back on board again, but, amidst all the confusion, the British boarded the ship. With the point of a sword at his chest, Helt had to yield and watch helplessly as the British prize crew looted the possessions of his crew.

The volunteer carpenter
At 1430 the *Jylland*, *Kronborg* and *Sværdfisken* were beaten and taken. But behind them, aground on the Refshale Shoal, there was still a pocket of resistance: the artillery barge *Rendsborg* was still firing. Her ensign and command pennant were still flying and Lieutenant Commander Egede had succeeded in grounding and mooring his ship in the position he had selected when he had been forced to pull out of the line early on in the battle.

From his new position, some three cables behind the *Kronborg*, Egede had been firing his nine guns since 1130, alternating between roundshot, barshot and grapeshot. He had the same streak of stubbornness as his grandfather, Hans Egede, the first missionary to Greenland, and he was more than satisfied with the performance of his crew.

Among the volunteers was the Copenhagen carpenter Henrich Stub, who distinguished himself as gun captain and who "with impeccable discipline and accuracy maintained constant fire. Finally, he was badly wounded but remained at his gun, with no signs of despondency but, on the contrary, great courage."

During the battle a boat came alongside the *Rendsborg*: in it were a bosun's mate and ten men from Nyholm. The fresh men were a source of encouragement for the crew, but they were unable to change the ship's destiny. Just before 1500 the *Rendsborg* had had it. Her gunwale was badly damaged, her hull had been holed in seven places under the waterline, her masts, rigging, rudder and bowsprit were in fragments and, having fired 551 shots, there was only ammunition left for another 49. Egede therefore threw his signal books and ship's papers overboard and struck his colours. But the British kept on firing at her for another ten minutes, which cost another four men their lives.

Thanks to her position on the shoal, a considerable number of able-bodied and wounded men could be taken ashore. With the longboat and pinnace, and boats from Nyholm, Egede managed to save more than half his crew before Captain Rose of the *Jamaica* and two lieutenants boarded the artillery barge and took Egede and his remaining crew prisoner.

The British southern flank

When the *Rendsborg* struck at 1500 the battle in the northern sector of the King's Deep was over. In the middle sector it had been for some time. But in the south the *Wagrien* and *Prøvestenen* were still firing.

The two blockships had put up a hard fight, but losses among their opponents varied. Nobody was killed or wounded aboard the four gun brigs. They had only arrived in the King's Deep in the course of the afternoon and they had positioned themselves where they could fire on the *Wagrien* and *Prøvestenen* without them being able to return fire with more than two bowchasers on each deck. The *Desirée* had also placed herself in a similar position, but she was bows on to Stricker's Battery, which could fire on her without fear of reprisal. However, the frigate only suffered damage to her hull, masts and rigging and a few guns. No one was killed and very few wounded.

The blockships' main opponents were the battleships *Isis* and *Polyphemus*. And here the *Wagrien*'s gun crews proved to be more effective than those of the *Prøvestenen*. The *Isis* sustained some of the greatest British losses – thirty-three men killed and a great many wounded. The *Polyphemus*, however, lost very few men, despite the fact that she was also within range of Stricker's Battery. After more than four hour's action she had only lost six men dead and twenty-five wounded. The gunners aboard the *Prøvestenen* were unpractised and many of their shots went too high.

Losses aboard the grounded *Russell* were also noticeably few; for one, the distance was great but, as could be observed from the deck of the blockship, the Danes were aiming too high. No men were killed and only a few wounded.

The *Bellona*, the other grounded ship-of-the line, however, took serious losses. Just after she went aground her captain was seriously injured. Sir Thomas Thompson, who had commanded the battleship *Leander* at the Nile and done battle with the French flagship *L'Orient*, was hit by a Danish shot that took away his left leg. He was taken below immediately and command passed to his second. Lieutenant Thomas Wilkes was full of admiration for the *Wagrien* and the other Danish vessels: "I will do them the credit to say that they fought well, far better than I have found the French or Spaniards; not a vessel surrendered till nearly all her men were either killed or wounded, and several of the ships received men from the shore during the Battle."

But it was their stamina Wilkes admired rather than their gunnery. The *Bellona* certainly suffered serious damage to her masts and rigging but few of the casualties – eleven dead and seventy-two wounded – were lost to the Danish guns. They were due to a much more dreaded factor – exploding guns, particularly on the enclosed lower deck. Such tragic incidents were usually due to human error rather than poor craftsmanship: in the noise and confusion of battle; two charges were sometimes accidentally loaded into the barrel, over-stressing the gun with calamitous results. Many were killed and wounded and the deck above the gun was shattered. An hour later the same thing happened to one of the guns aft, with the same terrible results.

Risbrich and the Wagrien

On board the *Wagrien* Commander Risbrich followed the battle and his crew's efforts, and those of his younger brother in the *Jylland*, from his post on the upper deck: "Defended ourselves to the best of our ability against the powerful enemy and kept up a steady and accurate fire with double shot against the enemy hulls. I could see that against such a superior force I had no alternative other than to attempt to destroy their guns to reduce the rate of fire. I gave orders not to use anything but roundshot when double-loading to avoid stressing my guns."

But not long after the battle began Risbrich realized that the King's Deep line had been broken just to the north of his ship.

"Towards noon, as the artillery barge *Rendsborg* – just to our north – had taken a bad beating, her cables shot away and drifting towards the Refshale Shoal, her British opponent hauled in on her spring and directed a broadside at our port quarter without us being able to return fire because of the attention we were paying to our main opponent. The frigate *Desirée*, of forty-four guns, had anchored close off the Prøvestenen Shoal and was firing on the *Prøvestenen* and *Wagrien* bows on, destroying our two foc's'le bow chasers. Also at about 1300, some smaller enemy ships and gun brigs had taken up position in the southern sector so that they too could fire on us."

The *Wagrien* was a puny ship to take on the *Edgar* and the *Desirée* at the same time. Nor could she withstand the combined fire power of the ships. "At that time I believed the enemy was using incendiary ammunition against us as there were several outbreaks of fire on the quarterdeck. I therefore ordered the senior gunner to fight fire with fire and load with incendiary shells from the lower deck and himself take charge of the gun that was to fire them. For some time I had hopes that they were having some effect as I observed unusually dense smoke from the *Isis*, which, however, was soon to dissipate."

Slowly but surely the British superiority began to make itself felt. "The enemy guns did not let up in their fierce attack and their fire was returned as eagerly as our waning strength permitted. In this situation, surrounded by enemy ships, we continued to defend ourselves until half past two, when all further resistance was futile. All our guns apart from three lay damaged and useless, most of the ship's side was holed. Almost half the men were dead or wounded and those still alive so weakened and exhausted that they could barely fight back. I could also see numerous armed boats passing between the enemy ships, which led me to fear that they would board us, which we were powerless to prevent. For these reasons I decided to abandon ship with the officers and as many of the men as we could get into the pinnace and longboat and surrender the battered hull and save as many as possible from being taken prisoner, which would be the inevitable outcome."

Risbrich was a cool-minded captain. He knew when the time had come to stop fighting. But he was also very much aware of what his duty was before he left his ship. "I left the surgeons aboard to care for the wounded as much as their limited resources could be of help. I ordered the carpenters to spike the upper deck guns facing the shore that could still be used to prevent the British from using them against us when they boarded. The starboard guns, facing the shore, on the lower deck were still resting on chocks as their carriages had not arrived when the British did. I also had thrown overboard as many filled cartridges and powder kegs as possible, rather than leave them to the enemy. When I had completed the last duty I could usefully perform I left the ship in the pinnace and Lieutenant Henne in the longboat, taking with us as many able-bodied and wounded as we could get into them. The English continued firing at the boats as we rowed ashore: when we left the ship, neither ensign nor pennant was flying as they had both been shot away and the *Wagrien* had long been fighting without either. Neither of the boats was hit, although some oars were shattered and we reached land safely."

Risbrich steered towards Quintus Battery, hauled the boats ashore and walked over to the Crown Prince, who at the time was watching the battle from Citadel Point, to present his report. The blockship had resisted the enemy for more than four and a half hours and Risbrich had saved almost half his surviving crew.

Little wonder that he was received by Crown Prince Frederik with "the most gracious welcome".

The Prøvestenen's *last shot*

Only one ship in the King's Deep line lasted longer than the *Wagrien* – the *Prøvestenen*.

Commander Lassen commanded his blockship from the upper deck, where his second, Lieutenant Commander Ravn, had charge of the guns. That duty was performed on the lower deck by Lieutenant Michael Bille.

She was given a hard time by her opponents. Fire broke out three times but each time the crew managed to get it under control and extinguish it. The ensign was twice shot away and the command pennant on the half mast once. Grapeshot fire against the un-protected upper deck had caused so much devastation among the crew by this time that Lassen ordered his men down to the lower deck to continue the fight.

Since the outbreak of the action Bille had been going from gun to gun, cheering up his men with his sword drawn until a shot ripped it out of his hand. The gun crews below were less exposed than their shipmates on the upper deck, but they were still deci-mated. Just next to where Bille was standing a shot passed through a man so that when he fell it was possible to see the deck through the hole. Bille stood paralysed at the horrific sight until one of the men grabbed him by the sleeve and pulled him gently away, saying, "It were best you did not look at that, Lieutenant."

Bille was given no reason to complain about his gun crews. "The people fought with the greatest spirit. Armed with sights, training tackle, handspikes and an experienced gun captain at every gun, I believe this crew could have achieved great things. In the early stages we suffered little damage, but in the middle of the battle it was much more serious. Breechings were shot away and we stopped the recoil with the anchor cable; the gunport halyards were parted and the ports closed; we cut them open where we could; the guns and their carriages destroyed; people decimated. Almost half the men had gone when the captain ordered the remaining men from the ravaged upper deck to be redistributed along the guns of the lower deck and we managed to keep up considerable fire. Contract Lieutenant Rosenkilde used the forrard guns well. The gun captain, layer and loader of his own and the neighbouring guns aft was Seaman Jacob Hansen. When our bows were raked he leapt forward, running the gun in and out from the port; and I believe it was he who had the honour of firing the last shot. At the midships guns Private Gorel was fighting alone, fuse in hand, wounded over one eye, aiming with the other, firing when a target presented itself; he was taking charge of four guns entirely on his own. Many pressed men, volunteers and naval conscripts (we had very few seamen) displayed great determination."

But the British superiority was too great. "Enemy shots continued to put men and guns out of action. Men were also taken from the guns to take the wounded below, put out fires on the orlop deck and throw overboard the powder from the forrard gun positions and, as time passed, the men lost their spirit and some left their posts. The two remaining guns were putting up but light fire against the four ships engaging us. No flags were seen to the north of us, nor, I believe, any gunfire, and the boats from our faithful neighbour, the *Wagrien*, were heading for shore. It seemed unjustified to allow more bloodshed. The captain ordered us to cease firing."

By now it was 1500. On the lower gundecks the survivors were beginning to collapse from exhaustion after levering the mighty 36-pounders around for more than four and a half hours. Only very few of the gun captains had ensured their guns were elevated properly and, from his observations through the gunports, Bille's impression was that too many shots were being aimed too high. And he could hardly avoid noticing that "some of the men who had fought well and hard by this time were keeping over to the starboard side", and that more and more were taking the opportunity when a man was taken below to sneak along with him.

Together with Lassen, Bille went up top to the devastated upper deck, where they could see that they would either have to abandon the *Prøvestenen* or be taken prisoner. A British brig and two armed boats were heading for the ship and the men simply did not have enough strength left to repel boarders. Lassen and Ravn therefore took to the boats with as many of their men as they could cram aboard and rowed for the shore, sent on their way by shots from the brig.

Michael Bille, who was slightly wounded, elected to remain on board. "I thought it only fitting to get ashore as many as possible but also that an officer remained to comfort the wounded as their hopes faded. I still held out hope that boats from the shore would come and pick them up. We were still fighting fires on the orlop deck and the carpenters were attempting to cut holes in the ship's side when the enemy gunfire stopped and boats escorted by a brig approached. I shouted for men to come up with grenades. Nobody answered. There were no boats on their way from shore. The people had lost all hope and almost none had the spirit to continue the pointless action. The officers approached with respect and promised we would be treated fairly, with no looting, and that I would be allowed to care for the wounded."

The last shot fired from the King's Deep line was fired by the Norwegian seaman Jacob Hansen from Tønsberg aboard the *Prøvestenen*. Shortly afterwards, the British, too, held their fire. The thick blanket of smoke slowly began to lift and drift northwards and the roar and thunder of the guns gave way to an eerie, almost unreal, silence.

Together with the last men of the *Prøvestenen*, Bille was rowed across the King's Deep to the *Russell*. He had been in battle from 1030 to 1515. Sitting in the British boat, he could see over his shoulder the Danish defence vessels, crushed, battered and silent, – not a flag to be seen flying from any of them.

In front of him were the Royal Navy ships-of-the-line, with masts and rigging showing the scars of battle but otherwise unharmed.

What he could not see from the boat, however, were two pinnaces making their way from the shore across the Refshale Shoal to Nelson's ship.

From the bows they were flying a white flag. On board were Crown Prince Frederik's aide and Lord Nelson's emissary.

Chapter 10

THE BATTLE OF COPENHAGEN – ACT III

NELSON'S EMISSARY

When Nelson went aboard Parker's flagship on 1 April he had been bursting with optimism. It would be a short scrap, and he would win.

Parker's Division had weighed at 1000 on 2 April, at the same time that Nelson's forces began to enter the King's Deep. With the *Defence*, *Ramillies* and *Veteran* in the van, Parker's Division began its long slog against wind and tide to the south, towards Trekroner Fort and the Danish northern flank. It was less than 6 miles to the King's Deep and the visibility was good. With the wind blowing the smoke away from the British ships, Parker had a clear view of the battle and could communicate with the other ships unhindered.

What he observed from his flagship as the morning wore on did not please him. He could see that the *Agamemnon* had stayed in the Hollander Deep and was taking no part in the battle. At 1130 the *London*'s signals officer reported that the *Bellona* and *Russell* had gone aground and had hoisted emergency signals. And by 1300 Parker could see no sign that the Danish vessels were being overwhelmed and taken.

In the light of this, he considered it most prudent to stop the action. At 1315, after almost three hours of fighting, signal No 39 was hoisted aboard the *London*. It was concise and impossible to misunderstand – "Discontinue the action." It was a general signal, that is to every commanding officer, not just Nelson. Attention was drawn to it with shots from the flagship.

Parker's signal is one of the most hotly debated in the history of naval warfare. Nelson neglected to mention it in his report and Parker did not speak of it. But it was sent, and it was received and understood by the ships in Nelson's Division. Parker never disclosed his reasons for ordering the action to be stopped. The theory that an agreement was reached in advance for Nelson to decide for himself whether to obey or ignore the signal has no foundation in source material and is contradicted by events.

The responsibility lay with Parker alone for ensuring that the fleet could sail onwards to the Baltic against Russia and Sweden. As Commander-in-Chief, it was his responsibility that there were ships, completely seaworthy and battleworthy ships, for the later operations against the League of Armed Neutrality. But since the fleet sailed from Yarmouth he had displayed astonishing doubt and uncertainty when it came to making decisions and taking risks. When he sent Signal No 39, he did not have, and could not have had, the data to evaluate whether the order made sense from a military point of view, nor whether it could even be followed. Had it been explicitly obeyed, it would have meant almost certain disaster for the British ships in the King's Deep.

When the signal was received Nelson was walking the *Elephant*'s quarterdeck with Colonel Stewart. The signals lieutenant reported receipt of the signal, but Nelson gave no response. When the lieutenant asked whether he should repeat it, Nelson just told him to acknowledge it. With that done, Nelson asked if his own signal - "Engage the enemy more closely" – were still flying. When he was reassured it was, he said, "Mind you keep it so".

When he was excited, Nelson had the habit of moving the stump of his right arm that was left after the amputation four years before. Now, swinging it agitatedly, he turned to Stewart and said, "Do you know what's showing on board the Commander-in-Chief? No 39!" When Stewart asked what it meant, Nelson answered, "Why, to leave off the action. Leave off action," he repeated and added with a shrug of his shoulders, "Now damn me if I do!" Turning to Captain Foley, he said, "You know, Foley, I have only one eye and I have a right to be blind sometimes." Putting his telescope to his blind eye, he exclaimed, "I really do not see the signal."

Behind the joking, which Nelson loved and for which he was loved in return, he was deadly serious. He decided, off the cuff, to ignore the orders of his superior officer and continue the battle. By leaving his own signal flying, he also showed his intentions to his own commanding officers. This was blatant insubordination that could lead to a court martial and the severest penalty the Articles of War could mete out – death. But Nelson knew what he was doing. Shortly afterwards, he explained his reasoning to Stewart: "Will Stewart, these fellows hold us a better Jug than I expected. However, we are keeping up a noble fire, and I'll be answerable that we shall bale them out in four if we cannot do it in three hours. At least I'll give it them till they are sick of it."

At that time Nelson could see for himself that the Danish defence line was almost beaten and, unlike Parker, he had full confidence in his commanding officers. He knew them and he knew they knew him and understood what made him tick. Only in the very north, therefore, was Parker's signal obeyed. Captain Riou ordered his frigates to cut their cables and pull out of the action, with the remorseful words, "What will Nelson think of us?" But in the King's Deep the British commanding officers followed Rear Admiral Graves' actions. When he was told of Parker's signal, he asked whether Nelson was repeating it. On being told that this was not the case, he just said, "Then we have nothing to do with it."

From the *Elephant* it was plain to see that some of the ships in the division first, hesitantly, repeated Parker's signal, only to haul it down when they saw Nelson was taking no notice of the Commander-in-Chief's orders.

To weigh and get under way in such disarray in the uncharted waters at the time would have been to invite disaster. What saved the British ships was the fact that their captains knew Nelson and his intentions intimately and trusted his judgement more than their Commander-in-Chief's.

Nelson's letter

Having bluntly refused to follow Parker's orders to break off the action, only shortly afterwards Nelson himself took an extraordinary initiative to the same end. He wrote a letter.

At 1345 he left the quarterdeck for the upper gundeck and walked out onto the *Elephant*'s stern gallery. Using the rudder casing to rest on, he wrote a letter with a conciliatory salutation – "To the Brothers of Englishmen the Danes." Standing beside him, the *Elephant*'s writer, Thomas Wallis, made a copy of the letter.

"Lord Nelson has directions to spare Denmark when no longer resisting but if the firing is continued on the part of Denmark Lord

Nelson will be obliged to set on fire all the floating batteries he has taken, without having the power of saving the Brave Danes who have defended them."

When he had finished the letter, he folded it and put it in an envelope on which he wrote, "To the Danish Government." Wallis made to seal it with a wafer but Nelson would have none of it. He wanted it sealed properly with wax. A man was therefore sent below to hunt out the wax and seal. He never returned; a cannon ball took off his head. Nelson sent another man in his stead. A wafer, still damp would indicate that the letter was sent in haste. A wax seal would reveal nothing.

Shortly before 1400 the letter was finally sealed. A boat was waiting on the starboard side and a few minutes later Captain Thesiger left the ship to deliver Nelson's letter.

It was very short and not very clear. What exactly did Nelson mean by the expression, "all the floating batteries he has taken" when, at that time, he had not taken a single Danish vessel? Was he expressing his intentions? And what did he mean when he wrote that he would "set on fire" the floating batteries and their men? Would he set them on fire after taking them, or would he fire on them with incendiary shells? Or would he send a fireship among them?

This was an extraordinary lack of clarity from a man renowned for expressing himself precisely and succinctly. Was he not thinking clearly when he wrote the letter or was he just being devious?

Nelson's motive

All these questions have been the object of speculation and debate since he sent that now famous letter. Nelson himself claimed that he had but a single motive – 'humanity'. He said that on 2 April and he kept on saying it. He was still saying it the day he died.

From the Danish point of view, however, the letter has always been interpreted as a *ruse de guerre*. His cynical threat did, after all, get him out of a very sticky military situation. The same interpretation was given by many among the Baltic Fleet, not by Nelson's enemies alone but also by many of his friends.

But Nelson was never in doubt: his motive was humanity. When Commander Lindholm went aboard the *Elephant* that afternoon to hear a fuller explanation of Nelson's motives, he was given the same answer – 'humanity'. After his audience with Crown Prince Frederik at Amalienborg Palace on 3 April Nelson made much of the Prince's gratitude for displaying such great 'humanity' during the battle. And when he wrote to Lady Hamilton on 9 April it was this royal gratitude for his 'humanity' that had saved Copenhagen from bombardment he wrote most about: "Nelson is a warrior, but will not be a butcher." He was indignant when he later read in Commodore Fischer's official battle report of doubts of his motives in sending an emissary ashore. He could not and would not, he claimed, fire on an opponent who could no longer defend himself. "When they became my prisoners, I became their protector. Humanity alone could have been my object."

In a letter to the British Prime Minister he justified his indignation at the accusation of adopting a *ruse de guerre*. When he sent his emissary, victory was already his. Continued action against the Danish vessels would have meant needless massacre. His only motive was one "which I trust in God I shall retain to the last moment, *humanity*." It was a virtue he did indeed defend until his dying day. On the morning of 21 October 1805, with HMS *Victory* in the van of the British fleet, when he took on the combined fleets of France and Spain at Trafalgar, Nelson wrote an entry in his diary: "and may humanity after Victory be the predominant feature in the British Fleet".

The situation in the King's Deep

The question is – had Nelson achieved victory when he sent his letter ashore? The answer lies partly in the analysis of the military situation in the King's Deep at 1400.

An hour earlier, the middle sector of the Danish line had fallen. The *Dannebrog* and *Hajen* were still firing, it is true, but only sporadically. At 1400 the remaining vessels were so damaged that half of them struck their colours within half an hour and the others managed to keep firing a gun or two for only another half hour. This was clear to those aboard the *Elephant* and to the professional observers ashore. At 1345 Vice Admiral Cronstedt wrote to the King of Sweden that the southern sector of the Danish line, from the *Prøvestenen* to the *Søhesten*, was demolished and that it was doubtful whether the northern sector could hold out much longer.

If victory is understood to mean the opponent was defeated, then Nelson had his victory when he sent his letter. But his objective was not to destroy the King's Deep line but to take out the ships in it, so that his bomb vessels could take up a safe position. However, until the Deep was completely cleared of all Danish vessels, he had not completed the task he had undertaken, and not won the victory

195

he had promised Parker. And when the letter went ashore he did not have anything like that control of the King's Deep. Far from it. He could see that the British boats sent to claim the Danish vessels as prizes were being fired upon, even though their colours had gone. That is what made Nelson lose his patience. As he saw it, he had two choices: either he could send a message ashore to put an end to this irregular fashion of conducting warfare or he would have to send his fireships against the Danish vessels.

But he had not reached his goal and Trekroner was still intact.

Humanity or ruse de guerre*?*

The real question is whether Nelson himself was so confident that he had achieved victory. His officers were not so certain, either about victory or Nelson's motive for sending an emissary ashore.

The man closest to Nelson when he made his decision was Colonel William Stewart. His evaluation was that, although Danish resistance had been overcome, Nelson's position was still tenuous. The shore batteries prevented him from seizing the out-fought Danish vessels and Trekroner Fort prevented him from weighing and sailing out of the King's Deep. This was the situation that prompted Nelson "to push his advantages no further". And that, he explained, is why he sent his letter; a letter Stewart believed "for style, ingenuity and presence of mind is unparalleled". In Stewart's opinion, sending the emissary was "a masterpiece of policy".

Such was the interpretation of a knowledgeable and sympathetic supporter, and he was not alone in his view. A staunch admirer of Nelson, Captain Fremantle, was also aboard the *Elephant* at 1400. He understood from Nelson that he was concerned about his damaged ships and how he was going to get them out of the Deep – and that was the reason for sending the emissary. In his opinion, the ceasefire was just as much to Nelson's advantage as it was to the Danes'. As far as the victory of 2 April is concerned, Fremantle wrote, "every merit is due to Lord Nelson for his policy as well as bravery on this occasion".

Nelson's greatest admirer in the Fleet heard him discussing the battle that evening, and there can be no doubt that when Captain Thomas Hardy of the *St. George* wrote to his brother-in-law in a letter three days later what he stated was indeed Nelson's own version of things: "His Lordship finding his little squadron very hard pressed by the Batteries after the ships had struck, the wind not sufficient to take off his Prizes and crippled ships, he very

196

deliberately sent a flag of truce on shore to say that his orders were *not* to *destroy* the City of Copenhagen, therefore to save more effusion of blood he would grant them a *truce* and land their wounded as soon as possible."

Hardy was full of admiration for Nelson's attack on the King's Deep line, which he described as "the most daring attack that has been attempted this war (the Nile not excepted)". But the loyal Hardy added, "The more I see of His Lordship the more I admire his great character, for, I think on this occasion, his Political management *was, if possible*, greater than his Bravery."

The doubt enveloping Nelson's motive for sending an emissary ashore during the battle was no short-lived affair. In 1809, eight years after he had stood by Nelson's side on the *Elephant*'s quarterdeck, and four years after Nelson died on board the *Victory* at Trafalgar, William Stewart wrote an account of the Battle of Copenhagen for the first official Nelson biography. He made a courageous attempt to get to the bottom of things. He was lenient and understanding, and he expressed himself with the delicacy of a diplomat of the old school. But despite his deep loyalty to Nelson and his memory, he had to admit that, at the time, Nelson had been highly conscious of the exposed position the *Ganges*, *Monarch* and *Defiance* were in, that he had abandoned any ideas of storming Trekroner Fort and that what he most desired was to get his ships out of the King's Deep while the wind was still favourable.

Stewart weighed his words with extreme care. But his conclusion was *not* that Nelson's motive was humanity. It was that "it was by no means improbable that Lord Nelson's observing eye pointed out to him the expediency of a prudent conduct."

If a person's motives for action are the articulate manifestation of what is uppermost in his mind, then Nelson's motive was undoubtedly humanity; he really believed what he said. But if later analysis of these motives shows a possible conflict of interest, then doubt can arise. Statements made by Stewart, Graves, Foley and Hardy indicate that all Nelson's professional instincts told him to put an end to the battle and get his ships out of the King's Deep while the going was good. This is the most probable explanation for his famous letter being such an enigmatic combination of humanity and cynical threat. Weighing these two alternative conclusions against each other, and deciding which should be given the benefit of that doubt, will continue to present a fascinating, albeit hopeless, task for the historian.

The Capitulation

The emissary's barge left the *Elephant* at 1400 with a white flag of truce flying in the bows. Six men pulled on the oars, with a quartermaster at the helm. In the sternsheets sat one of the Baltic Fleet's volunteer officers, the multi-lingual Captain Frederick Thesiger, with Nelson's letter addressed "To the Danish Government".

Nelson had wanted the letter delivered as a matter of urgency, without it appearing so. The fastest route to Copenhagen was also the most dangerous: up the channel between the fighting ships, where the water was whipped into foam by cannon balls, and then across the Refshale Shoal, where the shots from the shore batteries were flying thick and fast. Not surprisingly, therefore, Thesiger opted for a route that was longer but safer. He headed north up the Deep, in the lee of the *Elephant, Ganges, Monarch* and *Defiance*; safely out of the Deep, he steered in a cautious arc north about Trekroner Fort and down the Kronløbet Channel. It was a long, hard pull. Before the barge lay herself alongside the blockship *Elefanten* it was 1430.

It was therefore the decision of the guardship's commanding officer, Commander von Thun, as to what the final route of the barge would be, and ever since 2 April he has had to take his share of the blame that Nelson's ruse worked, because he did not refer Nelson to Commodore Fischer but directly to the Crown Prince. Neither then nor afterwards did von Thun receive any reprimand for his actions. Like all the other commanding officers, he was decorated with the campaign medal after the battle and his subsequent career took its normal course. Von Thun simply sent Nelson's emissary to the addressee on the envelope. He also allowed one of his officers to go aboard the barge and steer them safely down the Kronløbet Channel to Citadel Point and the Crown Prince.

Apart from functioning as the country's regent, Crown Prince Frederik was also supreme Commander-in-Chief of the Copenhagen defences. He had followed the entire battle at close quarters, first from Quintus Battery, where the British bombs began to fall in the middle of the day. As the battle moved north, he and his entourage moved to Sixtus Battery, where Lieutenant Commander Schrødersee had reacted to the Crown Prince's appeal for volunteers and taken command of the force sent out to assist the *Indfødsretten*. And when Parker's ships had closed on Trekroner

Fort and the blockships in the Kronløbet Channel, the Crown Prince moved camp once more to the Customs Quay and thence to Citadel Point, from where he had a clear view of the King's Deep and the waters north of the Fort.

The jetty at Citadel Point was therefore the destination Contract Lieutenant Lundbye had given to the British quartermaster. The men at the oars had a hard pull against wind and tide and it was 1500 before Thesiger handed Nelson's letter to a Danish officer, who immediately took it to the Crown Prince.

The Crown Prince's decision

What the Crown Prince could see at that time was far from comforting. The defence line was no longer firing and not one vessel was flying her colours.

The *Indfødsretten* had just struck and the *Dannebrog* was on fire. The last occasional shots were still coming from the south, with the *Wagrien*, *Prøvestenen* and *Rendsborg* still in their death throes. But it was plain to see that they had not long left. None of Nelson's ships, though, appeared to have suffered much. From the north, Parker's eight ships-of-the-line were approaching, with the first three already firing at the *Elefanten* and *Hjælperen*. Trekroner Fort was unscathed and still firing. But what was the value of that with the rest of the defences beaten into submission? The Crown Prince knew that the unfinished Fort was indefensible. Not long before, Commodore Fischer's aide had come ashore to report that he would defend the Fort to the last man but that it would be incapable of resisting an all-out attack.

This was the military situation when the Crown Prince received the emissary's letter, broke the seal and read, or was given a translation of, Nelson's message. The King's Deep line that had been there when Nelson wrote his letter was there no longer. His threat of burning the Danish vessels and their crews was no longer the deterrent it might have been, so it was neither Nelson's ruse nor the Crown Prince's kind heart that made him act as he did. Prince Frederik had the necessary military insight, he had the necessary information, and the decision he reached was objective and realistic. The fight was over, and it was lost. Further resistance from the Fort and the Kronløbet Channel squadron would not only be pointless, it would be politically unwise, because Nelson's letter hinted at negotiation. The battle was lost in military terms but perhaps not in diplomatic terms. If the Crown Prince were to avert the bombardment of his capital that the King's Deep line had failed to prevent, it would have to be done through talking. He therefore accepted Nelson's demands without reservation. He ordered a ceasefire and sent Lindholm out to the British ship to delve a little deeper into Nelson's motives for sending the letter.

The white flag

Shortly after 1500 Lindholm stepped into the British barge, which immediately shoved off and rowed the short distance to the frigate *Iris,* the most southerly of Steen Bille's ships in the Kronløbet Channel. Here he ordered the commanding officer, Commander Wessel Brown, to "send an officer to Trekroner Fort with orders from His Royal Highness the Crown Prince to cease fire forthwith". He also requisitioned a boat to take him out to Nelson.

At about 1530 an officer from the *Iris* landed at the Fort with the Crown Prince's orders to Olfert Fischer. He in turn repeated the orders to the *Elefanten* and *Mars*. The last Danish guns fell silent.

Lindholm boarded the *Iris*'s boat, also flying a flag of truce from the bows. The two boats set off across the Refshale Shoal for the *Elephant,* where Lindholm was ushered post-haste into Nelson's presence. Almost at the moment Lindholm reported that the Crown Prince had ordered a ceasefire a white flag was hoisted to the *Elephant*'s maintop, a signal for the British ships to cease hostilities.

The greatest victory

Lindholm thus achieved the first of his objectives, to bring an end to the fighting. The second was political. The Crown Prince had found Nelson's letter just as unclear as later historians – "it was coined in vague terms" – for which reason he instructed Lindholm, who spoke fluent English, to "hear his intentions and enquire of his reasons for sending the emissary". As soon as Lindholm presented that question, Nelson began talking politics. Lindholm requested an answer in writing and Nelson wrote his second letter of 2 April:

"Lord Nelson's object in sending on Shore a flag of truce is humanity, therefore consents that hostilities shall cease, till Lord Nelson can take his prisoners out of the Prizes, and he consents to Land all the Wounded Danes and to Burn or remove his prizes, Lord Nelson with Humble Duty to His Royal Highness begs leave to say that he will ever esteem it the Greatest Victory he ever gained if this flag of Truce may be the happy forerunner of a lasting and happy union between My Most Gracious Sovereign and His Majesty the King of Denmark."

At the same time as specifying his conditions for a ceasefire, Nelson repeated his personal appeal for negotiation. For any further political discussion, he referred Lindholm to his superior, Sir Hyde Parker.

With that answer, Lindholm returned to the shore. The Crown Prince instructed him to sail out to Parker with the Danish opening gambit in the political game that had now commenced: Denmark was willing to agree to an armistice and enter political negotiations.

Just before 1900 Lindholm went aboard the *London* and made the opening move. Parker responded by repeating the demand Britain had made before the outbreak of war: Denmark was to leave the League of Armed Neutrality and enter an alliance with Britain. Those were his terms for accepting an armistice.

The first two pieces on the board had been moved. As the Crown Prince's confidant, Lindholm was well aware of Denmark's political dilemma. He therefore offered his personal assessment to Parker that, if Denmark accepted the British demand, it would have to contend with much more dangerous enemies – the Russians, Prussians, Swedes and the French. This was a signal that Parker's terms were unacceptable. With mutual assurances of friendship and peace, the two naval officers bade each other farewell, with a promise that Lindholm would return the next morning with his government's answer.

Out of the Deep

Thus far, the ceasefire was assured until the morning of 3 April and both sides very much needed it.

Whilst Nelson waited impatiently for the Danish answer, he discussed the situation with Captains Foley and Fremantle and Rear Admiral Graves, whom he had hailed to come aboard the *Elephant*. It was as plain as a pikestaff that the Fort was still intact and towards the end of the battle they had been able to see the reinforcements being taken out to the Fort. Foley and Fremantle, therefore, argued against an attack on the Fort and advised Nelson to get his ships out of the King's Deep whilst the wind was favourable. And Nelson agreed.

So he had already decided what he would do if the Danish answer was positive. When it came, he did two things immediately: not only did he order a white flag of truce to be hoisted, he sent the general signal for all ships, with the exception of the *Ardent*, which was told to stay where she was close to the grounded *Bellona* and *Russell*, to weigh anchor and leave the King's Deep.

The eight ships-of-the-line cut their cables and springs at once and, under all the sail that was still useable, they sailed, with the current under their keels, to the safety of the Copenhagen Roads, where Parker's ships had anchored three miles north-east of Trekroner Fort. Their departure fully vindicated the concerns Nelson and his commanding officers had and their desire to exploit the ceasefire to get out of their tricky situation.

Four of the line of battleships, the *Edgar, Polyphemus, Glatton* and *Isis*, managed to leave the Deep with no problems. The *Isis* was badly damaged but her crew was in good spirits. As she passed the *Elephant* they gave Nelson a resounding huzza. The ships anchored with Parker's Division and, with assistance from the ships that had not been in action, the crews set to work repairing the battle damage to the hulls and rigging.

The other four ships-of-the-line did not have such an easy time of getting out of the King's Deep. The *Monarch* had taken the greatest losses on either side, and when the battle came to an end Midshipman Millard could see how much punishment she had taken.

Graves had signalled the *Monarch* to cut and sail. Her signal halyards were shot away and Millard had to climb the mizzen shrouds and wave the ensign as acknowledgement of the signal. "Our decks were choked with disabled guns; near half our complement were either killed or wounded; and there was not fore and aft one single brace or bowline that was not shot away; so that the sails could not possibly be directed one way or the other but hung on the caps as when we first anchored." The *Monarch* was not capable of manoeuvring and when her cable was cut she began drifting slowly to the north, only to run aground after a short time. And aground she stayed, within range of the Fort's guns. In her wake followed the *Ganges*, rigging in shreds and sails in tatters and very difficult to steer. With a splintering crash, she collided with the *Monarch*, the rigging of the two ships becoming entangled. She too touched the shoal but there was so much way on her that she kept on going, dragging the *Monarch* with her off the shoal. Once the *Ganges* had let go her other anchor, the crews managed to sort out the mess aloft, cutting the rigging to allow the two ships to escape each others clutches. Nelson had been so quick off the mark in ordering his ships to cut and sail, and the *Monarch* and *Ganges* so speedy in responding, that they were off Trekroner Fort and aground before the Crown Prince's order to cease fire had reached Olfert Fischer. So the guns at the Fort were still blazing away at the *Monarch* – before they suddenly stopped. Fremantle breathed a sigh of relief; if the firing had continued, both ships would have been lost.

The *Monarch* and *Ganges* were afloat again, more drifting than sailing out to the Copenhagen Roads, but the *Elephant* and *Defiance* were not so fortunate. They too ran aground at the northern entrance of the King's Deep Channel, still within range of the guns at the Fort.

No one aboard either of the British flagships was in any doubt that the two vessels were saved from obliteration by the Crown Prince's orders. Despite all efforts, the *Elephant* was not refloated until late in the evening and the *Defiance* not until the next morning.

The last ship to fall foul of the Middle Ground Shoal on 2 April was the frigate *Desirée*. When Nelson had sent the ceasefire signal Captain Inman left his position in the shallow waters south of the *Prøvestenen* and made for the shoal to render assistance to the *Bellona* and *Russell*. Whilst attempting to haul them off the shoal, she went aground herself and she was to be the last to get off. The *Bellona* and *Russell* floated off in the morning of 3 April and made north, out of the King's Deep. Not until that evening, however, had the hapless *Desirée* lightened ship enough for the crew to pull the frigate off the shoal.

But the battle in the King's Deep had ended on the afternoon of 2 April. Aboard the *Elephant*, Nelson watched his ships' efforts to get out of the waters that had caused him so many problems and disappointments. The reaction to so many days and nights of stress and strain were beginning to set in and the fate of the *Dannebrog* had affected him deeply, as it had Colonel Stewart. It was a physically and mentally exhausted admiral who left the *Elephant* that afternoon to be rowed across to the *St. George*. Nelson's last words when he left Foley and his crew were typical of the man – and the situation: "Well! I have fought contrary to orders, and I shall perhaps be hanged: never mind, let them".

WINNERS AND LOSERS

The rumble of the last cannon had faded. The battle was over, but not the war. The Copenhagen Roads were a hive of activity. Frantic efforts were being made to get the grounded ships afloat and repair the damage to the hulls, masts and rigging. Ships from both divisions were busy taking possession of the Danish prizes and transporting the crews across to British ships. Later in the afternoon Danish boats, too, appeared on the scene. In accordance with the terms of the ceasefire, they picked up their wounded and landed them at the Customs Quay from whence some were taken to hospital and others just went home.

On board the British ships, the shock wave of relief that always arose after a battle was spreading; men were beginning to realise they had come through it all with life and limbs intact. Nobody knew how their shipmates had fared during the battle, whether they were dead or alive. So it was a heart-wrenching event to be reunited – "as if you had not seen one another for 20 years". Aboard the *Polyphemus* they could see that the *Prøvestenen* had finally checked fire. Midshipman Alexander Nairne was sent to the lower gundeck to give orders for the blockship to be boarded and taken. This was greeted by three thunderous cheers.

The relief after the long, hard battle was also washing over the men in the *Monarch*. Young William Millard had had nothing to eat or drink since seven that morning and he was suddenly ravenously hungry and thirsty. With utter contempt for the rights of property, he broke into the gunner's locker. His harvest – a cheese, some potatoes and a sack of hardtack biscuits and, most welcome of all, a jug of cold water – was shared generously with all those in the vicinity.

British losses

Both sides had suffered dead and wounded, and damage to their ships. But the losses were different in numbers and nature. Losses in the British ships-of-the-line varied. By far the highest number of casualties were taken by the *Monarch*, with 56 dead and 164 wounded. Next on the list of death and destruction was the *Isis*, with 33 dead and 88 wounded. These high figures, however, were not due solely to Danish cannon balls; there had been several incidents of their own guns exploding. Other battleships also recorded heavy casualties: the *Edgar* 31 dead and 111 wounded; the *Ardent* 30 dead and 64 wounded; the *Defiance* 24 dead and 51 wounded. Other British ships-of-the-line had surprisingly low casualties: the *Elephant* only 10 dead and 13 wounded; the *Polyphemus* 6 dead and 25 wounded; the *Ganges* 7 dead and 5 wounded. In all, the British losses were 254 dead and 689 wounded, some of whom died of their injuries the day after the battle.

Damage to the ships was, generally speaking, limited. The British had lost not a single ship and, although several of the battleships took a beating in their masts and rigging, it was no worse that it could be repaired, and repaired quickly. This was the kind of work the officers and men were used to and their professional standards were high. When the *Ganges* left the King's Deep on the afternoon of 2 April her masts and rigging were badly damaged, but, two days later, Captain Fremantle could declare optimistically that his ship would be in just as good condition and just as seaworthy as when she had left Yarmouth.

The hulls of the British ships were almost unscathed: the Danes had fired too high. There were two exceptions to this, the *Monarch* and the *Isis*, but in both cases the hull damage was inflicted by their own guns exploding. Immediately after the battle it became clear that the damage was beyond what could be rectified in the Copenhagen Roads, allowing them to continue into the Baltic. Parker therefore ordered them home for repair in a naval dockyard.

But, at the end of the day, the Baltic Fleet could conclude that, although the Danes had put up tough resistance, their gun crews were amateurs by comparison. In less than a week the Baltic Fleet was seaworthy – and battleworthy.

Danish losses
Losses in men and wounded on the Danish side were higher.

Of the men aboard the 18 vessels in the King's Deep on 2 April 367 were killed and 635 wounded, 100 so seriously that they died in the days and weeks after the battle. While the battle was raging 171 men had been sent out to the line as reinforcement; of these 3 were killed and 30 wounded, 6 of whom also died later. 1,779 men, a third of the entire Danish contingent, were taken prisoner. The Admiralty had to give up on discovering the fate of 205 men; some were undoubtedly killed in action and unceremoniously dumped over the side. They did, however, know what happened to 66 of them: they were soldiers from the various regiments, probably German mercenaries who ended up fighting for the British after being taken as prisoners of war.

Many of those who disappeared without trace, though, were pressed men and volunteers who had gone, or run as fast as their legs could carry them, their separate ways as soon as their feet touched dry land.

One of them was Ole Hansen. He was a 34-year-old farm labourer who had been unable to find work near his home village of Ferslev, some 30 miles from the capital. So he had gone to Copenhagen and found a job with aquavit distiller Anders Rossing in Store Brøndstræde. During the night of 25 March he, like so many others, was taken by the press gangs and sent to the *Indfødsretten*. He had stood on board and heard the captain read the loyal oath, heard the words ringing through his head that he was to show "loyalty and fidelity to the King and his rightful successors" and that he, "as a brave and valiant Danish seaman and warrior", should risk "fortune, life and blood". Together with those around him, he had obediently promised that this he would, "in God's holy name".

On 2 April Ole Hansen had lived through the most terrible three hours of his life aboard the *Indfødsretten*. At the very last moment he managed to get aboard a boat just as the British boarded the ship. When he reached shore he had no food and only the clothes he stood up in. So he made his way in a daze to his employer, but Rossing refused to offer any help. He then walked the 30 miles back to his home and parents, only to be arrested by the local recruiting officer, even though he swore he intended to return to the King's service.

The punishment for what Ole Hansen and so many other stunned and shell-shocked men did after the battle was draconian. Ratings who deserted were to be hanged from the yardarm. But the cold, objective words of the Articles of War were one thing and flesh and blood another. The Admiralty dismissed the case with the statement: "By the gracious leniency of His Royal Highness, all charges in this case are dropped". Ole Hansen and the other volunteers and pressed men had no intention of deserting. But food and clothing, and a short break to gather their wits and get over the shock, were basic human rights.

The vanquished wrecks
Material losses and damage on the Danish side were also considerable. The Danish line had been made up of different types of vessel: custom-built defence vessels, converted barges, vessels from the breaker's yard and warships that still had a little life left in them.

On the morning of 2 April there had been 18 such vessels in the

King's Deep; 12 had surrendered and were taken as prizes in the positions where they had moored and fought: the ship-of-the-line *Holsten*, the blockships *Indfødsretten*, *Charlotte Amalie*, *Kronborg*, *Jylland*, *Wagrien* and *Prøvestenen*, the artillery barges *Søhesten*, *Svœrdfisken* and *Hajen*, and the converted cavalry barge *Rendsborg*. Also in this group was the *Dannebrog*, who struck her colours whilst still in position and only drifted northwards after the fire had parted her anchor cables.

The other six had all cut their cables and pulled out of the action. During the retreat the artillery barges *Aggershus* and *Nyborg* had sunk. They were later salvaged and the *Aggershus* remained on the Navy List, whilst the *Nyborg* was so badly damaged that she was broken up. The frigate *Hjœlperen*, signals frigate *Elven* and Fleet Battery No 1 managed to reach the shore and with such limited damage that they could remain in active service. In fact the *Hjœlperen* was warped out again to take up a new position at the entrance to the Kronløbet Channel, between the *Elefanten* and Trekroner Fort. The signals frigate, which was no longer needed, warped right in and passed through the boom. The Fleet Battery had drifted into the bay just south of the fishing hamlet Skovshoved, where she spent the night under the protection of the gunboat *Nakskov*. On 3 April she helped warp the artillery raft into the Kronløbet Channel.

The last of the vessels to cut and withdraw was the ship-of-the-line *Sjœlland*. Commander Harboe had anchored east of Trekroner Fort in a position where she did not interfere with the Fort's barrage of the *Defiance* and *Monarch*. He ordered the ensign to be hauled down and put his crew to discharging powder and shot. When hostilities ceased, his command pennant was still flying from the mainmast.

Commodore Olfert Fischer had watched the *Sjœlland*'s manoeuvres. He had considered having her towed north about the Refshale Shoal and into the Kronløbet Channel but had not had the boats necessary to do it. At 1800 Steen Bille had sent men from the *Danmark* to spike the *Sjœlland*'s guns. It was at this time that Harboe proposed that his ship be set on fire, a suggestion Bille rejected as she was too close to the Fort. Instead, he left orders that, if the British attempted to board, Harboe was to get his men into the boats.

And that very evening boats from the *Defence* did indeed try to board the *Sjœlland*, but they promptly withdrew when Harboe denied that he had struck his colours, pointing to his command pennant. The next morning Nelson was furious at what he regarded as a pathetic attempt by the Danes to escape being taken as a prize; the *Sjælland had* struck her colours and therefore, by definition, surrendered. He urged Parker to claim her and at 0900 on 3 April armed boats lay off the *Sjælland*'s starboard side. Harboe and his men, as ordered, then took to the boats on the port side, taking with them their signals book and the Articles of War. Shortly afterwards the Union Flag was flying from the *Sjælland*. Some hours later the gun brig *Harpy* towed her out to the other prizes in the Copenhagen Roads.

On the evening of 2 April the British had burned the *Rendsborg* where she lay on the Refshale Shoal. The other prizes were towed out to the Roads. Efforts to keep the *Indfødsretten* afloat were abandoned and on the morning of 4 April the British let her sink.

The prizes were too badly damaged to be of any use and what they had on board was of negligible value. So the British took what they needed in the way of rope, cordage and firewood, a few valuable bronze cannons, and set fire to the wrecks. This was normally done at night. From Copenhagen the people could see the flames licking at the night sky and hear the dull thuds of guns going off as the fire reached them

It is highly probable that the timing was a deliberate effort to exert some form of psychological pressure on the recalcitrant Danish negotiators. The last to go up in flames was the *Sjælland*, on the morning of 10 April and after the armistice was signed. The only prize the British kept was the ship-of-the-line *Holsten*. After inspection it was determined that she could be made seaworthy and Parker gave orders for her to be fitted out as a hospital ship. Together with the two badly mauled ships-of-the-line *Monarch* and *Isis*, she sailed for England and entered the Royal Navy as HMS *Nassau*.

Because of her shallow draft, she was used in the war against Denmark from 1807–14. By a strange twist of fate, she was one of the three British ships-of-the-line to take part in the Battle of Sjællands Odde on 22 March 1808, where Denmark lost her last battleship, the *Prins Christian Frederik*, and Peter Willemoes fell.

The Danish defeat

The battle of 2 April had a winner and a loser. Before it started, both sides had a clear and well-defined military objective. As Commander-in-Chief of the Defence Line, Commodore Olfert

208

Fischer's objective was to retain Danish control of the King's Deep in order to prevent bombardment of the fleet, the dockyard and the capital. Parker's and Nelson's objective was to gain control of the same water to do just that, or threaten to do it, so as to force Denmark to leave the League of Armed Neutrality and enter an alliance with Britain.

The battle was long and bloody, but from a military standpoint that was unimportant. According to these objectives, the result was clear: before the battle the King's Deep was under Danish control, after it under British control. The Battle of Copenhagen ended with a victory to the British and defeat to the Danes, just as Olfert Fischer had said it would and just as the Danish government had known it would.

From the shore that afternoon people could see the enemy bomb vessels taking up their positions in the King's Deep, out of range of the shore batteries and Trekroner Fort. With their massive 13-inch mortars they could hurl bombs and incendiary shells against the Naval Dockyard, Nyholm slips, the Citadel and most of Copenhagen.

The Crown Prince and his government knew they had lost and that they were powerless to prevent a bombardment, and so did Parker. That is why he was so uncompromising in maintaining his government's demand for Denmark to pull out of the League and change sides. Denmark was still in the vice-like grip of major politics. As Lindholm had intimated to Parker, Denmark's dilemma was that, although her military situation had changed drastically on 2 April, her political position remained the same; she was still bound as a member of the League and still obliged to show political loyalty to the Tsar and Bonaparte. Otherwise Sweden, with Russian help, would take Norway, and Russia and France would coerce Prussia to take Holstein, Slesvig and Jutland.

This, then, was the Gordian knot that Crown Prince Frederik and his advisers would have to unravel when they met on the evening of 2 April at the Commandant's residence in the Citadel to draw up a reply to Parker's demands.

Chapter 11

THE BATTLE OF COPENHAGEN – EPILOGUE

THE THREAT OF BOMBARDMENT

On the evening of 2 April the Crown Prince and his advisers were faced with a simple choice: either they could reject Parker's demands, thus invoking bombardment of the fleet and city; or they could concede to them and jeopardize the very existence of Denmark as a sovereign state. It was a desperate situation. In the week that followed, with the ceasefire being extended time after time at the last minute before the British carried out their threat, the desperate situation spawned desperate thoughts. The Crown Prince and Duke Frederik Christian, his brother-in-law, seriously considered sacrificing Trekroner Fort, the blockships and Steen Bille's squadron in a final hopeless battle. Their thinking was that the ships might just as well be put into action as be set on fire where they lay. They were still capable of inflicting damage on the British ships before they sailed on into the Baltic and that would be yet another demonstration of Denmark's unconditional loyalty to its allies in the League of Armed Neutrality. Christian Ditlev Reventlow, the most prominent member of the Privy Council, declared that the political situation could justify such a suicidal mission, but rejected it on humanitarian grounds. The thought remained but a thought, but it did reflect just how desperate the Crown Prince and his Privy Council were after the defeat and their full realization that the British could carry out a bombardment without the Danes being able to do anything to prevent it.

Even while the battle was being waged, five of the bomb vessels had reached their position in the King's Deep. The *Hecla* arrived half an hour after hostilities ceased and on the morning of 3 April, when the *Sulphur* let go her anchor, they were all in place and poised

210

for action. Together with their tenders, the seven bombs were anchored barely 2,000 metres from Nyholm slips and the dockyard. Their heaviest weapon, the 13-inch mortar, had a range of more than 4,000 metres, and they themselves were safe as houses, out of range of the shore batteries and Trekroner Fort. If the Danes took it into their heads to fight fire with fire and use mortars against them they could just up-anchor and move. They were also protected from boat attack by the frigate *Jamaica* and a few of the gun brigs that had positioned themselves between the bombs and their targets.

Steen Bille's defences

The Danish situation was hopeless. But what could be done was done.

On the evening of 2 April Commodore Olfert Fischer accepted that his injuries made it impossible for him to go on leading his forces effectively, suffering from concussion as he was. He therefore handed over command of what was left of the defences to Steen Bille, with the full approval of the Crown Prince and the Admiralty.

So it fell to Bille to try to regroup and prevent a bombardment. The Admiralty elected to take responsibility for the protection of Nyholm, Gammelholm and the fleet in the dockyard itself. The fire service was strengthened. Naval officers were seconded to assist the captains of the ships-of-the-line. And the ships' decks, to the horror of every naval officer who witnessed it, were covered in load after load of wet soil and manure.

The forces Steen Bille had taken over consisted of the Trekroner Fort, the blockships *Elefanten* and *Mars*, and "what was left of the defences of the Copenhagen Roads". Apart from a few minor vessels, 'what was left' was the frigate *Hjælperen*, already at anchor at the entrance to the Kronløbet Channel, and Fleet Battery No 1, that was once again being prepared for action.

Steen Bille was in no doubt as to how he would deploy his limited assets. He had two military objectives: to defend the Fort and to deny access to the Kronløbet Channel. The Crown Prince and the Admiralty gave their seal of approval on 4 April.

His plan called for the positioning of the *Elefanten*, *Mars* and *Hjælperen* at the entrance to the Channel, where they could fire on any British ship that tried to attack the Fort. He would also block the Channel by dumping large anchors in it. Finally, he wanted the Fleet Battery moored on the Refshale Shoal south of the Fort. As his contribution to the defence plan, the Crown Prince proposed

211

fitting the fleet's water tenders with guns and positioning them near the sunken anchors between the northern tip of the Refshale and Stubben Shoals.

The Fort was the defences' Achilles heel, as it had been before and during the battle.

Before the battle, work was being done to construct a heavy boom to block the entrance to the Fort's harbour. When it became obvious on 2 April that it would be impossible to finish this structure in time to be of any use, a thick iron chain was suspended from mole to mole. Just after the battle, orders were given to raise and strengthen the Fort's ramparts with sandbags, work which began on 4 April, along with the mounting of carronades in the battery.

The Fort had neither powder magazines nor quarters for the men and the vessel that had served as the magazine had been sunk during the battle. So a replacement was towed out. One of the most important factors was that the Fort was simply not big enough to quarter all the men necessary to repel an attack. A force of men was therefore held in reserve in the Citadel, with a flotilla of boats under the command of Lieutenant Fasting, ready to transport them from Citadel Point as soon as the signal was given from the *Danmark*, where Steen Bille was flying his pennant. And in case the Fort should fall into enemy hands, Bille ordered the boats in its harbour, apart from those that were absolutely essential, to be towed in to Nyholm.

And with this, Steen Bille had done everything he could to defend the Fort.

On the night between 5 and 6 April, barges were towed out of Nyholm with ten heavy duty anchors to block the entrance to the Channel. The blockships were at the highest state of readiness – they were cleared for action, lookouts were doubled and a guard boat patrolled throughout the night. On 5 April, Fleet Battery No 1 had been so well repaired that Sub-Lieutenant Peter Willemoes could hoist his command pennant and begin the long warp to his appointed position on the Refshale Shoal.

A hero's burial
Crown Prince Frederik was desperate to defend Copenhagen. The briefing he gave at Amalienborg Palace the morning after the battle showed just how desperate he was. He informed those gathered that he had requested negotiations: "But if the English do not accept

this offer, it is my hope that every man of honour will stand and fall at my side." He also informed that, if he should be killed, then military command would fall upon the recently appointed Governor of Copenhagen, Prince Friedrich of Württemberg. This was an appointment that had received the deepest political consideration: Prince Friedrich was Tsar Paul's brother-in-law.

Meanwhile, the capital prepared itself for bombardment. Fire watches and fire services were intensified. Those who were able evacuated themselves and their property to safety outside the city or to parts of town out of range of the British mortars. And on the morning of 7 April, when the ceasefire could be rescinded at any moment, the army's largest barracks was opened to the public.

Morale was high among most Copenhageners. They were convinced that the British had suffered great losses. The wave of patriotic fervour reached its peak on Easter morning: 5 April was the day when the dead were to be buried. With the bells of all the city's churches ringing, the burial procession moved off from the Naval Infirmary on Christianshavn at 1100. Carts bearing forty coffins were followed by a throng of people, with admirals at the fore; the procession continued through the North Gate and onwards to Holmen's Churchyard, the cemetery of the naval church. The burial was a carefully stage-managed event, with speeches and patriotic songs, with young girls dressed in white strewing flowers on the coffins and the crowds singing the most popular song of the day: "To arms, lo the enemy approacheth". But they could not avoid being reminded of the seriousness of the situation that day; from the churchyard the smoke and flames of yet another burning Danish prize ship out in the Roads were impossible to ignore.

Many took part in the ceremony. The Crown Prince, however, was not among them. He was in a meeting of the Privy Council. The previous day he had approved Steen Bille's defence plan, knowing full well that whatever defence they could cobble together was a pure facade; Copenhagen could not be defended by military means. If it was going to be done, it could only be done through politics. As the Commander-in-Chief, therefore, his rightful place was neither at Holmen's Churchyard nor at the Admiralty, it was in the Privy Council. And although Bille was making superhuman efforts with what little was available to him after the defeat, the fact is that it was not he who would be defending Copenhagen, it was Foreign Minister Christian Bernstorff.

During the evening of 2 April Crown Prince Frederik and his advisers had reached agreement on many things. They agreed that Denmark had lost the battle; they agreed that Denmark could put up no military defence against a bombardment and they agreed that Denmark was on the horns of the same political dilemma as before the battle. What they did not agree on was the policy they should now adopt. Should they bow to Parker's demands or should they reject them out of hand? Discussions went on until midnight and still they were deadlocked.

They reconvened at six the next morning to discuss further the issue of policy and the response they were to give Parker.

The Crown Prince was pale but composed when he opened the meeting with a description of how hopeless the military situation was and asked for the opinion of those present. The division was still as great as it had been the night before. The three oldest ministers were shaken by the defeat; they wanted peace at any price and begged the Crown Prince to accede to Parker's wishes. Bernstorff argued that Denmark should stick to its previous standpoint and continue to demonstrate the country's loyalty to its allies. If Denmark deviated from this policy, it would mean the loss of Norway, the Duchies and Jutland. Duke Frederik Christian backed Bernstorff.

So the deciding vote lay with Crown Prince Frederik. He made his very difficult decision at that meeting and stuck to it during the nail-biting week of negotiations that followed, despite the threat of bombardment and despite the repeated appeals from his oldest ministers to give in and save the capital and the fleet. But the Crown Prince's mind was made up: he insisted on a negotiable solution that would appease Tsar Paul and General Bonaparte.

To him it was essential that the Tsar received such reassurance at the same time as reports of the defeat. When the Russian envoy sent a courier to St. Petersburg that same day he took with him, therefore, a personal message from the Crown Prince to the Tsar: although the Crown Prince believed he had done more than enough to save Denmark's honour, he did not believe he had done enough for his allies and he would rather die under the ruins of his capital than give in to the British demands.

Big words, but very carefully considered. It would be catastrophic for Denmark if the Tsar were to begin doubting its loyalty.

And Frederik and Bernstorff knew the Tsar well enough to know the sort of language that appealed to him. As a political message, the signal was crystal clear.

Nelson at Amalienborg

The Crown Prince's answer to Parker's demands was an offer to act as intermediary between Britain and the members of the League of Armed Neutrality.

On the morning of 3 April Commander Lindholm and Lieutenant Captain Steen Bille went out to Parker and presented this invitation. Shortly afterwards, Nelson arrived. With him he brought his battle report, which he had dictated directly to Captain Fremantle; on his way he had visited the ships that had fought under his command the day before.

The gulf between Parker's demand and the Danish response was so wide that it really went beyond discussion on board the *London*. Instead, it was agreed that Nelson should go ashore that very afternoon to negotiate directly with the Crown Prince.

At around 1600 a barge pulled alongside the Customs Quay. Nelson and Hardy went ashore and, watched by curious Copenhageners, walked calmly down Amaliegade to Amalienborg Palace. They found the Crown Prince not at home. He was with his father, the King, at Rosenborg Palace. They passed away the time by enjoying a meal, after which they were presented to a group of people which included the King's brother. Nelson expressed in grandiloquent terms his admiration for the courageous resistance the Danes had put up and Britain's amicable feelings towards Denmark.

At that point Crown Prince Frederik arrived. For more than an hour the Crown Prince and Nelson, with the only other person present being Lindholm, engaged in a very candid political discussion that was to be decisive to the course of later negotiations.

The Crown Prince repeated his offer to act as go-between – an offer that Nelson categorically declined. Denmark could not act as intermediary in its own case. In return, he offered the Crown Prince a choice – either accept Parker's demands to leave the League and join forces with Britain or disarm the fleet. Prince Frederik, equally categorically, rejected the first alternative: that would mean war with Russia. But he was not so dismissive in principle at the idea of decommissioning his fleet and probed Nelson further as to what exactly he meant by disarmament.

At this juncture Nelson turned the negotiations in a quite different direction. Both he and Parker were aware that the Danish intransigence to their demands was founded on fear of reprisals from their allies. Nelson, however, was impatient to get into the Baltic before Russia and Sweden united their fleets. So he hinted that Sir Hyde Parker might consider waiving his explicit orders and agree to political negotiations between the two governments. In return, Denmark was to allow the British fleet to provision in Copenhagen and to suspend its obligation to Russia for the duration of the negotiations. If these conditions were met, Parker, he said, would agree to an armistice.

The Crown Prince accepted the first condition immediately; the second he was not prepared to discuss there and then; he would have to hear the opinion of the Privy Council. Nelson therefore agreed to an extension of the ceasefire until 5 April, by which time the Danes must make up their minds.

The talks between the two thus ended with an outline for a negotiable settlement that Denmark could accept without triggering a break with her allies. It also gave Denmark two priceless days.

Parker's ultimatum

But an outline for negotiations was far from a settlement.

On the morning of 5 April the Privy Council convened at Amalienborg Palace. The two differing viewpoints were still as far apart as before, and Minister of Finance, Count Ernst Schimmelmann, and Christian Bernstorff were now no longer on speaking terms. The Crown Prince listened to his Foreign Minister and stuck to the line he had taken on 3 April. The meeting ended with the appointment of two official negotiators: Commander Lindholm and Major General Ernst Frederik Walterstorff (brother of the commander of the gunboats), who, from his time as Governor General in the Danish West Indies, was just as fluent in English as Lindholm. They were sent out to Parker to be given further details of the outline for negotiations reached by the Crown Prince and Nelson.

Aboard the *London*, however, it transpired that the two parties interpreted the individual terms in a very different light. The Danes adopted a very restrictive idea of how the British fleet might provision itself whilst in Copenhagen, whereas Nelson, in his usual bluff fashion, claimed that "in a neutral harbour, we should be just as entitled to purchase cordage as a pair of stockings". What is more, the British wanted a greater reduction in the number of commissioned warships than the Danes would go along with. When it came to that most sensitive issue of all, Nelson demanded that Denmark, without reservation, withdraw from the League of Armed Neutrality. In the course of the ensuing discussion, Parker mollified the Danes by saying that it would be acceptable if Denmark would at least agree to putting its military obligations in abeyance for the duration of the negotiations.

But as accommodating as Parker was trying to be, the British had no intention of letting negotiations drag on interminably. Before the meeting, therefore, Parker had drawn up what he called his "ultimatum" and presented it to the two Danes towards the end of their discussion. He insisted on a written declaration from the Foreign Minister that Denmark was not obliged to support the combined Russian and Swedish fleets but could declare itself truly neutral, and that Denmark would allow the British fleet to provision itself in Copenhagen with everything it needed. The ultimatum was to expire the next day, 6 April, at noon.

War of nerves

The Privy Council met yet again to discuss the latest development and, yet again, the two camps were just as divided. And, yet again, the Crown Prince listened to his Foreign Minister and stuck to the original policy.

With his ultimatum, Parker had tried to force a binding agreement out of Bernstorff, but the latter was far too experienced a diplomat to fall for so undiplomatic a trick. In an elegant letter, in French, that was intended just as much for the Tsar's eyes, he assured Parker that Denmark had entered no agreements against the interests of Britain and that his fleet, once an armistice had been signed, was free to provision itself in Copenhagen with all the water, fresh food and medicine he required.

With this letter, and the authorization to promise, though only verbally, that Danish warships would not join the Russian and Swedish fleet during an armistice, Walterstorff and Lindholm returned to the *London* just one hour before the armistice expired.

In Parker's dining cabin they handed over Bernstorff's letter, which the admiral remarked was "a highly unsatisfactory note" that

217

he found unacceptable. The two Danes appealed to the admirals to understand their country's delicate position, but in vain. At this point Parker sat down and began studying a document the Danes assumed were his written orders and then asked Nelson to join him in the day cabin, where they had a lengthy conversation. When they returned, they both looked very serious and solemn, and Parker handed Walterstorff a letter addressed to Count Bernstorff. He also told them that, according to his orders, he was not empowered to sign an armistice but merely to make a provisional peace treaty with Denmark on Britain's conditions.

With a brush of his hand, Parker had swept all the pieces from the board. First, he had insisted on his original demands, then he had agreed to negotiate an armistice and now he had retracted to his original position of insisting on a political treaty. The Danes tried to back-track to the position of prolonged ceasefire without success and, in the heat of the moment, Lindholm exclaimed to Nelson that he "regretted that hostilities had ceased and that I will always regard the emissary sent by you as particularly unfortunate for Denmark; as we have no other choice than to accede to dis-honourable proposals or face a new and powerful enemy, then let us rather stand or fall as one man". But the admirals stood as firm as the Rock of Gibraltar. Denmark must make its choice: capitulation or war. Parker demanded an answer within twenty-four hours.

Their patience had reached its limit. Day after day Parker had postponed sending despatches back to London about the military victory, hoping each day that he would be able to supplement them with news of a political victory and now he would wait no longer. That afternoon the *London*'s captain, Robert Otway, boarded the *Cruizer* and sailed with Parker's victory report. In a supplementary letter Parker made it clear to the Admiralty that he very much doubted the possibility of reaching political agreement with the Danes: "The bombs are placed and will immediately commence their operations upon the answer to the last note of mine not having been complied with". Nelson was, for once, in complete agreement with Parker. Shortly after midnight the flames of three more of the prize ships illuminated the night sky as a warning to the Danes of what might lay in store for them. And at dawn on 7 April, Nelson personally inspected the seven bomb vessels in the King's Deep to reassure himself that everything was ready for the bombardment of Copenhagen.

Pen and sword

Parker's letter to the Foreign Minister was a genuine ultimatum: if Denmark refused to sign a treaty with Britain within twenty-four hours, based on the instructions Vansittart had referred to in his conversation with Bernstorff in mid-March, Parker would break off any further negotiations.

His letter was clear and unambiguous, but Bernstorff was a professional diplomat. He saw a loophole, one single point that was not entirely clear, and he exploited it immediately. In his reference to Vansittart's instructions, Parker had written in parentheses: "which the Admiral takes for granted have been communicated to the Secretary of State, Count Bernstorff".

These sixteen words saved Copenhagen from bombardment. Its saviour was Christian Bernstorff. With these words, he succeeded not only in extending the deadline beyond noon of 7 April, but also in manipulating Parker back to a negotiated solution that Denmark could accept.

On the morning of 7 April the Privy Council met yet again to discuss the response to Parker. Yet again it was divided into two camps, and yet again the Crown Prince stuck to the same political line. The two Danish negotiators were therefore instructed to reject any demand of a treaty and, in a letter to Parker, Bernstorff replied in his exquisitely polished French that he had the honour to inform the admiral that as he had no knowledge whatsoever of Mr Vansittart's instructions, he was obliged to await further information before he could answer the admiral's esteemed missive on behalf of the Government.

The two negotiators boarded the *London* at 1100 that morning and handed over the Foreign Minister's answer. What little patience Nelson had left was now exhausted. He had always regarded the Danish Foreign Minister as the evil spirit that had poisoned the good relations between Denmark and England, and he had told him so when the two had met face to face for a tense moment at Amalienborg Palace on 3 April. In Nelson's opinion, Bernstorff's letter was arrant nonsense "couched in the usual ambiguous diplomatic language". He later vented his anger on the British Prime Minister by saying, "I hate the fellow!"

Parker and Nelson informed the two Danes that their answer was completely unacceptable and criticized, in blistering terms, Bernstorff's refusal to negotiate with Vansittart. The Danes interrupted them and asked if Parker could give them Vansittart's instructions.

This seemingly innocent question marked a pivotal moment in the negotiations, and the entire situation, because Parker answered, "I find myself in a very difficult position as I have no copy of those instructions." He sat long in deep thought, until the Danes broke in and suggested that, in the light of this, perhaps it would be wisest to abandon a political solution and return to negotiations on a purely military armistice. Parker replied that "he was inclined to cease hostilities out of sheer humanity," despite the fact that this was in direct contradiction to his orders. The condition for such an armistice was that Denmark enter an alliance with Britain or disarm their fleet. When the Danes categorically rejected any idea of an alliance, the conversation turned to how much of the fleet should be disarmed.

During this part of the discussion Parker's secretary, Alexander Scott, was sitting at another table taking notes. He reached over and handed the admiral a piece of paper and said, "I believe I have set out concisely the points Your Excellency and these gentlemen have reached agreement on".

Scott had listened carefully and summarized what he perceived as Parker's conditions for reaching an armistice. Would Denmark formally undertake to stop its re-armament and leave its warships in their present state and would Denmark observe the strictest neutrality towards Britain and suspend its treaty with the other Nordic powers until the two governments had reached agreement or until Parker received new orders?

Parker read it through and showed it to Nelson, who accepted it as a valid basis for further negotiations. Walterstorff and Lindholm were of the same mind. They attempted, therefore, to clarify what was meant by "suspend". They also wanted to know the duration of the armistice, to which Parker replied that he wanted a long armistice of four months, with a further two weeks' notice of expiry.

At the time Parker wanted the negotiations to go no further. Instead, he asked Nelson and Colonel Stewart to negotiate the terms of the armistice with Walterstorff and Lindholm. Nelson agreed, as did Stewart when he was summoned. The two sides then parted, having agreed that Nelson and Stewart were to go ashore the next day at noon to conduct negotiations in Amalienborg Palace.

An armistice based on a previously agreed solution was clearly in Denmark's interest. The result, that Walterstorff and Lindholm returned with on 7 April, gave cause for great relief and exaggerated optimism that an armistice was assured. With the intercession of Countess Schimmelmann, the wife of the Minister of Finance, the schism in the Privy Council was healed and during the morning of 8 April Benstorff received the approbation of the Crown Prince and ministers for the Danish demands in the next round of negotiations. The armistice was to be a purely military agreement and for a limited period of time; this was crucial for the acceptance of Denmark's allies. The Fleet would not be given carte blanche to provision itself freely . It was to take on board no military stores in Copenhagen; the armistice period should be considerably shorter than the four months Parker was angling for and Denmark's suspension of her membership of the League of Armed Neutrality would expire with the end of the armistice.

An armistice based on a previously agreed solution was not, however, in Britain's interest.

Parker's orders were as clear as military orders can be. If Denmark rejected his demands – withdrawal from the League and alliance with Britain – Parker was to take or destroy the Danish fleet and its dockyards. Although he was empowered to spare Copenhagen from bombardment of military targets, it was only on receipt of the entire Danish fleet and its stores.

The victory of 2 April put Parker in the position where he could carry out these orders. But he did not.

He had several reasons for his actions, or lack of same. Like Nelson, he claimed one of them was 'humanity'. But the two admirals had other reasons as well – political, strategic and tactical.

Parker and Nelson agreed that a bombardment would be a politically unsuitable action; it would only push Denmark and Britain further apart and make Denmark rush even more eagerly into the arms of her allies.

Parker and Nelson saw that relations between the two countries were of long-term strategic importance. Parker's orders were to take him into the Baltic against Russia and Sweden; he would like to have his back free of the Danes before he set sail. British supply ships, despatch vessels and reinforcements must be able to pass through the Sound unhindered and the deep-draught three-deckers would be unable to pass over the Drogden Shallows whilst Denmark and Britain were at war as they would have to remove their guns to lighten ship. Somehow or other, Denmark had to be neutralized. Nelson was not the only one impatient to get on with the job and head east; so was Parker. On 7 April, while he waited for the Danish answer to his ultimatum throughout the morning, he had the waters around the Drogden Shallows sounded.

Parker and Nelson were also agreed on the tactical aspects of the issue. Both had serious doubts as to whether the bombardment could be carried out at all.

It was common knowledge that the effect of bombs and shells was uncertain. When Lord St. Vincent took up his post as First Sea Lord and had wanted a massive amphibious operation, it was because "shells thrown from ships are impotent weapons, and will be laughed at, when the first consternation is over". Be that as it may, he himself had given the sailing orders for a fleet whose ultimate weapon against Denmark, the military deterrent, was borne in seven small bomb vessels. In 1800 the very threat of bombardment had persuaded Denmark to accede to British demands.

As late as the afternoon of 6 April Parker had informed St. Vincent that he was ready to force acceptance of his demands by carrying out a bombardment. 24 hours later, however, both he and Nelson were convinced that such action would have no effect. The magazines at Nyholm were already empty and deserted; the Danish ships-of-the line being fitted out and armed had been warped out of the Dockyard and further down the harbour channel, in a line with considerable distances between each ship. This would mean that they would have to be set afire one by one and that the bomb vessels would have to hit a target just thirteen metres wide (the beam of a battleship) from a range of 2,800 metres. And with the bombardment completed, the bomb vessels would be out of action; they would have to be sent home to a dockyard for maintenance.

The two admirals were not the only ones with such doubts about the effectiveness of bombardment. On 6 April, while Parker and Nelson still believed they could bomb Denmark into submission, another experienced officer expressed his own reservations. Captain Fremantle was certain that the bomb vessels could inflict only limited damage and that a prolonged stay in the Copenhagen Roads would necessitate the Fleet having to return home for water and supplies.

As Commander-in-Chief, Parker therefore had many good reasons for deviating from his orders and seeking a negotiable outcome with the Danes.

The Tsar is dead

Early on 8 April Nelson and Stewart boarded a boat, together with Alexander Scott who was to act as their secretary, that was to be towed to Trekroner Fort by a British schooner, flying a white flag from the foretop. They were met by a Danish barge under the command of the *Danmark*'s second-in-command and the two boats were rowed in to the Customs Quay. They were soaked to the skin in the half-gale that was blowing, received by Lindholm and driven the short distance to Amalienborg Palace in a private carriage.

On arrival, the two sides got to work immediately on preparing an armistice. But it was a long-drawn-out affair and the deep and lengthy discussions of each single point showed just how much the Danes feared both Britain and Russia. As expected, the item on the agenda that took longest to get through was the duration of the armistice. On this point the two sides were a long way apart. The British wanted four months plus two week's notice, the Danes four to six weeks and a maximum of two months. Walterstorff and Lindholm made no bones of the fact that they feared the reaction of the Tsar. Nelson was no less candid: he needed four months to complete his business with the Russian fleet and return to take care of the Danes. The negotiations reached deadlock.

One of the Danes whispered to the other that hostilities should be re-opened, but Nelson understood enough French to get the gist of what they were saying and turned to Stewart and said in very peppery tones, fully aware that both Danes were fluent in English, "Renew hostilities! Tell him that we are ready at the moment; ready to bombard this very night!" The Dane apologized for the remark, but the two sides were just as far from agreement on this point as when the discussions were opened.

By this time it was the middle of the afternoon. The meeting was adjourned and the British contingent was escorted to one of the large royal chambers to be presented to the Court, a chamber they found completely empty of furniture because of the threat of bombardment. So, with the Crown Prince in the lead, they all ascended the grand staircase to the dining room. On the way Nelson took Stewart's arm and in a theatrical whisper said, "Though I have only one eye, I see that all this will burn very well!"

During the meal Nelson sat next to the Crown Prince. The atmosphere was relaxed and open, but the crucial negotiating point was still to be resolved. The Crown Prince and Nelson were to make an attempt after the meal.

At the correct juncture the two withdrew to another room, where they began their discussions in private. Time passed and those waiting outside realized that no agreement could be reached. At this point Commander Lindholm received a message that changed the basis for any negotiations out of all recognition. He went to the door of the chamber, opened it very quietly and walked in unannounced. With a poker face, he bent down and whispered in the Crown Prince's ear, "The Tsar is dead."

Victory at the negotiating table
The news that Tsar Paul was dead and that there was a new Tsar on the throne was a vital piece of information for the Crown Prince. It meant that the threat of immediate reprisals from Russia no longer existed. A new Tsar would need time to establish his power and formulate his policies. Without letting on to Nelson, who first heard the news two days later, the Crown Prince gave in to the British demands. He accepted an armistice of fourteen weeks and two weeks' expiry notice and Nelson left the chamber to resume negotiations.

The armistice, then, was a reality. At 1930 the negotiators could leave their table after Nelson and Walterstorff had signed the armistice document that effectively brought the war between Britain and Denmark to an end.

With everything virtually signed, sealed and delivered, Nelson, in his customary no-nonsense style, said to the Crown Prince as one officer to another, "Now, sir, that this is settled, suppose we write Peace instead of Armistice?" The Crown Prince received the remark with good grace and answered that he would be delighted with peace as an outcome but that it would have to be approached cautiously if a new war were to be averted.

When Nelson returned to the *St. George* late on the evening of 8 April, soaked to the skin and fatigued, what he brought with him was an armistice, and a purely military armistice at that.

This was exactly what the Danes had wanted. In the preamble to the document, it was made quite clear that the following text comprised a purely military agreement and that it had been entered to save Copenhagen from bombardment. The meat of the seven paragraphs was that the Danish fleet was not to be further armed, that the British fleet may provision itself with non-military supplies in any Danish harbour in the fourteen weeks of the armistice, and that Denmark for that period of time suspended its obligations as member of the League of Armed Neutrality.

On the morning of 9 April Nelson, Stewart, Walterstorff and Lindholm met aboard the *London* to sign and seal the armistice document. Sir Hyde Parker then ratified it in his position as the British Commander-in-Chief and Nelson went ashore with the document to receive similar ratification from the Crown Prince. It was 1800 before Nelson returned to his ship, physically exhausted and shivering with fever. And half in defiance, he summarized the result: "Under all circumstances I am sure our armistice is a good thing".

Early the next morning Colonel Stewart set off overland to London as a courier. With him he took the political result of the Battle of Copenhagen. He also took the truth of what had happened since the Baltic Fleet left Yarmouth a month before, at least Nelson's version of the truth.

THE LOST WAR

The armistice included a clause that the 1,800 or so Danish prisoners of war on board the British ships were to be brought ashore.

Together with fifty-nine men from the *Prøvestenen*, *Wagrien* and *Jylland*, Michael Bille had been taken aboard the *Russell* on the afternoon of 2 April. For the first few days he had been full of resentment towards Captain Cuming because he had refused to allow him to visit his wounded on board the *Prøvestenen*. But Bille had thawed out somewhat since then. Cuming treated him with courtesy; he was given permission to write to Marie, in French, because of the censoring of letters from the Danes that the ship's amicable chaplain was put in charge of; and in the wardroom he managed to brush up his English to the level that one of the officers burst out, "By God, if this gentleman is given one more glass of wine he will end up speaking better English than I do myself."

On 10 April the prisoners were informed of the armistice. The next day Lieutenant Commander Grove came on board and signed for eighty-six prisoners of war – to Bille's angry dismay, fourteen soldiers elected to stay and enter British service. Bille and his men were put ashore in the fishing village of Taarbæk just north of Copenhagen. He requisitioned two carriages for the wounded and the few clothes they had managed to save, and they marched back to the city as a ship's company. "We were met with such unexpected satisfaction and warmth on the beaches and along our route to Copenhagen that it lifted our spirits and renewed our eagerness to fight for country and right."

For Michael Bille and the men from the *Prøvestenen*, the war was over, but not for Denmark and Britain. The Fleet still had an appointment in the Baltic. Months of intense diplomatic and military activity were to pass before the war came to an end and peace was once more a wonderful reality.

Parker and Nelson in the Baltic

Parker could now sail into the Baltic against Denmark's allies. On 9 April he ordered the bomb vessels and their tenders out of the King's Deep; the sounding of the Drogden Shallows was intensified and the *London* lightened ship by removing guns and stores to allow her to pass over them. The brig *Speedwell* was ordered to proceed north and patrol off the Kattegat island of Hjelm to inform Rear Admiral Totty, who was expected with reinforcements, to follow Parker to Køge Bay and thence to Reval. The brig *Harpy* was told to remain in the Copenhagen Roads and act as observer to ensure that Denmark complied with the conditions of the armistice and to inform British ships of the Fleet's rendezvous point north of the Danish island of Bornholm. The frigate *Amazon* was sent under a white flag to Karlskrona to inform the Swedish governor of the armistice and offer Sweden a similar solution to the conflict.

On 12 April the wind changed to a northerly. The next day the Fleet passed through the Hollander Deep and over the Drogden Shallows, where the *London* twice went aground but without remaining so, and out into the deeper water of Køge Bay, where they went to anchor. The following day the *Amazon* came tearing up from the south. Captain Sutton had sighted the Swedish squadron at sea: seven ships-of-the-line, three frigates and a brig. Parker immediately sent a message to Nelson, whose flagship was still in the Copenhagen Roads being lightened prior to her passage over the Drogden Shallows, and asked him once more to transfer his command to the *Elephant*. Nelson wasted not a moment. He went on board immediately, together with the *Bellona*'s master, Alexander Briarly, in a six-oared boat. It was 1800 when they left and for the next six hours the crew rowed like men demented, urged on by Nelson, who swore that if they did not reach the Fleet before it sailed he would follow it in that very boat, all the way to Karlskrona if necessary. But he did reach the *Elephant* and the Baltic Fleet headed south on the hunt for the Swedish battle squadron.

This squadron, meanwhile, had received warning they had been sighted. When Parker reached Karlskrona on 19 April it was only to see the entire squadron safely at anchor in the skerries, and once more he was plagued by doubt and uncertainty. His plan had been to make for Reval. He now feared that the Swedish squadron would sneak out in his absence, make a fast run up the Sound and block the passage of Rear Admiral Totty's ships. So he decided to remain north of Bornholm, from where he could keep an eye on the Swedes and the entrance to the Baltic.

The Fleet did not stay there for long. On 22 April the Danish naval cutter *Le Petit Diable* arrived with a letter to Parker from the Russian envoy in Copenhagen. At a time when the new Tsar Alexander believed the Fleet was still in the Kattegat, he informed Parker that he had opened negotiations with Britain and that, as a result, he expected him to refrain from any hostile act towards any member of the League of Armed Neutrality and await new orders from London. When Parker, almost at the same time, received news from British diplomats in Berlin and Hamburg that confirmed that talks between Britain and Russia were imminent, he decided to meet the Tsar's request. The Fleet weighed and sailed back to Køge Bay.

And there it was that Parker received the most unexpected order of his life. Until then the orders and letters he had received from London had supported him in his venture. Lord St. Vincent had congratulated him on his victory of 2 April and Parliament had passed votes of thanks to him and his Fleet. But Colonel Stewart had had more in his baggage than the armistice document when he arrived in London. He had Nelson's version of Parker's leadership of the fleet. On 5 May Stewart returned to the Fleet. Parker's new orders were to hand over the Baltic Fleet to Nelson's command immediately.

Despite Parker's concerns and procrastination, St. Vincent and the Cabinet had supported him loyally as Commander-in-Chief. Parker's report that he intended to sail through the Great Belt, however, shocked St. Vincent to the core. Now he had been told that on 2 April Parker had been within a hair's breadth of grasping Britain a defeat from the jaws of victory, and the armistice he had ratified, in the Cabinet's opinion, came nowhere near what could be termed reasonable conditions in the light of the victory at Copenhagen. The Cabinet, though, elected to approve the armistice, unsatisfactory as it may have been, but it had lost any confidence in Parker's abilities. St. Vincent ordered him home, prematurely and in disgrace.

On 5 May, therefore, Parker's flag was hauled down from the *London*'s mainmast and that very afternoon he left aboard the frigate *Blanche*.

Nelson took over command of the Baltic Fleet at a time when the situation of high politics was far more complicated than when Parker had sailed from Yarmouth. The Fleet's operations were now curtailed by rapidly changing political developments. But the Fleet was to feel almost immediately that it was under new command. Nelson's first signal was to prepare to weigh and on 6 May the Fleet entered the Baltic for the second time. North of Bornholm, he left a squadron of seven ships-of-the-line under Captain Murray and delivered a letter to the governor in Karlskrona of the consequences of the Swedish squadron leaving the skerries. He also left the bomb vessels, gun brigs and fireships off the island. With the remaining eleven ships, Nelson set course for Reval to demonstrate the presence of the Fleet in the Baltic.

On 12 May Nelson anchored his division off Reval, where he could observe that the Russian squadron had been withdrawn to Kronstadt, but his stay was to be a short one. The new Tsar could not enter negotiations with Britain under any circumstances whilst one of her squadrons was in Russian waters. Nelson was given a sharp reminder to remove himself forthwith and he had enough political acumen to know when not to question an order. When a senior Russian naval officer came aboard the *St. George* on 20 May to make him aware of the new Tsar's friendly attitude towards Britain, he also had the common sense to know when to fall into line and take his position in the diplomatic counterpoint, and issued an official declaration that the Fleet had no intention of hostile acts towards Russia.

At that time the politicians had taken over and the Baltic Fleet had served its purpose. It returned to Køge Bay and on 19 June Nelson handed his fleet over to Rear Admiral Pole and returned home on the brig *Kite*. The Fleet remained there until 21 July, when it weighed anchor and sailed for England, but not through the Sound. It went south into the Baltic and then west and north through the Great Belt, where it gained extensive navigational data that would prove to be invaluable six years later when the British returned to Danish waters.

Break with the allies

When the Baltic Fleet left Yarmouth on 12 March Britain had stood alone against Europe. Less than a week later this political constellation was cracking. On 21 March, the same day that the British land forces defeated the French army in Egypt, the British Foreign Secretary opened peace negotiations with France. On 24 March a British courier set off in haste from the Foreign Office with important despatches that would pave the way for a political understanding with Russia. Lord Hawkesbury had no way of knowing that Tsar Paul had been murdered that very morning in his fortress palace in St. Petersburg. Nor could he know that Paul's son, the new Tsar Alexander, had decided that same morning to seek a political understanding with Britain. The Tsar's courier was already on his way on 25 March with this message.

The Commander-in-Chief of the Baltic Fleet did not know it either, and nor did the Danish government. The most vital of information could not be sent any faster than a horse could gallop or a despatch vessel sail. So the Battle of Copenhagen had to be fought, even though it was politically meaningless. What Denmark was fighting for no longer existed on 2 April. The Tsar of Russia, whom Denmark feared more than the Baltic Fleet, was no longer in the land of the living, but that information did not reach Copenhagen until 8 April. Only the day after, when the armistice had been signed, could the Danish government get to work in readjusting to the new political situation.

With Tsar Paul's death and the reshuffle in high political constellations, the League of Armed Neutrality fell apart. Denmark was reduced to a powerless political bystander whilst the League was dissolved and the great powers rearranged the map of Europe after eight years' war.

The first break was with Sweden. King Gustav had taken the line that the armistice was an act of treason against the League of Armed Neutrality and decided to exploit it to weaken Denmark's position in St. Petersburg. The political objective behind this cynical act was an attempt to acquire Norway. As early as 11 April the Swedish

King ordered two diplomats to keep themselves ready for a mission intended to gain support for the plan in St. Petersburg, Berlin and Paris. The King himself prepared the plans for an invasion of Norway and later for a lightning attack on Copenhagen while the Danish fleet was still immobilized after the armistice. But it was a plan that never saw the light of day; it did not receive the backing of the major powers. This time the Danes were in blissful ignorance of the intentions of the Swedes, but they did know the Swedes were no longer their allies.

Nor was Prussia. Denmark herself had coerced Prussia into the League and chosen to operate in Northern Germany, where Prussia had important political interests. Prussia withdrew from the League of Armed Neutrality the moment news of the Tsar's death reached Berlin. Before April was out they demanded that Danish troops withdraw from Hamburg immediately. Denmark had no option but to do as they were told and watch impotently as Prussia maintained her occupation of Hanover and the Duchy of Lauenburg.

Unconditional surrender

Sweden and Prussia were important to Danish foreign policy, but Russia was decisive. The sporadic reports from St. Petersburg were therefore gone through with a fine toothcomb in Copenhagen. On the surface of it, Denmark had every reason to feel optimistic. Tsar Alexander had given them an assurance that he would stand by his father's promises and that he and his allies would bring peace to Europe. But, whatever the circumstances, Denmark had to cut its political cloth to the requirements of Russia. The government therefore declared its willingness for the Tsar to negotiate with Britain on behalf of the members of the League. But political observers who were long in the tooth (and the Danish envoy in St Petersburg, Count Danneskiold-Løvendal, was not one of them) spent a lot of time considering the fact that the Russian Foreign Minister consistently neglected to inform his country's allies of the progress of negotiations with Britain.

Tsar Alexander's move had alerted the British to send one of their most experienced diplomats to St. Petersburg and on 27 May Lord St. Helens arrived. His prime task was to reach an agreement with Russia on the principles of neutrality. At the very first meeting the Russian Foreign Minister, Count Panin, informed him that Russia wished to withdraw from the League of Armed Neutrality but in such a way as to take into account the prestige of the Tsar and

Russia's continued dominance over the Nordic powers. The Count went even further and promised that Denmark and Sweden would accept whatever solution Britain and Russia reached.

With this political willingness, it took only six meetings before the British Ambassador and the Russian Foreign Minister had reached a mutually acceptable agreement. Russia withdrew its support for the three principles of neutrality that represented such a threat to Britain's superiority at sea: the right of neutral countries to transport war contraband; to transport cargoes for belligerent nations; and the right of convoys to refuse to be visited and searched on the high seas. But he also made sure that the Anglo–Russian Convention of 17 June was worded in such a way that the Tsar could claim to Denmark and Sweden that he had adhered to the articles of the League of Armed Neutrality, although with certain modifications.

Only when the convention had been finalized was it presented to the Danes and Swedes, with the Tsar's insistence that they accept it immediately and unconditionally. The Swedish King accepted at once; his plans for the annexation of Norway were dependent on maintaining good relations with Russia. Denmark, on the other hand, attempted to avoid such a humiliating defeat for its policy of offensive neutrality. It tried to reach a compromise through direct negotiations between Bernstorff and Lord Hawkesbury.

At the end of May Christian Bernstorff travelled to London to negotiate with Britain the return of the captured Danish ships and occupied colonies. Whilst he was there he was informed by Crown Prince Frederik that the Tsar had sold them out in terms of the principles of neutrality and instructed him to try and reach better conditions through personal talks with the British Foreign Minister. The treachery the Crown Prince found hardest to swallow was the abandoning of the highly prestigious issue of the immunity of neutral convoys.

The mission was a total failure, partly because Hawkesbury had been able to gain access to Bernstorff's correspondence, even to those parts that were in code, and so was always in a position of knowing what his opponent's instructions were. But what really sealed the fate of the attempt was the fact that Bernstorff had nothing to offer and nothing to threaten with. As far as Britain was concerned, the treaty with Russia was ideal. It gave her all the rights she had been squabbling with the neutral countries about for more than a hundred years. Lord Hawkesbury could only regretfully inform the Danish Foreign Minister that Britain felt bound by her promises to the Tsar. Bernstorff had to return home having achieved nothing.

Meanwhile the Russian envoy had been putting more and more pressure on the Danish government for speedy and unconditional acceptance of the Anglo–Russian convention. In total political isolation, and with its ships taken and colonies occupied, Denmark could do nothing but surrender. On 26 September, Lieutenant Fasting, who had commanded the artillery barge *Aggershus* on 2 April, set sail for St. Petersburg in the despatch schooner *Ørnen*, with instructions to Count Danneskiold-Løvendal to sign Denmark's acceptance of the Anglo–Russian neutrality convention.

The signature was given in a period of great festivity, during the celebrations of the Tsar's coronation. In Prince Kurakin's palace, on 23 October, the Danish envoy put his name to the document and crowned the defeat of Crown Prince Frederik's policy of offensive neutrality.

CURTAIN DOWN

The war had ended – for now. In a Europe dominated by the major powers, Denmark had endeavoured to have some influence on her own destiny. The Crown Prince and his government made a conscious effort to play in major league politics. But when the situation became perilously dangerous, they had been unable to extricate themselves and pull out again. In the critical winter months of 1801, when they saw themselves as being between the devil and the deep blue sea, all they managed to achieve was to choose the lesser of two evils – war with Britain. And it was a war they would lose on 2 April. The price of defeat was that Denmark had to abandon definitively the principles of neutrality it had defended for more than a century – destroyed after just three years of the policy of offensive neutrality.

When Danneskiold-Løvendal signed Denmark's unconditional surrender in Moscow, the Revolutionary Wars had come to an end. At that time, the belligerent parties had negotiated themselves towards the basis for a peace settlement; and although no treaty to that effect was signed by France and Britain until March 1802 in Amiens, all hostilities on land and at sea ceased in October 1801. So the loss of the principles of neutrality were not really felt by Denmark.

232

But in May 1803, war broke out again. Bonaparte had used the time of peace to catch his breath and prepare the final onslaught against Britain. The new and bitter war between the ruler of the continent and the ruler of the waves was not to be resolved for another twelve years, at the Battle of Waterloo in 1815.

So it was not until May 1803 that Denmark needed to take another look at a policy of neutrality. Denmark complied strictly to the terms of the convention it had accepted in the autumn of 1801. Not only did it not reassert the rights it had lost, but it kept a very low profile in its exploitation of neutrality during this period of intensified aggression between Britain and France. With the outbreak of war, the Danish government banned ship owners from operating directly from Asia to Europe under the Danish flag – the kind of neutrality speculation that, more than anything else, had brought Denmark into conflict with Britain.

So when disaster revisited Copenhagen again in 1807, Denmark was entirely without blame – which it was not in 1801. The massive conflict between Britain and France had ended in a military stale-mate. In October 1805, Nelson had crushed the combined fleets of France and Spain at Trafalgar. In December of the same year, Napoleon conquered Austria at the Battle of Austerlitz. In October 1806, he humiliated Prussian military power at the Battle of Jena. And on 21 November, in Berlin, he issued his famous declaration on the blockade of the Continent – cessation of any form of economic involvement with Britain; now she was to be starved into submission. Napoleon assured himself the overriding condition for the success of this blockade by driving the Russian army back through Poland and humiliating the Tsar at Friedland, just a hundred kilometres from the Russian border. This was something that made the Tsar sit up and think and he began making overtures to France. And unlike the parallel situation in 1801, this under-standing would be reached on France's terms.

On a floating pavilion on the River Njemen, the French Emperor and the Russian autocrat entered an agreement that together they would force the remaining maritime states – Denmark, Sweden and Portugal – into joining the blockade against Britain. One result was the Tilsit Treaty of 7 July 1807.

Another was the fact that Copenhagen had once again become the focal point of the aggression of the major powers.

On 6 August, to his great consternation, the Danish envoy in Paris was presented with Napoleon's ultimatum: join the blockade and go to war with Britain – or do not, and go to war with France. On the very same day, a British emissary arrived at Crown Prince Frederik's headquarters in Kiel. He, too, presented an ultimatum: enter an alliance with Britain or go to war with her.

British spies at Tilsit had passed back the message to the Cabinet that the Tsar had entered negotiations with Napoleon. For Britain, it was absolutely imperative that the Danish fleet did not fall into Napoleon's hands. The Cabinet was also anxious to execute a lightning attack against Copenhagen to warn the Tsar not even to contemplate a peace treaty with France.

The expectation of the British Cabinet in advance was that Denmark would say no to Britain's demands – by which refusal the Danish fleet would immediately come under British command or be surrendered as mortgage for Denmark's neutrality. So it came as no surprise that Crown Prince Frederik dismissed both demands out of hand. And when British troops went ashore at Vedbæk, halfway up the coast between Copenhagen and Elsinore on 16 August 1807, to persuade (and, if necessary, to force) the Crown Prince into reconsidering his position, Whitehall received something of a surprise – he declared war. But Denmark was totally unprepared to go to war. The British surrounded the Danish capital, without the slightest resistance, from land and sea. General Arthur Wellesley, later the Duke of Wellington, dispersed the Zealand peasant militia regiments near Køge in what has come to be known as the Battle of the Clogs. Copenhagen was then subjected to three nights of bombardment and under pressure from the city's inhabitants, the commandant had to request a ceasefire. At the core of the capitulation on 7 September was the condition that the entire fleet and its stores were to be surrendered to Britain – as property. In record time, the British armed and fitted out the Danish fleet, which for political reasons had been left decommissioned so as not to antagonise the British – and on 20 October, it left Copenhagen. Before its departure, the British had destroyed a ship-of-the-line in drydock and three on the slips. They took with them fifteen ships-of-the-line, fifteen frigates, seven brigs and numerous minor vessels – probably the most successful combined operation of its era.

In that situation, Denmark's only ally was Napoleon – and he was the only one that would guarantee the return of the Danish fleet and territory when Britain was defeated. So Denmark allied herself with France.

In an attempt to transport French-Spanish troops to Zealand for a planned invasion of Sweden, Denmark's last ship-of-the-line, the *Prins Christian Frederik*, which in 1807 was in Norway, was lost in the Battle of Sjœllands Odde on 22 March 1808. Among the casualties was the Danish hero of 2 April 1801, Peter Willemoes.

Napoleon was defeated but the biggest loser in the Napoleonic Wars was Denmark. In 1813, the last year of the wars, King Frederik VI had to declare Denmark bankrupt; in 1814, he had to surrender Norway to the King of Sweden. Denmark was ruined and destroyed after seven years of war and had to forge for herself a place in the new Europe of peace and balance of power that emerged with the Vienna Congress in 1814–15. In the coming decades, the Danes followed how government after government throughout Europe adopted the principles of neutrality in their trade and shipping treaties; principles that had led to the Battle of Copenhagen. And in 1856, they were finally acknowledged and generally accepted at the Paris Peace Conference.

But only few of the survivors of 2 April were to see the belated restoration of Denmark's honour. Most of the men who fought that day had died long since. Michael Bille died in 1845 and was buried on 2 April, a date never to be forgotten, in the naval churchyard of Holmen's Church. In Denmark the feeling that day was that this was the end of an era – the last of the famous names of the battle in the King's Deep was no more.

There were others still alive, most of them in their 80s, who had fought that day, been decorated and could relate to adoring, wide-eyed grandchildren of the day they stood not so far from Peter Willemoes and fired a 36-pounder against Lord Nelson for a morning. But not many.

In 1856, the Battle of Copenhagen was history.

REFERENCES

Abbreviations: *Adm:* Danish Admiralty; *Disp:* The Dispatches and Letters of Lord Nelson, publ. N.H. Nicholas; *Logs:* Logs of the Great Sea Fights 1794–1805, II, publ. By T.S. Jackson; *Millard:* W.S. Millard: The Battle of Copenhagen; *NMM:* National Maritime Museum, Greenwich; *PRO:* Public Record Office; *RA:* Rigsarkivet (Danish National Archives); *Reports:* Reports from the Danish War Archives (Meddelelser fra Krigsarkiverne), publ. by C.T. Sørensen; *Stewart I:* William Stewart's diary in the Cumloden Papers; *Stewart II:* William Stewart's account from 1809, printed in Disp. IV, pp 299–327.

Unless otherwise specified, all Danish sources are to be found in the Danish National Archives (RA).

ONE GREY MORNING IN MARCH
O. Feldbæk: Lieutenant Bille of the Prøvestenen; census 1801.

DENMARK AND HIGH POLITICS
This chapter is based on O. Feldbæk: The Anglo-Danish Convoy Conflict; and Denmark and the Armed Neutrality. For the section on the *Freya* affair, research included the logs of the frigates *Prévoyante*, *Terpsichore*, *Nemesis* and *Arrow* (PRO; 51/1313, 1325, 1340 and 1346).

DRESS REHEARSAL FOR WAR
O. Feldbæk: Denmark and the Armed Neutrality.

BRITAIN ATTACKS
Strategy and tactics
Spencer's preparations: correspondence from St. Vincent 7/12, Whitworth 18/12, Parker 11/1, Lt. Frederick Thesiger 16/1 to Spencer (Spencer's Papers IV, pp 274–8); and St. Vincent 17/1 to Evan Nepean (Naval Miscellany, I, pp 331–2).
Dundas and the cabinet: correspondence from Dundas 9/1 to Evan

Nepean (State Letters, PRO), Thomas Grenville 13/1 to Lord Buckingham (St. Vincent Letters, I, pp 51–2).

Military planning: St. Vincent Letters, I, p 59; correspondence St. Vincent 13, 15, 24/1 and 9/2 to Evan Nepean (NMM); Nelson 17/1 to Spencer (Disp., IV, p 274); St. Vincent 17/1 to Evan Nepean (Naval Miscellany, II, pp 231–2); Dundas 23/2 to the Admiralty and the Duke of York (State Letters, PRO).

Parker's orders: Parker's log 25–28/2 (PRO); and Parker 26/2 to Nelson (NMM).

Gathering of the Fleet: Pope pp 157–9; Stewart I, p 1; Parker's log (PRO) and his letters to Evan Nepean (Admirals' Despatches, PRO); and Parker 10/3 to Rear Admiral Graves (NMM).

Nelson and Parker: Nelson 6, 7/3 to Lady Hamilton (Morisson II, pp 125–7); Nelson 7, 11/3 to Troubridge (Naval Miscellany, I, pp 415–16, 419); Nelson 11/3 to Alexander Davison (Disp., VII, p 203); Stewart II, p 300; St. Vincent 10, 11/3 and 5, 17/4 to Parker (St. Vincent Letters, I, pp 85–91).

The Fleet puts to sea
Parker's log 12/3 (PRO); Parker 12/3 to Evan Nepean (Admirals' Despatches, PRO).

Destination Denmark
Passage: Parker's log (PRO); Nelson's log (NMM); Parker 15, 18, 23/3 to Evan Nepean (Admirals' Despatches, PRO); Capt. Fremantle 17/3 to his wife (Wynne Diaries, III, p 31); Nelson 21/3 to Troubridge (Naval Miscellany, I, p 423).
Near disaster: Pope pp 217–42; Reports, I, p 108.
Blazer: log (PRO).

Turbot diplomacy
Naval Chronicle, 37, pp 446–7; note from Parker to Nelson (Letters from Parker to Nelson, NMM); Pope, who does not know of the note, rejects it (p 263) as apocryphal.
Nelson's plan: Nelson 16/3 to Troubridge (Naval Miscellany, I, pp 420–1); Nelson 16/3 to Alexander Davison (Disp., IV, p 294).
Meeting with Parker: Nelson 19/3 to Troubridge (Naval Miscellany, I, pp 421–2); Nelson 19, 20/3 to Alexander Davison (Disp., VII, pp 203–4).

Sound or Belt
The diplomats: Vansittart 21/3 to Parker (St. Vincent Letters, I, pp 61–2); Parker's log 22, 23/3 (PRO); Parker 23/3 to Evan Nepean (Admirals' Despatches, PRO).

23 March: Parker's log 23/3 (PRO); Nelson's log 23/3 (NMM); Stewart I, pp 7–8; Naval Chronicle, 37, p 447; Nelson 24/3 to Parker (Disp., IV, pp 295–8); Nelson 29/3 to Troubridge (Naval Miscellany, I, pp 424–5); Vansittart 8/4 to Nelson (Morisson, II, pp 135–6).

24 March: Nelson's log 24/3 (NMM); Stewart, I, pp 9–11; Tomlinson Papers pp 306–7; Parker 24/3 to Nelson (Letters from Parker to Nelson, NMM); Parker 6/4 to Evan Nepean (Admirals' Despatches, PRO); Nelson 24/3 to Parker (Disp., IV, pp 295–8); Nelson 8/7/01 to Parker (NMM); Vansittart 8/4 to Nelson (Morisson, II, pp 135–6).

New orders: *Jamaica*'s log (PRO); Dundas 14/3 to the Admiralty (State Letters, PRO); Admiralty 15/3 to Parker (Disp., IV, pp 294–5); Parker 24/3 to Evan Nepean (Admirals' Despatches, PRO).

25 March: Parker's log 24/3 (PRO); Nelson's log 25/3 (NMM); Domett 4/5 to Admiral Bridport (British Museum); Otway's memoirs (Disp., IV, p 301).

Cannon of Kronborg
25 March: Stewart, I, p 12.

26 March: Parker's log 26/3 (PRO); Nelson's log 26/3 (NMM); Fremantle 29/3 to his wife and Lord Buckingham (Wynne Diaries, III, pp 36–40); *Elephant*'s log (PRO).

27 March: Parker's log 27/3 (PRO); Nelson's log 27/3 (NMM); Pope, pp 294–5; Millard, p 82; Parker 27/3 to Col. Stricker (RA, Foreign Department, England I e. Correspondence concerning hostilities with England).

28 March: Stricker 28/3 to Parker (Admirals' Despatches, PRO); Kronborg optical telegraph log 28/3 (RA); Parker 28/3 to Nelson (Letters from Parker to Nelson, NMM); *Sulphur*, log (PRO); Nelson 28/3 to Capt. Bertie (*Ardent*) (Disp., IV, p 298).

29 March: Parker's log 28, 29/3 (PRO); Nelson's log 29/3 (NMM); Parker 29/3 to Stricker (as 27/3); Parker 29/3 to Nelson (Letters from Parker to Nelson, NMM); logs of *Discovery*, *Hecla* and *Sulphur*. (Logs, PRO); Millard, p 82.

Fear has wide eyes
Parker's log 22, 23/3 (PRO); Parker 23/3 to Evan Nepean (Admirals' Despatches, PRO); Nelson 24/3 to Parker (Disp., IV, p 297); Stewart, I, p 7; also Frantzen: Sømorterer, p 100, and Eriksen and Frantzen: Det danske artillerimateriel under Napoleonskrigene (Danish artillery during the Napoleonic Wars).

30 March: Parker's log 30/3 (PRO); Nelson's log 30/3 (NMM); Stewart I, pp 13–14; Stewart II, pp 301–2; Tomlinson Papers p 308; Reports, I, p 159; Millard pp 83–4.

COPENHAGEN FORTIFICATIONS

Calm before the storm

Squadrons and disarmament: general copy book, orders 28/8–8/9 and 13/10/00; also Bergersen, II, p 132.

Expectations of peace: general copy book, orders 18, 25/9; secret instructions, 22/9 and 21/11/00.

Armament 1801: Wleugel's calculation 21/11 and orders to district recruiting officers and Danish and German Chancelleries 22, 24/11/00 (general copy book).

Expedited armament: orders 8, 11, 22/12/00 (general copy book) and resolution 8/12 (minutes); Reports, I, pp 54–55.

Defence Plan

Planning orders: Adm. 27/12 to Defence Commission and Hohlenberg (general copy book); Defence Commission's report on Trekroner Fort 21/11/00 (Søkrigskancelliet, Royal Resolution).

Defence Commission's Plan 8/6/1784: Defence Commission of 6/1/1777, Proposals 1784–1837.

Preliminary plan: Defence Commission 29/12/00 to General Commissary, with appendix of Hohlenberg's analysis (28/12) of the floating defences; Adm. 5/1/01 to Fischer (general copy book).

Emergency plan: Original plan of 21/1 with chart of defences missing from archive – unsuccessful in locating either plan or chart; nor can they be reconstructed from the Defence Commission's own archives, which were destroyed by fire in Holmen dockyard in 1853. The reconstruction here is based on minutes in the Decision Log 1801 (General Commissary), supplemented with information from the Defence Commission's summary (26/1) of the navy's artillery (Dockyard Captain – Letters and drafts received 1740–1801); Fischer 28/11/02 to Crown Prince Frederik (Reports, I, pp 164–7).

Race against time

Defences outside Copenhagen: Reports, I, pp 48–179; Bergersen, II, pp 215–98.

Scythes: Moltke 21/3 to Crown Prince Frederik (Reports, I, p 111).

Southern border: O. Feldbæk: Denmark and the Armed Neutrality, pp 143–45.

Copenhagen defences: Reports, I, pp 48, 126–7, 130–6, 151–3.

Norwegian squadron and defences: Resolution 29/12 (decision log); plan 29/12 with Royal Resolution of 2/1/01 (Adm. Royal Resolutions); minutes 30/12 and 19/1/01; orders 30/12 and 19/1/01 (general copy book).

Artillery plan: 26/1 (Dockyard Captain. Letters and drafts 1740–1801); Adm. 9/2 to Army Office (general copy book).

Dockyard Captain: Hohlenberg 2/2 to General Commissary and statements by Dockyard Captain 5/2 (General Commissary – my thanks to Maria Ekberger for drawing my attention to this reference).

Battle squadron: minutes 14/3; Adm. 14/3 to commanding officers and 19, 26/3 to commanding officer Naval Academy (general copy book).

Plan and despair

Dockyard Captain and Holmen Medal: Louis Bobé: August Hennings' diary (1934) p 206; plan 26/1 with royal consent 29/1 (Adm. Royal Resolutions).

Trekroner Fort: Adm. 5/2 to von Thun (general copy book); Army Office 12/3 to Adm.(minutes); report from Meyer 11/7/01 (personal dossier); Reports, I, p 148. A report from Meyer on Trekroner Fort as of 2/4/01 was sought in vain. Stricker's Battery: minutes 12/1/01; Adm. 12/1 to Army Office (general copy book); Reports, I, p 141.

Temporary fort: Dockyard Captain 9/1 with accompanying resolution and Defence Commission 2/2 to Adm. (decision log); L.J. Flamand: Mindeskrift, p 135; H.C. Bjerg and J. Schou Hansen: Vragene i Øresund (Wrecks in the Sound) p 31; resolution 9/2 (minutes).

Abandoning of plans for temporary fort: resolutions 9, 21/2, and Adm. 26/2 to Runge, Branth and Dockyard Captain (minutes); Adm. 19/2 to Regulating Committee (general copy book); plan 26/2 with royal consent 27/2 (Adm. Royal Resolutions); Defence Commission 27/2 to Adm. with accompanying resolution (decision log).

Sjælland and Holsten: East India and West India captains 2/2 to Adm. (minutes); Defence Commission 2/2 with accompanying resolution and Dockyard Captain 5/2 to Adm. (decision log); Adm. 23/2 to Riegelsen and Arenfelt and 28/2 to Fischer (general copy book); Fischer 28/11/02 to Crown Prince Frederik (Reports, I, p 164).

Olfert Fischer: letter 28/11/02 to Crown Prince Frederik (Reports, I, p 164. Apart from some trivial errors, the printed letter is in accordance with the original in the National Archives. The Crown Prince's Command Office, Adm. Received Correspondence, 1802:1265). The letter was written eighteen months after the events and is clearly on the defensive. It must be regarded as a reliable source because Fischer categorically refers to two prominent members of the Defence Commission as witnesses, and because it would have been far too risky to lie about the Commission's negotiations as the minutes were still available to the Crown Prince. They were lost in a fire in 1853.

Wleugel: statement 3/8/01 (copy minutes 1801. Engineering Corps).

Defence line forms up
Norway squadron: Reports, I, pp 77–79; minutes 26, 28/2 and 9/3; Adm. 28/2 and 9, 10/3 to commanding officers (general copy book); logs of *Danmark* and *Trekroner* 8–23/3.
Elefanten: orders 5/2 to von Thun (general copy book); minutes 17, 27/2; log 7/2–5/3.
Gunboats: general copy book 17, 19, 23, 28/2; minutes 21/2.
First moorings: resolution 2/2 (minutes); Adm. to commanding officers, Dockyard Captain and Army Office 2, 4/3 (general copy book).
Fischer: 12/3 to Crown Prince Frederik and Adm. (Adm. Received Correspondence).
Second moorings: resolution 12/3 (minutes); Adm. 12/3 to commanding officers, Dockyard Captain, Army Office and Danish Chancellery (general copy book); Fischer 23/3 to Adm.
Elven and *Viborg*: Adm. 23/3 to Lt. Cdr. Holsten (general copy book); *Elven* and *Viborg* logs 21/3.
Søhesten, Sværdfisken and Fleet Battery No 1: Adm. 21/3 to commanding officers and 23, 24/3 to Dockyard Captain (general copy book); resolution 23/3 (minutes).
Hajen: resolution 30/3 (minutes); Adm. 30/3 to Sub-Lt. Müller and Dockyard Captain (general copy book); C. Lange: J.N. Müller's account, p 328.
Gun carriages: Report from Dockyard Captain, 9, 10, 12 /3 with resolution 16/3 (decision log); L.J. Flamand: Mindeskrift, p 139.
Augustenborg: O. Feldbæk: Denmark and the Armed Neutrality, p 106.

Dramatis Personae
Manning of the defences
Fischer: *Hjælperen*'s watch and quarter bill, 21/3.

Commanding officers and wardrooms
Estimate 9/7 with royal consent 10/7 1801 (Søkrigskancelliet. Royal Resolutions. Reproduced as appendix in P.C. Bundesen: Mindeskrift). O. Bergersen (II, p 317–19) has questioned the reliability of this official overview of manning levels, and numbers of casualties, wounded and captured. He gives no apparent reason why the Admiralty should have reported higher figures than was the case, and his own adjustments are not convincing. As the watch and quarter bills of all the vessels were lost, the Admiralty's estimates must be regarded as the best and most reliable figures of manning levels on 2/4.
Appointments: minutes and general copy book, supplemented with Topsøe-Jensen and Marquard: Søofficerer; J. Teisen: Contract Lieutenants.

Brøer: Fischer 23/3 to Adm. (Adm. Received Correspondence).
Runge: O. Feldbæk: Lt. Bille, pp 93–95.
Willemoes: minutes, 4/4.
Fischer: 23, 24/3 to Adm. (Adm. Received Correspondence).

Mates from merchant navy
Dahl: minutes 23/3.

Regulars and national servicemen
Regulars: Bergersen, II, p 574.
Recruiting of national servicemen: Adm. 17, 22, 24/11, 6, 30/1 and 6/2 to Dockyard Captain and recruiting officers (general copy book); minutes 5, 29/1 and 16/2.
Norwegian seamen: F.C. Smith 5/1 to Adm. (decision log); C. Bernstorff 7, 24, 31/1, 28/2 and 21/3 to envoy in Stockholm; and notes from Swedish Foreign Minstry n.d. (Mid-January); 5/3 to envoy (RA, Foreign Ministry, Orders Sweden and diplomatic archives. Sweden III. Acts concerning Neutrality Treaty); cash and supply accounts of transport of drafted men through Sweden 1801; Bergersen, II, pp 297–8.

Soldiers at sea
Adm. 9/2 to Army Office (general copy book); minutes 4/3; list of soldiers serving 2/4/01.
Fischer: Dockyard Captain 22/3 to Adm. (Adm. Received Correspondence).

Volunteers
Broadsheet 18/3; A. Nørlit: Tvangsudskrivning (The Press) pp 372–80; minutes 16, 18/3; Knud Waaben: A.S. Ørsted og negerslaverne i København (A.S. Ørsted and the slaves in Copenhagen), Juristen, 12, 1964; Fischer's log 22/3; 'Ismail the Indian' 3/6/01 to Crown Prince (Kommercekollegiet. East India journals, 1801:93); volunteer roles of defences 1801; cash accounts for volunteers 1801.
Fischer: *Elefanten*'s log 19/3.

Pressed men
Minutes 23, 31/3; Adm. 31/3 to all recruiting officers, Commander Naval Squadron in Glückstadt and Danish and German Chancelleries (general copy book); A. Nørlit: Tvangsudskrivning (The Press) pp 372–80; List of pressed men 1801.

Enough?
Manning regulations: 20, 28/2 (general copy book); Dockyard Captain 22/3 and Fischer 28/3 to Adm. (minutes).

Elven: Lt. Cdr. Holsten 4/3 to Adm.; Adm. 9/3 to Holsten (*Elven*'s log).
Doubling: minutes 23/3; Fischer's log 26/3.

COPENHAGEN ROADS

Orders and signals from Fischer: Most of the defence vessels' logs were lost along with the ships. Searches in English collections were unfruitful. Unless otherwise specified, portrayal of life on the Copenhagen Roads is based on Fischer's log.

Fischer's defence
Wagrien and Prøvestenen: Risbrich's notes in Some Diary Entries (Royal Library) and Naval Archives, 8, 1836, pp 414–16.
Single line: Fischer 23/3 to Adm.; *Elefanten*'s log 17, 23/3; *Elven*'s log 25/3; *Danmark*'s log 30/3; Holsten n.d. to Adm. (*Elven*'s log).

Gunboats
Logs of *Danmark*, *Viborg*, *Stege* and *Odense*; resolution 26/3 (minutes); Adm. 26/3 to Fischer and Steen Bille (general copy book).
Bille's squadron: *Danmark*'s log; Steen Bille 26/3 to Adm. (minutes); Crown Prince Frederik 23/3 to Steen Bille (private archives).

Gun drills
Hjælperen's log; C.F. Allen: Battle of Copenhagen Roads, p 59, note 1; Risbrich 28/3 to Fischer (Some Diary Entries, Royal Library); Fischer 23, 28/3 and Crown Prince Frederik 28/3 to Adm.; J.F. Bardenfleth: Draft p 5.
Chief gunner: Lassen 18/1/02 to Adm.(personal dossier); P.J. Jørgensen: Medal recipients pp 41–2.
Gun carriages and crew: *Elefanten*'s log 24/3; Risbrich 28/3 to Fischer (Some Diary Entries, Royal Library); resolution 28/3 minutes); Adm. 28/3 to Dockyard Captain(general copy book).

State of readiness
Oath: *Elefanten*'s log 25/3.
Crown Prince's visit: Logs of *Mars*, *Hjælperen*, *Danmark* and *Trekroner* 26/3.
Awards: *Elefanten*'s log 25/3
Readiness orders: Fischer's log; *Elefanten*'s log.
"Small vessel": Fischer n.d. to Hohlenberg (Dockyard. Files and incoming correspondence 1740–1801).
Standing orders: Fischer 23/3 to Adm.; resolution 23/3 (minutes); Adm. 23/3 to Fischer (general copy book).

Enemy in sight
Nidelven and *Sarpen*: logs of *Nidelven* and *Mars*; Steen Bille 26, 29/3 to Fischer; Steen Bille 29/3 to de Tengnagel (*Danmark*'s log).
Fleet Battery No. 1: *Danmark*'s log 30/3; H.F. Kiær: En øjenvidneberetning (An eyewitness account) pp 149–52.

Much honour, little hope
Defences 30/3: Fischer 28/11/02 to Crown Prince Frederik (Reports, I, p 164); J.F. Bardenfleth: Draft p 13; H.G. Garde's discussion in Den Dansk-Norske Sømagts Historie (The History of Danish-Norwegian Naval Power) pp 346–9.
Doubts about Trekroner Fort: Steen Bille 26/3 to Adm. (*Danmark*'s log).
Thermopylae: G. Poel: Johann Georg Rists Lebenserinnerungen, I. Gotha 1884 p 165.

DENMARK'S ALLIES
France
O. Feldbæk: Denmark and the Armed Neutrality pp 127–32.

Russia and Prussia
Prussia: ibid pp 123–27.
Russia: ibid pp 91–98.

Danish-Swedish mistrust
Swedish politics: ibid pp 85–7 and 95–8.
Cronstedt's first mission: Gustav IV Adolf 1/2/01 to Crown Prince Frederik (RA, Foreign Affairs Department, Sweden, I, a, correspondence between and concerning the Swedish royal family, I); Cronstedt 22/2 to Gustav IV Adolf (Uppsala University Library); Cronstedt 22, 26/2 to General Toll (Lund University Library).
Helsingborg: O. Feldbæk: Denmark and the Armed Neutrality p 264; Cronstedt 26/3 to Gustav IV Adolf (Uppsala University Library).

Admiral in a tight spot
Cronstedt's second mission: W. Odelberg: Carl Olof Cronstedt pp 236–60); Gustav IV Adolf 22/3 to Crown Prince Frederik (RA, Foreign Affairs Department, Sweden I a, correspondence between and concerning the Swedish royal family, I); Cronstedt 26, 30, 31/3 and 1, 2/4 to Gustav IV Adolf (Uppsala University Library); Gustav IV Adolf 30/3, 3, 7, 8, 9/4 to Cronstedt (War Archives, Helsinki).
Helsingborg batteries: O. Feldbæk: Lieutenant Bille p 97.

Swedish ships in the King's Deep
Karlskrona squadron: W. Odelberg: Carl Olof Cronstedt pp 236–60; Svenska Flottans Historia (History of the Swedish Navy) II p 548.

Pilots: Lt. Cdr. Løvenørn 14/3 to Adm.; resolution 23/3 (minutes); Adm. 16/3 to Løvenørn (general copy book).

BATTLE – PROLOGUE
Last three days
Seamarks 30/3: Nelson 30/3 to *Ardent* and *Bellona* (RA, Nelson's Order Book); *Elephant*'s log (PRO); Stewart I, p 15.
Reconnaissance 30/3: Nelson's log 30/3 (NMM); Stewart I, pp 14–15 and II p 302; H.G. Hutchinson: Nelson at Copenhagen p 235; Extract of a letter from on board the *Ganges* (Naval Chronicle, V p 338); Parker 6/4 to Evan Nepean (Admirals' Despatches, PRO); logs of *Elephant* and *Eling* (PRO); logs of *Mars*, *Elefanten*, *Hjælperen* and *Nidelven*.
London 30/3: Parker's log 30/3 (PRO); Nelson's log 30/3 (NMM); Stewart I, p 15 and II, p 302; Nelson 30/3 to Lady Hamilton (Morisson II, p 132).

Clear for action
Danish activity 30/3: Fischer's log; logs of *Danmark*, *Trekroner* and *Nidelven*.
Aquavit: *Elven*'s log 30/3; O. Feldbæk: Løjtnant Bille. p 93.

Council of war
Reconnaissance and council of war: Nelson's log 31/3 (NMM); Stewart I, pp 15–16 and II, p 303; Parker 6/4 to Evan Nepean (Admirals' Despatches, PRO); Nelson 31/3 to COs of original ten ships-of-the-line (RA Nelson's Order Book); Fremantle 4/4 to Lord Buckingham (Wynne Diaries III, p 43); Domett 4/5/01 to Admiral Bridport (British Museum).
British activity 31/3: Nelson 31/3 to COs of original ten ships-of-the-line (RA Nelson's Order Book); Stewart I, p 15 and II, p 303; H.G. Hutchinson: Nelson at Copenhagen p 325; logs of *St.. George*, *Veteran* and *Ramillies* (PRO); Nicholas Tomlinson 4/6/01 to Evan Nepean (Tomlinson Papers, pp 308–9).

Old blue trousers
Danish activity 31/3: Fischer's log; logs of *Elefanten*, *Mars*, *Danmark*, *Trekroner*, *Hjælperen* and *Elven*; Søren Wendelboe 1/4 to his wife (S.B. Bojesen: Fra Slaget på Københavns Red, pp 249–50); L.J. Flamand: Mindeskrift p 218.

Prepare to weigh
British activities 1/4: Parker's log 1/4 (PRO); Nelson's log 1/4 (NMM); Parker 6/4 to Evan Nepean (Admirals' Despatches, PRO); Stewart I,

pp 15–17; Millard, p 84; Nicholas Tomlinson 4/6/01 to Evan Nepean (Tomlinson Papers pp 308–9); logs of *London, Desirée, Elephant, Harpy, Teaser, Discovery, Sulphur, Hecla* and *Eling*.

Final precautions
Danish activity 1/4: Fischer's log; Cronstedt 1/4 to Gustav IV Adolf (Riksarkivet Stockholm); Mecklenburg 25/6/01 to Crown Prince Frederik (Reports, I, pp 160–63); C. Lange: J.N. Müller's report pp 328–9; Søren Wendelboe 1/4 to his wife (S.B. Bojesen: Fra Slaget på Københavns Red, pp 250–51); A. Lindvald: Kong Christian VIIIs dagbøger, pp 23–24; H.G. Garde: Den Dansk-Norske Sømagts Historie (Danish-Norwegian Naval Power) pp 355–6. Under the circumstances, Dudley Pope's critique (p 329) of Fischer's passivity as "a grave mistake" is unreasonable. From the Danish point of view, H.G. Garde also criticised the fact that the Danes sent no fireships into action. He explains his point by referring to the Crown Prince's "kind-heartedness". In fact, Crown Prince Frederik was not opposed to the use of fireships; however, no Danish fireships were available and even if there had been, it would have been a foolhardy venture to deploy them close to the moored defence line.

Southerly wind and victory
British activity evening of 1/4: Stewart I, p 17 and II, pp 303–4; Millard p 84; *Jamaica*'s log (PRO); logs of *Otter* and *Zephyr* (Logs pp 133–35); Pope pp 354 and 377. The account of Nelson's stalwart friend Hardy being aboard the *Elephant* the night before the battle and surveying the waters around the southerly Danish blockships is probably apocryphal. It first appears in the report Stewart wrote for Clarke and M'Arthur's biography of Nelson of 1809, a time when Nelson and Hardy were inseparable in the public eye. The *St. George's* log makes no reference to the captain having left his ship; and in his candid letter to his brother-in-law of 5/4 (Broadley and Bartelot: Nelson's Hardy, pp 63–65) Hardy does not speak of being together with Nelson on 1/4; on the contrary, the letter implies he was on board his own ship at that time.
Nelson's supper: Stewart II, p 304.

NELSON'S PLAN
Planning: Parker's log 30/3 (PRO); Stewart, I, pp 17–20 and II, pp 304–7; Millard p 84; Nelson 2/4 to his COs (Nelson's Order Book, RA); Nicholas Tomlinson 4/6/01 to Evan Nepean (Tomlinson Papers pp 309–10). Nelson's plan exists in several virtually identical versions (Disp., IV, pp 304–7; Stewart, I, pp 18–20; Wynne Diaries, III,

pp 45–7; Nelson's Order Book in RA; one copy in Admirals' Despatches, PRO).

NELSON'S IMPROVISATION
Preparation: logs of *Defiance* 1/4 and *Polyphemus* 2/4 (Logs, pp 100 and 95–99). The times recorded in *Polyphemus'* log are thought to be some fifteen minutes ahead of Copenhagen time, see O. Feldbæk: Historikeren og Tiden (The historian and time).
Monarch: Millard, pp 84–5.

Uncharted waters
Navigation problem: Stewart, I, pp 20–1 and II, p 307; William Stewart 6/4/01 to Sir William Clinton (NMM); *Cruizer*, log 2/4 (Logs, p 125); Nelson about 29/6/01 to St. Vincent (Disp., IV, p 499); Alexander Nairne 28/7/01 to James Nairne (NMM).

Victims to Middle Ground Shoal
Agamemnon log 2/4 (Logs, p 113); Nelson 4/4 to Fancourt (Disp., VII, pp 204–5); logs of *Discovery, Explosion, Hecla, Sulphur, Zebra, Biter, Bouncer, Sparkler, Teaser, Volcano* and *Force* (PRO and Logs, p 127–31).
Loss of ships: logs of *Polyphemus, Bellona* and *Russell* (Logs, p 97–8, 105–6 and 111); Alexander Nairne 28/7/01 to James Nairne (NMM); William Anderson n.d. (late May 1801) to his parents (D.B. Smith: Midshipman W.G. Anderson, p 243).

Nelson's presence of mind
Shorter line: Stewart, II, pp 307–8; Fremantle 4/4 to Lord Buckingham (Wynne Diaries, III, p 42); Extract of a Letter from on board the *Ganges* (Naval Chronicle V, p 339); *Polyphemus'* log (Logs, p 97).
Minor vessels: Nelson 3/4 to Parker (Disp., IV, p 314); Stewart, I, p 21–22; logs of *Amazon, Blanche, Alcmene, Arrow* and *Dart* (Logs, p 119 and 121–4); *Desirée*, log (Logs, p 120 and PRO).
Distance: reports of the distances between the combatant lines varies somewhat. In his letter to Sir William Clinton of 6/4 (NMM), Stewart estimates it to be more than 2 cables, or in excess of 400 yards. Rear Admiral Graves' secretary, Robinson Kittoe, who made a series of extremely accurate sketches and highly detailed notes for a representation of the battle estimated the distance to be 3 cables (Pope p 324). Several Danish and British accounts tend to report a shorter distance – thus making the action more dramatic. The actual distance was probably about 400 yards, possibly a little greater at the northern end of the King's Deep.

BATTLE – ACT I
First shots
Fischer's signals: Fischer's log.
Hajen: C. Lange: J.N. Müller's report, p 329.
Risbrich: Arkiv for Søvæsen (Naval Archives), 1836, p 418; Robinson Kittoe's notes (Pope, p 324).

British war machine
Edgar: Stewart I, p 21; Arkiv for Søvæsen (Naval Archives), 1846, p 104; Millard, p 86.
Ardent: Branth 13/4 to Fischer (personal dossier).
Ganges: Fremantle 4/4 to Lord Buckingham (Wynne Diaries, III, p 42); Extract of a Letter from on board the *Ganges* (Naval Chronicle, V, p 339).
Monarch: Millard, pp 86–7; H.G. Hutchinson: Nelson at Copenhagen, p 326.
Defiance: master's log (Logs, p 100).

Raking
Prøvestenen: Mecklenburg 25/6/01 to Crown Prince Frederik (Reports, I, p 162).
Wagrien: Arkiv for Søvæsen (Naval Archives), 1836, pp 416–17.
Sværdfisken: Sub-Lt. Sommerfeldt 14/4 to Fischer (personal dossier).
Kronborg: Lt. Bille 12/4 and Contract Lt. Helt 13/4 to Fischer (personal dossier and Adm. Received Correspondence 1801:823).
Hajen: C. Lange: J.N. Müller's report, p 330.
Aggershus: Fasting 3/4 to Fischer (personal dossier).
Charlotte Amalie: Kofoed 5/4 to Fischer (personal dossier).

Line is broken
Rendsborg: Egede 14/4 to Fischer (Adm. Received Correspondence; 1801: 848); *Explosion*'s log (Logs, p 129).
Wagrien: Arkiv for Søvæsen (Naval Archives), 1836, pp 416–17.

Gunboats in action
Gunboats: logs of *Danmark*, *Flensborg*, *Langesund*, *Nakskov*, *Odense*, *Staværn*, *Stege* and *Viborg*; Fischer's log; Fischer 3/4 to Adm. (personal dossier); Sub-Lt. Grove 21/7/01 to Adm. (personal dossier).
Shore batteries: Col. Mecklenburg 25/6/01 to Crown Prince Frederik (Reports, I, p 162).

COLLAPSE OF THE MIDDLE SECTOR
Nelson: Stewart, I, pp 20–4 and II, p 308; Stewart 6/4 to Sir William Clinton (NMM).

Monarch: Millard pp 87, 89.

Dannebrog's destiny

Dannebrog: Fischer's log; Fischer 3/4 to Adm. and 28/11/02 to Crown Prince Frederik (Reports, I, pp 164–7); Bardenfleth submitted report 4/4 to Adm. of Braun's verbal reports (Adm. Received Correspondence 1801:756); Braun's comments are given in Louis Bobé: August Hennings' dagbog (1934) p 198; J.F. Bardenfleth: Draft pp 7, 9; Lindholm 2/5/01 to Nelson (Disp., IV, p 347). Six of the eight Danish journals surviving recorded the time of *Dannebrog* blowing up to be 1630. Because of his concussion, Fischer delegated the drafting of the official report of 3/4, intended for public release, to the CO of the Naval Academy, Capt. H.C. Sneedorff (H.G. Garde: Den Dansk-Norske Sømagts Historie (Danish-Norwegian Naval History), p 395. Among other sources, this report was published in P.C. Bundesen: Mindeskrift, pp 68–72 and in O. Bergersen, II, App. 9. It is thought that immediately after the battle there were mutterings in naval circles that he should have relinquished when he was wounded (Lindholm 2/5/01 to Nelson, Disp. IV, p 346). The same feelings are recorded in L. Bobé: August Hennings' dagbog (1934) p 156 – undoubtedly with Steen Bille as the source.

First withdrawal

Elven: *Elven*'s log; Lt. Cdr. Holsten 3/4 to Fischer (Adm. Received Correspondence 1801:756), n.d. to Adm. (*Elven*'s log), and 25/7/01 to Adm. See also Fischer's log, *Danmark*'s log and J.F. Bardenfleth: Draft, pp 7–8, for a more likely time of *Elven*'s cutting her cables than the ship's own log.

Aggershus: Fasting 3/4 to Fischer; P.J. Jørgensen: Medal Recipients, p 9; C.F. Allen: Slaget på Københavns Red, pp 66–67.

Sub-Lt. Willemoes

Fleet Battery No. 1: Hohlenberg's report 28/12/00 on Fleet Batteries (Adm. Received Correspondence 1800:3122); H.F. Kiær: En øjen-vidneberetning (An Eyewitness Account), p 149; Willemoes 2/4 to Fischer (Adm. Received Correspondence, 1801: 756); Willemoes n.d. to his family (S. Birket Smith: Et brev fra P. Willemoes, 1801 p 95–96); J. Bardenfleth: Draft, p 9; logs of *Danmark*, *Trekroner* and *Mars*; List of pressed men. The origin of the Willemoes legend is covered by Christian Bruun in Admiral Lord Nelson and Peter Willemoes (1882).

Millard of the Monarch

Monarch: Millard pp 87–89.

Death sentence for desertion
Sjælland: Harboe 5/4 to Fischer, together with highly detailed information about conditions on board during the battle that emerged in the questioning of the accused and of a considerable number of witnesses in the courts martial of Schultz and Westerholt (Supreme Admiralty Court. Acta criminalia militaria. 1798–1802).

Müller and Nelson
Hajen: extract of Müller's report (Adm. Received Correspondence 1801:848); William Stewart 6/4 to Sir William Clinton (NMM); J.N. Müller's personal account, certainly given after 1830 and presumably to J.L. Flamand for his Mindeskrift of 1848, as Müller was in Copenhagen in 1847. (L.J. Flamand: Mindeskrift, pp 217–26; C. Lange: J.N. Müller's account, pp 327–35). Müller's account appears to be based on contemporary notes and memories and is only slightly influenced by the long interval between the events and his drafting of the account.

Beaten but not taken
English boats: Millard, p 90.

BATTLE – ACT II
Northern flank
Nelson: Nelson 22/4 to Lindholm (Disp., IV, p 345).

Charlotte Amalie
Kofoed 5/4 to Fischer (personal dossier); Stewart I, p 23.

Where is the rascal?
Monarch: Millard pp 90–91.

When all hope is lost
Søhesten: Middelboe 15/4 to Fischer (personal dossier).

Arenfelt of the Holsten
Arenfelt 9/4 to Fischer (Supreme Admiralty Court. Acta criminalia militaria. 1798–1802. Provost martial against Westerholt); Fischer to Adm. 3/4 (personal dossier) and 13/4 (Adm. Received Correspondence. 1801:823); Fischer's log; J.F. Bardenfleth: Draft , p 7.

Riou's squadron
Logs of *Amazon, Blanche, Alcmene, Arrow, Dart, Otter* and *Zephyr* (Logs, pp 119–24, 133 and 135); J.F. Bardenfleth: Draft, p 8; Stewart I, p 22 and II, p 309.

Early withdrawal
Hjælperen: Log and reference to Lillienskjold's report (Adm. Received Correspondence. 1801:890a). The time of the withdrawal recorded in her log – 1530 – is quite misleading, cf *Danmark*'s log.

Assistance to the Indfødsretten
Medal commendation from Lt Thode 25/7/01 (personal dossier); supplementary report from stores assistant Packness n.d.; report from Contract Lieutenant Meinertz 13/4; statements from Sub-Lts. Lützen and Nissen 4/4 (Adm. Received Correspondence: 1801:952, 823:1 and 984); Fischer 3/4 to Adm. (personal dossier); logs of *Hjælperen* and *Elefanten*.

Ships in Kronløbet Channel
Trekroner Fort: Fischer 3/4 to Adm.(personal dossier); J.F. Bardenfleth: Draft, p 11. We know precious little about the fort during the battle. A report from the CO, Major Meyer of the Marine Corps, was sought in vain. According to Steen Bille the fort fired with heated shot on 2/4 (Louis Bobé: August Hennings' dagbog, 1934, p 48).
Elefanten and Mars: own logs; logs of *Defence, Ramillies* and *Veteran* (PRO); Søren Wendelboe 2/4 to his wife (S.B. Bojesen: Fra Slaget på Københavns Red, p 251); List of volunteers in the defences 1801; list of pressed men 1801.
Steen Bille's squadron: logs of *Danmark* and *Trekroner;* Steen Bille 4/4 to Adm.(Adm. Received Correspondence 1801:719); Johan Wilhelm Jansen's log of Battle of Copenhagen (Regional Archives, Aabenraa).

Battle on southern flank
Shore batteries: Mecklenburg 25/6/01 to Crown Prince Frederik (Reports, I, pp 160–63); *Desirée,* log (Logs, p 120).

Deck was running with blood
Edgar and Ardent: own logs (Logs, pp 103–4 and 113–14); Murray's account n.d. of *Edgar*'s losses (NMM. CRK/14).
Jylland: Branth 13/4 to Fischer (personal dossier). Copy – possible draft – in private ownership reproduced in P.J. Jørgensen: Medal recipients, pp 14–15. Report from Wleugel 4/4 to Fischer; letters of commendation from Branth 19, 23, 24/4 and 9/7 (personal dossier).

Just the two of us left
Sværdfisken: Sommerfeldt 14/4 to Fischer (personal dossier).
Kronborg: Lt. Bille 12/4 (personal dossier) and Contract Lt. Helt 13/4 (Adm. Received Correspondence. 1801:823,3) to Fischer; Torgius Petersen: Mit levnesløb (Marinens Bibliotek); enquiry held to investigate discrepancies between the two reports (Adm. Received

Correspondence 1801:1010) that explain the situation on board when the colours were struck.

Volunteer carpenter
Rendsborg: Egede 14/4 to Fischer (Adm. Received Correspondence 1801:848) and his letter of recommendation to the Admiralty 16/4, and to Fischer 19/4 (personal dossier).

British southern flank
Polyphemus: log (Logs, pp 114–15); Alexander Nairne 28/7/01 to James Nairne (NMM.AGC/22)
Isis: log (Logs, pp 118–19)
Russell: log (Logs, pp 110–13)
Bellona: log; Edward Daubeny 4/4 and Capt. Thompson 25/4 to James Daubeny (Logs, pp 105–10); William Anderson n.d. (summer 1801) to his parents (D.B. Smith: Midshipman W.G. Anderson, pp 241–45); Lt. Wilkes 3/4 to unknown addressee (NMM.AGC/W/2).
Desirée: log (Logs, pp 120–21 and PRO); Millard p 86.
Biter, Bouncer, Force and Sparkler: logs (PRO).

Risbrich and the Wagrien
Risbrich 3/4 to Fischer (Adm. Received Correspondence, 1801:757); extracts of Risbrich's diary (Arkiv for Søvæsen – Naval Archives), 8, 1836, pp 416–18); commendations and personal dossiers 11, 18, 19/4 (personal dossiers).

Prøvestenen's last shot
Lassen 5/4 to Fischer, officers' personal dossiers 18/4 and commendations for ratings 18/4/01 and 18/1/02 (personal dossiers); Lt. Bille 18/4 to Lassen (personal dossier), O. Feldbæk: Lt. Bille på Prøvestenen; and Bille's obituary (Arkiv for Søvæsen, 1846, p 104).

BATTLE – ACT III

Discontinue the action
Parker's situation: Parker's log (PRO; reproduced in Logs, pp 89–90); logs of *Defence, London, Raisonable, Ramillies, St. George, Saturn, Veteran* and *Warrior* (PRO).
Parker's signal: Parker's log (PRO); *London*'s log (PRO); O. Feldbæk: Historikeren og Tiden, pp 39–41.
Nelson's reaction: Stewart I, p 24 and II, pp 308–9, and Stewart 6/4 to Sir William Clinton (NMM).
Nelson's ships: L.V. Harcourt: Diaries of George Rose, I, p 348; Stewart I, p 24 and II, p 309.

Nelson's letter
The original (RA. Udenrigsdepartementet – Foreign Department. Correspondence concerning outbreak of hostilities with England 1801) is reproduced in P.C. Bundesen: Mindeskrift, p 60 and Pope, p 388. The envelope has been lost. The address is referred to by Lindholm (Account 8/4/01. Lindholm's private archives). Circumstances surrounding its despatch: Disp., IV, pp 310–11; Stewart I, p 24 and II, p 310; *Elephant*'s log (Logs, p 93).
Emissary: O. Feldbæk: Historikeren og Tiden, p 42.

Nelson's motive
Nelson's second letter 2/4 (original in RA. Udenrigsdepartementet – Foreign Department. Correspondence concerning the outbreak of hostilities with England 1801. Reproduced in P.C. Bundesen: Mindeskrift, p 65); Hardy 5/4 to his brother-in-law (Broadley and Bartelot, pp 63–5); Nelson 9/4 to Lady Hamilton (Morisson, II, p 136); Nelson 22/4 to Lindholm (Disp., IV, pp 344–6); Nelson 8/5 to Henry Addington (Disp., IV, p 360) The Trafalgar Prayer is quoted from O. Warner: Nelson's Battles, p 189. The Danish tradition: O. Feldbæk: De danske søofficerer og 'dolkestødslegenden' om slaget på Reden.
Cronstedt: 2/4 to Gustav IV Adolf (Riksarkivet, Stockholm).
Fireships: Stewart II, p 310. The information is not contemporary and originates from 1809. It is reinforced, however, by the fact that Nelson did have fireships at his disposal and according to his plan had decided to use them.

Humanity or ruse de guerre?
Stewart: Stewart I, pp 23–4 and Stewart 6/4 to Sir William Clinton (NMM).
Fremantle: Fremantle 4/4 to his wife and Lord Buckingham (Wynne Diaries, III, pp 41–44). Cf Stewart II, p 311.
Hardy: Hardy 5/4 to his brother-in-law (Broadley and Bartelot, pp 63–65).
Stewart's conclusion: Stewart II, p 311.

Capitulation
Emissary: O. Feldbæk: Historikeren og Tiden, pp 42 and 45–6; *Elephant*'s log.
Trekroner Fort: Fischer's log 2/4; Fischer 3/4 to Adm. (personal dossier); O. Feldbæk: Denmark and the Armed Neutrality, p 156 with references.

Crown Prince's decision
Lindholm's mission: eyewitness account by Wessel Brown 15/4
(Supreme Admiralty Court. Acta criminalia militaria. 1798–1802.
Provost martial against Niels Westerholt); Lindholm's account 8/4
(private archives, reproduced in C.C. Zahrtmann: Genlyd, pp 174–5);
Fischer 3/4 to Adm. (personal dossier); logs of *Elephant* and *Mars*;
Nelson's second letter is in RA. Udenrigsdepartementet – Foreign
Department. Correspondence concerning outbreak of hostilities with
England 1801 (reproduced in P. C. Bundesen: Mindeskrift, p 65).
Lindholm's written questions to Nelson and copy of Nelson's second
letter addressed "To the Government of Denmark" are in
NMM.AGC/8. Ms. 9176.
Nelson's assets: Stewart I, p 25 and II, p 311; Millard p 90; Parker's log
(PRO).

White flag
Isis: log (Logs, pp 117–8).

Out of the Deep
Monarch and Ganges: list of losses (Disp., IV, pp 316–8); Millard p 91;
Stewart I, p 25; Fremantle 4/4 to Lord Buckingham (Wynne Diaries,
III, p 43).
Elephant and *Defiance*: logs and Graves 3/4 to John Graves (Logs, 93–4,
100–1 and 103); Stewart I, p 25.
Desirée, Bellona and *Russell*: logs and *Volcano*'s log (PRO and Logs,
105–7, 110–13 and 132).
Nelson's words on leaving the Elephant: Stewart II, p 312.

WINNERS AND LOSERS
Polyphemus: Alexander Nairne 28/7/01 to James Nairne
(NMM.AGC/22).
Monarch: Millard, p 92.

British losses
Parker's log 4/4 (PRO); list of casualties in Parker's report 6/4 is
missing but is probably identical to the list of losses in Disp., IV, pp
316–9. The losses recorded in each ship's log vary slightly but do not
contradict the overall casualty list.
Ganges: Fremantle 4/4 to Lord Buckingham (Wynne Diaries, III, pp
43–4).

Danish losses
Report 10/7/01 (Søkrigskancelliet. Royal Resolutions 1801) is given as
an appendix to P.C. Bundesen: Mindeskrift. Cf discussion above.

Ole Hansen: Adm. Register Received Correspondence 1800–01, no. 749. Cf Bergersen II, pp 586–7 and Frederik V's Søkrigsartikelbrev (Articles of War), §536 and §566.

The vanquished wrecks
Danish vessels: Logs of *Hjælperen* and *Nakskov* 2/4.
Sjælland: Harboe 5/4 to Fischer (personal dossier); *Danmark*'s log 2, 3/4; Nelson 3/4 to Parker (Disp., IV, p 331); Fischer 28/11/02 to Crown Prince Frederik (Reports, I, p 165–66).
Prizes: Parker's log 4/4 (PRO) and information contained in the British ships' logs. Parker burned the prizes because he did not have the crews to man them (Parker 30/4/01 to Evan Nepean. Admirals' Despatches PRO).

Danish defeat
Captain Peter Fyers of the Royal Artillery: Memo regarding bombardment of Copenhagen, with a sketch plan (NMM, n.d. but probably 4/4).

BATTLE – EPILOGUE
Threat of bombardment
Last resistance: Duke Frederik Christian of Augustenborg 4/4 to Princess Louise (Schleswig-Holsteinisches Landesarchiv. Primkenauer Archiv); Christian Ditlev Reventlow's reservations 5/4 (Reports I, pp 276–78).
British ships: *Teaser*'s log 4/4 (PRO); Captain Peter Fyers: Memo regarding bombardment of Copenhagen (NMM).

Steen Bille's defences
Change of command: Fischer 3/4 to Adm. (personal dossier and Adm. Received Correspondence 1801:701); Fischer 28/11/02 to Crown Prince Frederik (Reports I, pp 164–7); resolution 4/4 (minutes); Adm. to Steen Bille 4/4 (general copy book).
Defence of battle squadron: secondment of officers 7/4 (Adm. Received Correspondence 1800–01); despatch from French envoy 4/4 (Archives des affaires étrangères, Paris. Correspondance politique. Danemark).
Trekroner Fort: *Defence*, log 5/3–25/4 1801 (Naval dockyard's delivery 1945, No. 421); daily orders 4/4 (Reports I, p 148); resolution 4/4 (minutes); Steen Bille 8/4 to Crown Prince Frederik (Reports I, p 158); *Mars*, log 6/4.
Vessels and boom: Adm. 4, 5/4 to Steen Bille (*Danmark*, log); resolution 4/4 (minutes); Steen Bille 5/4 to Crown Prince Frederik and 6/4 to Dockyard Captain (*Danmark*, log); *Hjælperen*, log 2–9/4.

Hero's burial
Daily orders: Reports I, p 147; Crown Prince Frederik 4/4 to Major General Rantzau (Reports I, p 173).
Evacuation: Daily orders 7/4 (Reports I, p 149).
Funeral: Berlingske Tidende 6/4 and *London*'s log 5/4 (PRO).

DIPLOMAT AND ADMIRALS
Negotiations 2–7/4: unless otherwise annotated, the account is based on O. Feldbæk: Denmark and the Armed Neutrality.
Despatch to Tsar: Lizakevich 3/4 to the Tsar by courier (RA. Danica microfilm).

Nelson at Amalienborg
Nelson 3/4: Nelson's log (PRO); Hardy 5/4 to his brother-in-law (Broadley and Bartelot, pp 63–5); Fremantle 4/4 to Lord Buckingham (Wynne Diaries III, p 42).
Reactions 6–7/4: Parker's log 7/4 (PRO); Nelson's log 6–7/4 (NMM); Parker's two letters 6/4 to Evan Nepean (Admirals' Despatches, PRO); *Force*'s log 7/4 (PRO).

War of nerves
Nelson and Bernstorff: Nelson's log 7/4 (NMM); Nelson 4 and 9/4 to Henry Addington (Disp. IV, pp 335, 341).

Pen and sword
Armistice negotiation: unless otherwise annotated, the account is based on O. Feldbæk: Denmark and the Armed Neutrality.

ARMISTICE
British motives: Parker's log 7/4 (PRO); Parker 9/4 to Evan Nepean (Admirals' Despatches, PRO); Nelson 9/4 to Henry Addington (Disp. IV, pp 339–41).
St. Vincent: St. Vincent 9/2/01 to Evan Nepean (NMM).
Fremantle: Fremantle 6/4 to Lord Buckingham (Wynne Diaries III, pp 48–9).

The Tsar is dead
Amalienborg: Nelson's log 8, 9/4 (NMM); Nelson 9/4 to Henry Addington (Disp. IV, pp 339–41); Stewart II, pp 326–7; Recollections of A.J. Scott, pp 72–73.
Armistice: Danske Traktater efter 1800 I, 1877, pp 13–15.

THE LOST WAR
Prisoners taken ashore: Various diary entries about 2/4/01 (Kgl. Bibliotek); Arkiv for Søvæsen (Naval Archives) 1846, p 105; Lt. Bille 18/4 to Lassen (personal dossier).

Parker and Nelson in the Baltic
Parker's log (PRO); Nelson's log (NMM); letters from Parker and Nelson to Evan Nepean (Admirals' Despatches, PRO); Disp. IV, pp 342–420; Pope: The Great Gamble, pp 449 ff.

Parker's recall: The Admiralty rejected Parker's demand for an official investigation; therefore the reasons underlying his recall are difficult to document. But for significant cause see St. Vincent 4/4 to Evan Nepean (NMM); St. Vincent 17/4 to Parker (St. Vincent Papers I, pp 89–91); L.V. Harcourt: The Diaries of George Rose I, pp 347–8; St. Vincent 21/4 to George III (A. Aspinall: The Later Correspondence of George III, III, pp 517–18); St. Vincent Papers I, pp 62–3 and 76–9. On relations between Nelson and Parker see Nelson 8/7/01 to Parker and Parker's reply of same day (NMM.CRK/14), Parker 26/7 and 28/8 to Nelson (NMM.CRK/9); John McArthur 18/8/01 to Nelson (NMM.CRK/8). Cf Pope: The Great Gamble pp 507–18. This situation probably reveals the reason for the Cabinet's refusal to issue a medal for the Battle of Copenhagen – cf Disp. IV, pp 524–30.

Curtain down
Foreign policy: O. Feldbæk: The Anglo-Russian Rapprochement, and O. Feldbæk: Denmark and the Armed Neutrality.

Bibliography and Printed Sources

Bibliography

Printed in Copenhagen unless otherwise specified.

Allen, C.F.: *Slaget på Københavs Red den 2. april 1801.* Dansk Folkekalender, 1842.

Bardenfleth, J.F.: *Udkast til en militær beskrivelse over slaget på Københavns Red den 2. april 1801.* 1801.

Barfod, H.: *Vor flåde i fortid og nutid,* I. 1941.

Bergersen, O.: *Nøytralitet og krig. Fra Nordens væpnede nøytralitet saga. En sjømilitær studie,* I-II. Oslo 1966.

Beutlich, F.: *Norges sjøvæbning 1750–1809.* Oslo 1935.

Biering, K.: *Viser og digte i anledning af slaget på Københavns Red i 1801.* Almanak, 1:4, 1966.

Bille, S.: *Det danske flag i Middelhavet i slutningen af det 18. århundrede. Et bidrag til den danske marines historie. Uddraget af gehejmestatsminister admiral Steen Billes efterladte papirer.* 1840.

Bistrup, H.: *Slaget på Reden i dansk historie.* Tidsskrift for Søvæsen, 115. 1944.

Bjerg, H.C.: *Diskussion om slaget på Reden.* Marinehistorisk Tidsskrift 3/1970.

Bjerg, H.C. & Schou Hansen, J.: *Vragene i Øresund efter 1801 og 1807.* Marinehistorisk Tidsskrift 1/1974.

Bjerg, H.C.: *Dansk marinehistorisk bibliografi 1500–1975.* Marinehistorisk Selskabs Skrift no. 12. 1975.

Bjerg, H.C. & Erichsen, J.: *Danske orlogsskibe 1670–1860. Konstruktion og dekoration.* I-II . 1980.

Bojesen, M.: *Slaget på Reden.* Tidsskrift for Søvæsen, 113. 1942.

Bojesen, M.: *Slaget på Reden.* Tidsskrift for Søvæsen, 115. 1944.

Borg, E.: *Den danske marines uniformer gennem tre århundreder.* 1974.

Briand de Crèvecoeur, E.: *Olfert Fischer. Københavns modige forsvarer.* 1944.

Briand de Crèvecoeur, E.: *Nogle beretninger vedr. 'The Royal Artillery' ved København 1801.* Tidsskrift for Søvæsen, 121. 1950.

Broadley, A.M. & Bartelot, R.G.: *Nelson's Hardy. His life, Letters and Friends*. London 1909.

Bruun, C.: *Admiral Lord Nelson og Peter Willemoes*. 1882.

Bundesen, P.C.: *Mindeskrift om slaget på Reden den 2. april 1801*. Tidsskrift for Søvæsen, 72. 1901.

Clarke, J.S. & M'Arthur, J.: *The Life and Services of Admiral Lord Nelson*. London 1809.

Dalhoff-Nielsen, S.: *Slaget på Reden*. Tidsskrift for Søvæsen, 113. 1942.

Dalhoff-Nielsen, S.: *Slaget på Reden*. Tidsskrift for Søvæsen, 115. 1944

Ekberger, M.: *Københavns sødefension i foråret 1801*. Marinehistorisk Tidsskrift 1/1984.

Elling, C.: *Frederik VIII.s palæ på Amalienborg*. 1951.

Eriksen, E. & Frantzen, O.L.: *Det danske artillerimateriel under Napoleonskrigene 1801–1814*. 1985

Evers, C.V.: *Slaget på Reden i danks historie*. Tidsskrift for Søvæsen, 114. 1943.

Feldbæk, O.: *Dutch Batavia Trade via Copenhagen 1795–1807. A Study of Colonial Trade and Neutrality*. Scandinavian Economic History Review, XXI. 1973.

Feldbæk, O.: *The Anglo-Danish Convoy Conflict of 1800. A Study of Small Power Policy and Neutrality*. Scandinavian Journal of History, II:3. 1977.

Feldbæk, O.: *The Anglo-Russian Rapprochement of 1801. A Prelude to the Peace of Amiens*. Scandinavian Journal of History, III:3. 1978.

Feldbæk, O.: *Denmark and the Armed Neutrality 1800–1801. Small Power Policy in a World War*. With Danish summary. 1980.

Feldbæk, O. & Justesen, O.: *Kolonierne i Asien og Afrika*. 1980.

Feldbæk, O.: *Ostindisk konvoj i den florissante handelsperiode*. Handels- of Søfartsmuseets Årbog. 1981.

Feldbæk, O.: *The Foreign Policy of Tsar Paul I, 1800–1801. An Interpretation*. Jarhbücher für Geschichte Osteuropas, XXX. 1982.

Feldbæk, O.: *Danmarks historie, 4*: Tiden 1730–1814. 1982.

Feldbæk, O.: *De danske søofficerer og 'dolkestødslegenden' om slaget på Reden*. Fortid og Nutid, 1983.

Feldbæk, O.: *Historikeren og Tiden. Eller: Hvad var klokken den 2. April 1801*. Festskrift til Kristof Glamann. 1983.

Feldbæk, O.: *Kærlighed til fædrelandet. 1700-tallets nationale selv-forståelse*. Fortid og Nutid, 1984.

Flamand, A.J.: *Mindeskrift om Danmrks hædersdag den 2. april 1801*. 1848.

260

Frantzen, O.L.: *Træk af søartilleriets historie 1786–1855.* Våbenhistoriske Årbøger, XXV. 1979.

Frantzen, O.L.: *Sømorterer.* Våbenhistoriske Årbøger, XXVI. 1980.

Frantzen, O.L.: *Truslen fra øst. Dansk-norsk flådepolitik 1769–1807.* Marinehistorisk Selskabs Skrift no. 16. 1980.

Frantzen, O.L.: *Den danske flådes karronader.* Maritim Kontakt 3. 1982.

Frantzen, O.L.: *Artilleriets materiel.* Dansk Artilleritidsskrift, 1984.

Garde, H.G.: *Efterretninger om den dansk-norske sømagt,* IV. 1835.

Garde, H.G.: *Den dansk-norske sømagts historie 1700–1814.* 1852.

Grandjean, B.L.: *Roepstorffs puncheboller.* Kulturminder. 1960.

Harrel, V.O.: *Mindesablerne for slaget på Reden og deres baggrund.* Våbenhistoriske Årbøger, XI. 1962–64.

Herbert, J.B.: *Life and Services of Admiral Sir Thomas Foley, G.C.B. Rear-Admiral of Great Britain.* Cardiff 1884.

Holm, E.: *Har admiral Cronstedt været forræder i 1801 og hindret, at Sverige dengang kom Danmark-Norge til hjælp?* Historisk Tidskrift, VIII:3. 1910.

Holm, J.C.: *1801–2. April–1951.* Nordisk Numismatisk Unions Medlemsblad, april 1951.

Ipsen, P.: *I anledning af 150-årsdagen for slaget på Reden 2. april 1801.* Tidsskrift for Søvæsen, 122. 1951.

James, W.: *The Naval History of Great Britain,* III. London 1837.

Jeppesen, H.: *Matroser til den dansk-norske flåde 1770–1802.* Norsk sjøfartsmuseum. Årsberetning 1981. Oslo 1982.

Jørgensen, P.J.: *Modtagerne af medaljen for slaget på Reden 2. april 1801.* 1976.

Kennedy, L.: *Nelson and his Captains.* London 1976.

Kjølsen, F.H.: *Så kæmped de helte hin anden april.* Tidsskrift for Søvæsen, 147. 1976.

Laws, M.E.S.: *The Royal Artillery at Copenhagen 1801.* Journal of the Royal Artillery, October 1949.

Lindeberg, L.: *De så det ske. Englandskrigene 1801–1814. Slaget på Reden. Guldalder. Statsbankerot.* 1974.

Lindsay-MacDougall, K.F.: *Nelson Manuscripts at the National Maritime Museum.* Mariner's Mirror, 41. 1955.

Lundsgaard, I.C.: *'Copenhagen' den 2. april 1801.* Marinehistorisk Tidsskrift 1/1971.

Lütken, O.: *Om Peter Willemoes.* 1883.

Mackaness, G.: *The Life of Vice-Admiral William Bligh.* New York 1935.

Mackesy, P.: *War without Victory: the Downfall of Pitt, 1799–1802.* Oxford 1984.

Mahan, A.T.: *The Life of Nelson. The Embodiment of the Sea Power of Great Britain*. I-II. London 1897.

Marcus,G.J.: *A Naval History of England*. II. *The Age of Nelson*. London 1971.

Marcus, G.J.: *Heart of Oak. A Survey of British Sea Power in the Georgian Era*. London 1975.

Monrath, E.C.: *Slaget ved København den 2. april 1801*. Nordisk Penningmagazin. 1842.

Nyrop-Christensen, H.: *Mindehøjtideligheder fra Frederik VI.s tid. Omkring H.C. Knudsens heroiske tableauer*. Studier fra Sprog- og Oldtidsforskning, 274. 1970.

Nørlit, A.: *Tvangsudskrivning og presning af mandskab til flåden og defensionen (1800–07)*. Historiske Meddelelser om København, 3:5. 1942.

Odelberg, W.: *Carl Olof Cronstedt. Levnadsteckning och tidsskildring*. Helsinki 1954.

Pedersen, P.: *Om termometerstanden i København fra 1767–1853*. Meddelser fra Det Statistiske Bureau. 2nd collection. 1855.

Pope, D.: *The Great Gamble. Nelson at Copenhagen*. London 1972.

Ramshart, P.: *Efterretninger om det bekendte af den danske flådes tjeneste 1752–1807*. 1808.

Rasmussen, H.J.: *'The Royal Artillery' ved København 1801*. Tidsskrift for Søvæsen, 121. 1950.

Schultz, J.H.: *Den danske marine 1814–1848*. I-II. 1930–32.

Seidelin, K.H.: *Krig for havenes frihed*. I. 1801.

Soldin, S.: *Krigen mellem Danmark og England*. 1801.

Soldin, S.: *Patriotiske handlinger af danske og norske. En eksempelbog for ungdommen*. 1806.

Southey, R.: *The Life of Nelson*. London 1813.

Steensen, R.S.: *Flåden gennem 450 år*. I-II. 1961.

Svenska Flottans Historia. II. O. Lybeck (ed.). Malmø 1943.

Saabye, E.J.: *Bemærkninger til 'The Royal Artillery' ved København 1801*. Tidsskrift for Søvæsen, 121. 1950.

Taylor, A.H.: *The Battle of Copenhagen April 2nd 1801*. Tidsskrift for Søvæsen, 122. 1951.

Teisen, J.: *Månedsløjtnanter 1801–14*. Tidsskrift for Søvæsen, 132. 1961.

Thomsen, B.: *Marinekorpset 1798–1816*. Marinehistorisk Tidsskrift 4/1972.

Thomsen, B.: *De dansk-norske kanonbåde 1780–1850*. Marinehistorisk Tidsskrift 3/1975 & 4/1975.

Thostrup, B.: *Hædersmedaljen for slaget på Reden.* Tidsskrift for Søvæsen, 115. 1944.

Topsøe-Jensen, T.A. & Marquard, E.: *Officerer i den dansk-norske søetat 1660–1814 og den danske søetat 1814–1932.* I-II. 1935.

Unger, G.: *Varför ingrep ej svenska flottan vid överfallet på Köpenhamns redd i 1801?* Nordisk Tidskrift. IX. 1933.

Warner, O.: *Lord Nelson: A Guide to Reading.* London 1935.

Warner, O.: *Nelson's Battles.* London 1965.

Winge, M.: *Søetatens syge- og kvæsthuse.* Marinehistorisk Selskabs Skrift no. 113. 1976.

Zahrtmann, C.C.: *Genlyd fra 1801.* Nyt Arkiv for Søvæsenet, I. 1842.

PRINTED SOURCES

Anonymous: *Extract of a Letter from on board the Ganges, off Copenhagen, dated April 4th.* Naval Chronicle, V. 1801

Asperne, T.S.: *HMS Jamaica, 6 April 1801 to his Father.* Naval Chronicle V. 1801.

Aspinall, A.: *The Later Correspondence of George III.* III. Cambridge 1967.

Berlingske Tidende: *'De til Forsendelse med Posten alene privilegerede københavnske Tidender'.* 1800–01.

Bille, S.: *Biografiske erindringer om admiral Steen Billes liv.* Arkiv for Søvæsnet, XII. 1840.

Birket Smith, S.: *Et brev fra P. Willemoes om slaget på Reden 2. april 1801.* Danske Samlinger, 2:6. 1877–79.

Bojesen, S.B.: *Fra slaget på Københavns Red.* (Assistant surgeon Søren Wendelboe, the *Elefant*) Historisk Månedsskrift for folkelig og kirkelig Oplysning, X. 1887.

Bullocke, J.G.: *The Tomlinson Papers.* Navy Records Society, LXIV. London 1935.

Carlsen, O.: *J.F. Clemens' beretninger om 1801 og 1807 i breve til Johan Bülow.* Historiske Meddelelser om København, 2:3. 1927–28.

Collegial Tidende for Danmark og Norge. 1800–01.

Cumloden Papers. (Lieutenant Colonel William Stewart). Edinburgh 1871.

Feldbæk, O.: *Løjtnant Bille på Prøvestenen. En nyfunden kilde til slaget på Reden.* Fund og Forskning, XXV. 1981.

Fremantle, A.: *The Wynne Diaries,* III. (Captain Thomas Fremantle, Ganges). London 1940.

Harcourt, L.V.: *The Diaries and Correspondence of the Right Hon. George Rose*. I. London 1880.

Hutchinson, H.G.: *Nelson at Copenhagen*. (Lieutenant Colonel William Hutchinson) Blackwood's Edinburgh Magazine, CLXVI. 1899.

Jackson, T.S.: *Logs of the Great Sea Fights 1794–1805*, II. Navy Records Society, XVIII. London 1900.

Kiær, H.F.: *En øjenvidneberetning fra Willemoes' flådebatteri*. Tidsskrift for Søvæsen, 130. 1959.

Kong Frederik den Femtes Søkrigsartikelbrev 8. januar 1752. Second edition. 1811.

Lange, C.J.: *J.N. Müllers beretning om hans deltagelse i slaget 2. april 1801*. Norske Samlinger, II. 1860.

Laughton, J.K.: *The Naval Miscellany*, I. (Nelson to Sir Thomas Troubridge) Navy Records Society, XX. London 1902.

Laughton, J.K.: *The Naval Miscellany*, II. (St. Vincent to Evan Nepean) Navy Records Society, XL. London 1902.

Layman, William: *Naval Biography*. Naval Chronicle, XXXVII. 1817.

Linvald, A.: *Kong Christian VIII.s dagbøger og optegnelser*, I. 1799–1814. 1943.

Millard, W.S.: *The Battle of Copenhagen (being the experience of a Midshipman on board HMS Monarch, told by himself)*. Macmillan's Magazine, June 1895.

Minerva. 1800–01.

Morisson, A.: *The Hamilton and Nelson Papers*, II. London 1894.

Naish, G.P.B.: *Nelson's Letters to his Wife and other Documents 1785–1831*. Navy Records Society. London 1958.

Nicholas, N.H.: *The Dispatches and Letters of Vice-Admiral Viscount Nelson*, IV and VII. London 1845 and 1846.

Petersen, A.: *Bidrag til historien om 2. april 1801, efter en optegnelse af L. Engelstoft* (Hertug Frederik Christian af Augustenborg). Danske Samlinger, I. 1865–55.

Richmond, H.W.: *Private Papers of George, Second Earl Spencer, First Lord of the Admiralty 1794–1801*, IV. Navy Records Society LVIII. London 1924.

Recollections of the Life of the Rev. A.J. Scott, D.D., Lord Nelson's Chaplain. London 1842.

Smith, D.B.: *Letters of Admiral of the Fleet the Earl of St. Vincent whilst First Lord of the Admiralty 1801–1804*, I. Navy Records Society, LV. London 1932.

Sørensen, C.T.: *Meddelelser fra Krigsarkiverne*. Published by the General Staff, I. 1883.

Index

269